FROM OUR IMMIGRANTS WITH LOVE

Created and compiled by
JOAN S. FOLLENDORE

Racz Publishing Company
P.O. Box 287
Oxnard, CA 93032

First Printing, June, 1977

Library of Congress catalog card number: 76-20977
ISBN: 0-916546-03-9
Printed in the United States of America

FOREWORD

It is overwhelming to think of the number of ships that crisscrossed the oceans to bring all the people to the United States. Imagine the courage and faith those first arrivals had. They risked everything that had been home to them. They risked their lives and their children's lives. What drew them from their families and ties in their homeland to a strange, unsettled country? Some had been drawn by steamship and railroad ads. But the best ad of all was an "American letter" from someone who was already there.

Each one brought his gift to the new land, and it is still a new land--new to him, and relatively new in age, also. As the newcomers keep arriving, they continue to give, for that is how they get. That is the life process. The more one contributes, the more one gets out of life.

This is an anthology, or collection of stories, of some of those contributions made by the immigrants to the United States. Its purpose is to instill pride in your ancestry and to create an awareness of your neighbor's enrichment of the U.S.A. "You don't live in a world all alone. Your brothers are here, too." as Dr. Albert Schweitzer put it.

The writers of this book are not trying to teach you history, geography, or economics. They just want to tell you about some people who followed Emerson's suggestion, "The great use of life is to spend it for something that outlasts it."

We hope that this will lead you to recognize that the "oneness" of American life and culture was made possible only by the contributions of "many."

It is true that anyone living on the North or South American continents may be rightly called an American, but in this book the name is used to mean a person residing in the United States of America, and "America" refers only to the land area that is now the U.S.A. By "Indians," we mean American Indians, not the East Indians from India. We hope that these definitions will not offend any readers.

In the formative years of the United States, gifts were brought by many whose names have been lost to history. It is generally known from which country important gifts have come. We regret not always knowing the name of the individual who first gave us each generous gift, but we hope that learning from which country it came will make you feel a part of the lives and concerns of many others, and see that we all represent something significant and beautiful.

3

CONTRIBUTING AUTHORS

Elizabeth M. Birks
Howard L. Cleveland
Lelia K. Fligelman
Joan S. Follendore
Marilyn D. Hall
Evelyn Isaacs
Irene L. Jerison
J.H. Jack Kimberly
Mable Corinne Parrish
Jeanne Pieper
Lillian H. Post
Loretta Roberts
M.J. Saperstein
Joyce B. Schwartz
Virginia Stevenson
Nedra Woolf

ILLUSTRATIONS

Corinne Lilyard-Mitchell

CONSIDER OUR STRENGTH

It's the freedom to write, to speak, and to pray;
To think as we chose; to work and to play.

It's the nation we've built, with laws that are just;
It's the faith that sustains us: "In God we trust."

It's the spirit and pride we share in our name;
It's our love for the land our forefathers claimed.

It's the cities and farms from New York to L.A.;
It's the homes where we live the American way.

It's our memories of great men; great women too;
It's our search for tomorrows when dreams can come true.

It's the power we muster, when goals have been set,
By acting together to meet each new test.

It's the pursuit of new knowledge to build an alliance
Of the values we cherish with the outreach of science.

It's the fields and the mines, the forests and waters,
But greatest of all--our sons and our daughters.

Consider our strength.
Consider it well.

Reprint courtesy of: "The National
Association of Conservation Districts"

DEDICATION

To our Lord, who through my husband, Lee, gave me the perseverance to complete this project.

To the goals that our immigrants reached so that these fine writers could record their contributions for our families to treasure always.

TABLE OF CONTENTS

FROM

OUR

IMMIGRANTS

WITH

LOVE

1

AFRICA

by

LILLIAN H. POST

Although the figures show that there have been only about 87,000 immigrants to the United States from Africa, this book would never be complete without the story of the Negro people who were brought by force to work as slaves. It has been estimated that some twenty million black people were enslaved during the 17th through 19th centuries and of these twenty million, more than a million were delivered to the shores of what is now the United States and sold in the market places to the settlers and plantation owners.

Unlike most immigrants who made the trip with hope of a new and better life, the Negroes were brought with chains on their ankles, bundles of supplies on their heads, and fear and despair in their hearts. Their strong and healthy bodies created a work force which enabled the Colonies to become powerful in the world of trade. Their love of rhythm and their unconquerable spirits created a whole new era in the field of music. They left a legacy that ranges from haunting spirituals to bright and ritualistic dances; from colorful tapestries to beautiful sculpture; from architecture to agricultural techniques.

Some of these slaves became cowboys, Indian fighters, soldiers, sailors, tradesmen, factory workers, domestic workers, and entertainers but most were field workers. Some of their children became congressmen, governors, musicians, authors, poets, orators, inventors, and shop owners although many remained in the fields.

Not all of the first black people from across the Atlantic were slaves. Historians say that Negroes have been in the New World since 1501. At least thirty black people were with Balboa when he discovered the Pacific Ocean, and they helped build the first ships on the Pacific Coast. The most famous of the Black explorers was Estavanico, who was born on the Moroccan coast of North Africa. He was a servant of Dorantes de Carranze, a member of the expedition of Panfilo de Narvaez, who, with a force six hundred strong, journeyed to the New World seeking land and gold. Through desertion, starvation, shipwreck, and Indian attacks, the six hundred men dwindled to eighty and then to only four. Estavanico was one of these four survivors who moved northward from Mexico in search of the legendary Seven Cities of Gold. As they traveled through the country, they became famous for their "mysterious" healing powers. The Seven Cities of Gold were never found . . . only an adobe pueblo. However, Estavanico is credited with discovering New Mexico. Indian legends still tell of the black Mexican who traveled among their tribes, healing the afflicted.

Some of the early Black immigrants were indentured servants, selling their services for a period of years, in return for freedom and a plot of land where they could live and enjoy the same privileges the settlers had. The first wheat crop harvested in the colonies was grown by a Black freedman (a slave who had obtained his freedom) on a piece of land given him when he became free.

Many white people emigrated as indentured servants also; but mainly from Europe. This labor supply was adequate for the small farming, household work, and simple manufacturing in the early colonies. Then it was discovered that the soil in the eastern and southern colonial states was excellent for the growing of tobacco, rice, and indigo (a plant of the pea family from which blue dye, such as that which was used in the Confederate soldiers' uniforms, is obtained). The landowners found there were not enough indentured servants to do the work on the farms, and those who were there left when their periods of servitude were over. The landowners' attempts to enslave the Indians were unsatisfactory inasmuch as the Indians were not physically able to do the heavy work. They would catch white man's illnesses and die; or escape into the woods.

In the meantime, Negro slaves had been bought from traders on the coast. The landowners quickly discovered that such slaves could fill their labor requirements. The black man was strong and healthy; he was generally immune to the fevers common to the South; and he could be found easily because of his color. And last, but not least, he was considered a heathen who should be converted to the church.

IN THE BEGINNING

The first black people who were brought to the colonies as slaves were traded for food by the captain of a Dutch warship anchored at Jamestown, in August of 1619. This trade involved twenty Negroes. Shortly thereafter, the first Negro child was born into slavery in the colonies. He was named William Tucker, in honor of a local planter. By the time the last slave ship delivered its cargo to the United States at Mobile, Alabama in 1859, there had been born into slavery more than 10,000,000 little "William Tuckers."

At the time of the Revolutionary War, many Negroes joined the Continental army and fought against the British. Some of these black people had been brought to the colonies on British slave ships. They fought at Lexington, at Concord, at

Bunker Hill, at Trenton, at Brandywine, and at Saratoga. Two Negroes, Prince Whipple and Oliver Cromwell, were with George Washington when he crossed the Delaware River on Christmas Day, 1776. Tack Sisson actually crashed through a door with his head, enabling the Revolutionary forces to capture a British General at Newport, Rhode Island. Lemuel Hayes, who later became a distinguished minister, joined the brigade which stopped the British forces in the north, at Ticonderoga.

The spying by a Negro soldier named Pompey made possible the victory at Stony Point. Deborah Gannett, disguised as a man and using the name of Robert Shurtliff, served with the Massachusetts Regiment. She performed many official duties and the State of Massachusetts honored her with a resolution that reads: "She discharged her duties as a faithful and gallant soldier." She was issued the same pay as the men who served along with her.

Many Negroes also served in various capacities in the Colonies' first Navy. They were among the crews of the coastal vessels that defended Georgia, the Carolinas, and Virginia. They fought on the Patriot, on the Liberty, on the Tempest, and on the Dragon. Caesar Terront piloted Virginia's vessel, the Patriot, and was cited for his gallantry in action. At age fourteen, James Forten was a powder boy on the Royal Louis, a ship that participated in a victory over several British vessels. He was later captured and the British offered him a home in England along with his freedom. He refused and was finally released to the United States.

A very few of the early slaves were fortunate enough to have an opportunity to learn to read and write. Those who did were generally household servants with masters or mistresses who taught them. Some of these slaves became famous for their literary abilities. The first black author was probably Jupiter Hammon, a slave owned by the Lloyds of Lloyd's Neck, New York. His first published work (1761) was an 88 line poem entitled, "An Evening Thought, Salvation by Christ." He wrote and published many pieces of work, most of which carried an intense religious ferver.

TALENTED CHILD

The second book by an American woman was written by a Negress, Phyllis Wheatley, who was brought to the colonies from Africa with her mother when she was a child. She and her mother were sold separately from the slave block in Boston. John Wheatley, a rich merchant and tailor, saw her standing on the block, clad only in a small cloth, and shivering in the cold wind. Overcome with compassion for this frightened little girl, he bought her and took her home to be a servant girl for his wife. As was the custom, she was given the family name of Wheatley and was christened Phyllis. The kind Mrs. Wheatley taught little Phyllis to read and write. Within a year and a half, she could read the Bible and the classics (the literature of the ancient Greeks and Romans). She was writing her own poetry when she was only 14, and her first published work was a book of poetry entitled *Poems on Various Subjects, Religious and Moral.* Much of her poetry had a religious tone and was dedicated to the era in which she lived and to people who were prominent then. She was a guest of George Washington one time, and she traveled throughout Europe. When her owners, the Wheatleys, passed away, she married a man who was not successful. What money she had earned or inherited from the Wheatleys did not last, and she died in poverty.

A book written by Gustavus Vassa is probably one of the most authentic accounts of the life of a Negro during the period of slavery in the United States. Born in Guinea on the west coast of Africa, he was kidnapped when he was a boy and placed aboard a slave ship headed for the British West Indies. He was sold at a slave auction to a Virginia planter who, in turn, sold him to a sea captain. Vassa spent two years as a slave with the sea captain and was given an opportunity to learn to read and write. At the end of these two years, he was sent to England where he became a household slave in the home of two ladies who insisted he learn to read the Bible. He had many owners over the next several years. Finally he became the slave of a Quaker merchant in Philadelphia, from whom he was permitted to purchase his freedom. In 1789, his autobiography, *The Interesting Narrative of the Life of Olaudah Equiana or Gustavus Vassa,* was published. It is of interest to note that he used his African name, Olaudah Equiana, in the title. This book was so popular that it went through eight printings.

A fight for freedom which went all the way to the United States Supreme Court, and tested the very foundations of the Constitution was waged on behalf of Joseph Cinque, an African prince who was kidnapped and sold into slavery. He was shipped from Africa to Havana, Cuba, where he was purchased by a plantation owner from the island of Principe. Cinque, together with thirty-eight other slaves, was loaded into a vessel for shipment to his new master's home. While the ship was at sea, the slaves worked themselves free of their chains and overpowered the crew. They ordered the captain to take them back to Africa, but the sly man steered the ship in a zigzag fashion and they were not aware that he was not headed for Africa until they landed in the harbor in New York City. Cinque tried to negotiate for passage to Africa for himself and the other thirty-eight black men, but he was unsuccessful. All thirty-nine were arrested and put in prison.

This was one of the first real tests of our laws, and the courts which uphold them. It was to prove that justice does prevail, and that every man has the right to fight in the courts for his freedom. It was a milestone for the black man in the United States.

14

The United States District Attorney for the State of New York declared that Cinque and the thirty-eight other Negroes should be turned over to the Spanish government, which governed Cuba. A committee of Abolitionists (those who were against slavery) took up the cause and filed suit, charging that the thirty-nine Negroes were being held illegally and demanding that they be freed and allowed to return to Africa. The court found in favor of the Negroes. The Justice Department appealed to a higher court and the appeal was denied. Finally, the appeal came before the United States Supreme Court. John Quincy Adams, previously President of the United States, defended the shipboard revolt, citing as his reason the right of every man to be free. The Supreme Court found in favor or Cinque and the other thirty-eight Negroes and permitted them to return to Africa.

The Industrial Age in Europe in the middle of the 18th century resulted in a demand for cotton. With the invention of the cotton gin by Eli Whitney, the southern states could produce enough cotton to ship to the growing European market. Many workers were needed to plant and harvest the crops, and the landowners looked to Africa and the slave trade for their labor supply once again. There followed a period of oppression and depression for black Africans, which was to terminate only with Civil War.

By 1890, the cotton industry had peaked, and farm equipment, had been invented, replaced many workers. The next thirty years saw more than two million Negroes leave the farm areas and migrate to the cities, where they found whatever work they could in factories, shops, stores, and other businesses.

MUSIC

The culture of African immigrants has intertwined with the cultures of immigrants from other lands, and this has enriched the United States through the development of a unique and creative society.

The sad spiritual songs of the slaves, such as Goin' Home and Deep River (these with reference to dying and going to heaven), became popular with the general public and were sung by everyone. The songs of the slaves gradually dropped the religious overtones and became the blues (songs with words that vividly portray sadness and dejection, such as Mood Indigo and St. Louis Blues). With the birth of the blues, the tempo of the music changed, and jazz (music with a fast, syncopated beat) developed. It has been played by orchestras and dance bands, sung by black and white, and danced to by young and old.

There were no musical instruments to accompany the singing of the spirituals by the slaves, as they worked in the fields. However, they made simple drums and oftentimes played these when they sang in the evenings or on Sundays. Eventually the traders brought musical instruments from Africa. Among these were the xylophone, the violin, the zither, the harp, and the flute. Most people believe that the guitar originated in Spain, but historians say an instrument with the features of the guitar was used in Africa as early as 1000 B.C., and that the Moors from North Africa introduced it into Spain during the Middle Ages.

A natural characteristic of the slaves was for them to move their hands, feet, and bodies in accompaniment to the rhythm of the songs. They sang as they worked in the fields, and their work movements followed the tempo of the music. As they sang at their gatherings in the evenings and on Sundays, they kept time to the music by shuffling or moving their feet, swinging their arms, and swaying their bodies. The movements were ritualistic. When the sprirituals evolved into the "blues," these movements became more rapid and, with the introduction of "jazz," there came a great deal of handclapping, quick stamping of the feet, and more vitality in the body movements. Then came Swing, The Jitterbug, Rock and Roll, and the current, very athletic dances that are enjoyed the world over.

The clothing worn by the Africans has found a market in the United States as seen in the Daishiki (a cotton, pull-over shirt in vivid colors made for men, but worn by many women), the Gandura (a full, flowing robe worn by both men and women), the D'Jellaba (a hooded, lightweight garment from Morocco in North Africa), the Caftan (a long tunic worn with a wide belt or girdle), and the Gele (a long piece of material used for a wrap around the head in bandana fashion). Materials with bright colors in tie-die patterns (a sun-burst effect) and silkscreen, as well as hand-blocked motif have become popular.

Beautiful glazed pottery, delicately carved spoons and knives, golden filigree (lockets and other pieces of jewelry made from thin gold wire carefully intertwined into patterns), woven mats and tapestries . . . all of these products have contributed to our pleasure and happiness.

FAUNA AND FLORA

No zoo would be complete without the hippopotamus, the rhinoceros, the zebra, the camel, the giraffe, or the water buffalo, as well as the elephant and the lion . . . always a highlight in our famous circus performances. These animals have been shipped to our shores from Africa and have been a delight to young and old alike.

Their greatest contribution to our after-school crowd has been the peanut butter sandwich. Although Africa did not invent the sandwich, it did introduce to the world the basic product of wheat. The peanut originated in South and Central America, but was carried to Africa by the traders. Later merchants brought harvested peanuts to the colonial states from Africa. It took our combined talents to develop the peanut butter sandwich. They have also provided us with dates (not the Saturday night kind) and various spices.

Although coffee comes to us primarily from Brazil, old legends tell of goatherds in Ethiopia discovering that their herds stayed awake all night after they had eaten the leaves and the berries from certain bushes which grew wild in the fields. Coffee was first used as a food, then as a wine, and even as a medicine before it was used as a beverage. As a beverage, it was introduced into America in the 1600's and has been a principle part of our daily diet since that time.

A small, flowering plant that has given great pleasure to our mothers, our aunts and our grandmothers, is called the African Violet. Although it is not really a violet, it was given that name here in America. This plant, with its delicate pink and violet colored blossoms, grows wild in Africa. It is an indoor plant here in America, and it is so popular that many communities have women's clubs dedicated to the study and raising of different varieties, such as plants whose blossoms have fluted edges, unusual colors, etc.

Many celebrities in the field of sports, as well as in the field of entertainment, have immigrated to the United States. Gary Player, an outstanding golfer, has traveled the golf circuit for some time. Three running champions; Filbert Bayi, Ben Jipcho, and Mike Boyt, emigrated from Kenya.

Rita Hayworth and John Daly are from Johannesburg, South Africa, and have added excitement and flavor to movie and television screens. So have Errol Flynn and Merle Oberon, who emigrated from Tasmania. Omar Sharif is from Alexandria, Egypt and Cyril Cusack and Glynis Johns are from South Africa. Claudia Cardinale is from Tunisia; and that master of mystery and intrigue, Basil Rathbone, who emigrated from South Africa years ago, can still be seen and enjoyed in old movies shown on television. The charm of each of these talents will linger on.

As we look back on history over the past four hundred years, we discover that the African immigrants have left an indelible impression on every facet of life in the United States. I know that many of them look back on those years as a humiliating experience; but each and every one has made a profound contribution to the culture of the United States.

2

AMERICAN INDIANS

by

JOAN S. FOLLENDORE

Without the friendship of the Indians, it is doubtful that the first immigrants from across the Atlantic would have survived.

Columbus really misnamed the Indians. He thought he had gone three-fourths of the way around the world and landed in East India, a part of Asia. But maybe he was only a few thousand years too late for it is said that the first people to migrate to North America were the Indians. They supposedly immigrated at least 10,000 years ago from Asia, crossing over to what is now Alaska and traveling on to settle all over North and South America. These first Indians settled a few here and a few there, because there was so much fertile land. They established a strong farming life without hurting the environment.

One Indian chief said: "We never cut down a tree. Our tribe only used dead branches or trees that had fallen. We found harmony with the natural world. We never killed for sport, only for food, and then we used every part for some necessity, like clothing, utensils, and even the dried skins for our teepees." The United States, the most successful agricultural country in the world, began with the Indians' food growing knowhow; and their willingness to share their knowledge with the strangers who came to live in their land. In the Colorado River valleys, the Indians developed flood farming. The modern application of this is irrigation, and it has revolutionized farming by allowing the production of crops (which could not survive otherwise) in some drier climates.

The Indians used herbs (small plants and roots) for many purposes. They discovered that about two hundred of them, including quinine, made good medicines, many of which are still used today. They taught the early settlers how to use them to cure illnesses. This is a good example of the high development of the Indian civilization, hundreds of years ago. This must be why the familiar Indian greeting "How" developed. Whenever a settler saw an Indian, he must have asked, "How?"

Rubber processing had been developed by the Indians before the Pilgrims arrived, and maple syrup goes back to that time too, thanks to Indian immigrants.

Hiawatha, a 16th century Iroquois Indian chief, is revered by some people today just as others revere Christ, Buddha, or Confucious. The religion of the Indians is as moral, as sacred, and as noble as any in history. Hiawatha is said to have used miraculous powers to protect his people from the evil forces of nature. History tells us that he taught the Iroquois the arts of medicine, farming and navigation.

The late President of the United States, John F. Kennedy, once wrote: "The League of Iroquois [five Indian nations--organized by Hiawatha almost 400 years ago] inspired Benjamin Franklin in his planning the federation of the American States." The principles Hiawatha used in the formation of the League of the Iroquois were used as a model for the Constitution of the United States.

SPORTS AND BALLET

Two Indian superstars in athletics are Charles Bender and Jim Thorpe. Charles (Chief) Bender, a Chippewa Indian, was elected to the National Baseball Hall of Fame in 1953. He was one of the best clutch pitchers the game has seen. His coach, Connie Mack of the Philadelphia Athletics, started him in all five of the World Series the Athletics were in when Chief was with the team.

In 1950, Jim Thorpe, whose mother was a Sauk Indian, was chosen by sportswriters as the greatest male athlete and the outstanding football player of the first half of the 20th century. He played professional baseball as an outfielder and also was an outstanding boxer, wrestler, bowler, swimmer, golfer, and marksman. Incredible!

In the arts, Maria Tallchief, America's first native prima ballerina, is world-reknowned and has stated;

> I've done something for the image of the American Indian, but I don't think of myself that way. My contribution is as a dancer, an American dancer, the first to enter the rarified world of ballet . . . to attain the position I did in that very European world. When I first went to the Ballet Russe (de Monte Carlo), they thought the only thing Americans could do was chew gum. Of course, they didn't know I'd been dancing at Boy Scout benefits and rodeos since I was four. And now I find people who are envious of me as if I never worked for all of this, as if it were something someone handed me.

She feels there is a great need for a high school degree to be offered in the fine arts. She believes that the best way to acquire discipline is through the arts--because of the dedication the arts, through its firm structure, requires of a person.

"Structure gives the only freedom there is. You can only have freedom in structure," she adds.

WILL ROGERS

When you talk about the American sense of humor, a prime example is Will Rogers of Cherokee Indian ancestry who "never met a man he didn't like." I am sure that every man he met felt the same way about him. He brought laughter out of the most serious of listeners by putting a humorous edge on the daily news of one of his country's saddest eras--the great depression of the 1930's. His happy-go-lucky attitude was seen in every area of show business of his time and his "common sense" remarks are quoted to this day. To memorialize his great contribution to the United States, a statue of him stands in the Capitol, Washington, D.C.

One of his timeless ancedotes is:

> If sentiment in November is strong enough against the President, why the other side can nominate Shirley Temple and win with her. In this country people don't vote for--they vote against. You know that. And this year it will be for, or against the President.
>
> The other fellow won't cut any figure, no matter who is running. The whole thing will depend on conditions. If things have picked up, and continue to pick up right up to election time, why, the other party can go ahead and hold that convention, but it will be just for exhibition purposes only.
>
> And they can charge admission, and take the money and send the candidate they nominate on a four-year tour of the world, or something. --June 9, 1935.

MUSIC

"Oscar Pettiford is without doubt one of the greatest bass players in the world," wrote one critic. Born on an Indian reservation, one of twelve children, all with musical ability, Oscar said, "I studied tailoring in case the music business ever got too tough." He was a composer of original jazz numbers, and became internationally famous for his mastery of the bass and cello.

There are many more American Indians who have made lasting contributions to the U.S., like one of the country's most popular blues singers, Mildred Bailey.

Maybe everyone doesn't agree that they should be referred to as "the original immigrants to America," and we surely don't have a record of what they brought with them 10,000 years ago, but that is not important. What is important is that they learned how to live in a new land, and shared that knowledge with new arrivals, thereby saving many lives from the clutches of starvation and exposure to a strange climate.

The Indians continue to give of their talents, and we must give them past due thanks for granting us a legacy of sharing.

3

AUSTRALIA

by

JOAN S. FOLLENDORE

Girls in the early years of the 20th century didn't go swimming. They went bathing. The reason they didn't swim was because the clothes they wore in the water were too bulky and heavy. They consisted of knee-length sailor suits, pleated and belted, of wool material over pleated bloomers of the same heavy wool. Their sailor collars were trimmed with braid and stars. They wore heavy cotton stockings and soft-soled slippers. Their ruffled caps matched their suits. No one could swim in this clothing.

ANNETTE KELLERMANN

When Annette Kellermann went swimming in a one-piece bathing suit that we would call a leotard and tights, cut out at the shoulders to allow her arms to be seen, people were shocked! At that time it was daring to show an ankle.

Annette was an Australian. She was not healthy as a child and her legs were slightly deformed. She corrected this handicap by swimming and diving.

Annette didn't mind that in her revolutionary black swimsuit every line of her figure showed. She was twenty-two when a doctor took her measurements and declared that she was the most perfectly formed woman he had ever seen! She stood five feet, three-fourths of an inch, weighed 137 pounds, had a waist of 26 1/4 inches, and her hips taped at 37 3/4 inches!

She was proud of her figure and posed for many photographs standing poised on the diving board, arms upraised, ready to leap into the water.

Annette made her home in the U.S. for some years. She contributed numerous articles to women's magazines, all telling about the great benefits to be derived from swimming and diving.

Evidently these articles made their impression. The girls discovered that when they removed the pleats and shoes and collars they were more comfortable in the water and instead of just wading around looking pretty, they actually could swim and dive as Annette did!

Annette was a great showperson and gave public demonstrations that brought her money and fame.

She invented formation swimming and trained a group called AquaBelles, pioneers of water ballet as we know it now.

Girls of today, accustomed to the brief, backless one-piece bathing suit and the bikini and the freedom of movement they provide, probably have never even heard of Annette Kellermann. The magazine articles she wrote in 1915, 1917, and 1918 are to be found only in the most complete libraries, and then the pages are musty and likely to be mildewed. Articles published before that time are not even listed in periodical reference books!

Her black-clad figure disappeared from the public scene years ago and the proportions of her body, of which she was so proud, are a thing of the past also. No winner of a Miss America or a Miss Universe contest in the past decade has weighed as much as 137 pounds!

But through her efforts she made women conscious of the beauty of a healthy body and she led the way out of their cumbersome clothing.

In her own way, Annette Kellermann set women free.

Her life story was beautifully shown to the world in the 1953 movie, Million Dollar Mermaid, starring Esther Williams.

It's a long way from Australia to the bikini.

Thank Annette Kellermann for shortening the distance.

Some noted Australian immigrants who are entertainers include: popular singing star, Helen Reddy; fine actor, Cyril Ritchard; and well-known actress, Joan Sutherland.

ELIZABETH KENNY

Sister Elizabeth Kenny left the Australian bush in 1940 hoping to persuade doctors in the United States that their traditional methods of treating infantile paralysis resulted only in crippling and deforming the children.

The title "Sister" is not that of a religious order. It is given to Australian Army nurses and corresponds to the rank of First Lieutenant.

Elizabeth Kenny was born late in the 19th century--at a point in time when society decreed that a woman's place was in the home. Nice girls fainted easily and let men make decisions for them. Queen Alexandra of England had fallen from her horse and broken her hip. The accident left her with a slight limp. Girls of the British Empire copied her walk, feeling that it made them more feminine and queenly. "Down under," this walk was dubbed "The Australian Halt."

Elizabeth Kenny didn't limp. She was a tall, strong girl who had never fainted in her life.

"But my brother Bill was not like me," she recalled in later years. "He was always puny and weak, and he tired so easily that he often had to be carried home from school on an older student's back. Two of my mother's eleven children had died, and we were all worried about Bill."

Elizabeth wanted to help Bill. She read every medical publication she could find that discussed muscles and body structure. She outlined a course of exercises for Bill that he followed faithfully. He became an outstanding young athlete.

Elizabeth was always eager to be of help to others. One year, when she was in her late teens, Australian farms in her community overproduced to such an extent that there was no demand at all for the crops. The farmers were frightened and discouraged. They couldn't pay their bills.

Elizabeth took it upon herself to cure the situation. She sent letters to seventeen supply houses in the nearby city describing the food that was available. Seventeen telegrams came back in reply with so many orders that the farmers couldn't fill them.

The farmers loved Elizabeth, but the young people of the area were furious with her. She had dared to work out a problem herself, instead of giving it to a man to do. She wasn't being womanly. She wasn't "nice."

Hurt and angry, Elizabeth wept. "I'm going to be a missionary and go to India!" she declared.

The family doctor was sympathetic but more practical.

"Our people in the bush need you as much as the Hindu people do," he told her. "Why don't you become a nurse?"

Elizabeth entered a hospital for nurses training and completed the course. Then she spent months delivering babies in the farmlands and treating various illnesses and injuries.

A CRISIS AND A TURNING POINT

When a call came in for help one afternoon from an outlying farm there was nothing to suggest to Elizabeth that this case was to change her life and the lives of thousands of children.

She was simply informed that she was needed. She knew the people who had summoned her. She had delivered their beautiful little daughter two years before and, more recently, their son. The little girl was a special pet of the young nurse.

Elizabeth had not expected to find anything particularly serious when she arrived at the farmhouse.

What greeted her there prompted her to send a rider to the nearest town to telegraph her friend, Dr. Aeneas McDonnel. She had no idea how to cope with what she had found.

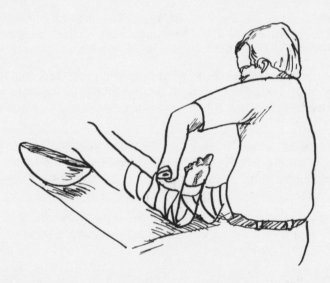

The two-year-old was lying feverishly and in pain, with rigid arms and legs pulled into grotesque positions. Before long the baby boy was afflicted and before day's end four other children needed her help, all suffering with the same terrifying illness. The farmers called it "the cow disease."

Dr. McDonnell wired back promptly and the message brought despair to Elizabeth. He said, "Infantile paralysis. No known treatment. Do the best you can."

Elizabeth remembered what she had learned while she was studying about muscles to help Bill. She saw that the children's muscles were causing the problem. To relax the rigid little limbs and ease the pain she tore woolen blankets into wide strips, wrung them out in hot water, and wrapped them around the small arms, legs, and backs. All six children recovered and their arms and legs resumed their normal functioning.

Dr. McDonnell was so impressed by her success that he urged her to pursue her method and teach it to others.

"But it will take great courage," he warned. "It is going to be a rough, hard road for you!"

Dr. McDonnell was a true prophet. Elizabeth, a mere woman and nurse, was not acting at all as a "nice" girl should.

A HARD ROAD TO SUCCESS

She was snubbed by the medical profession.

"Do you think a nurse is to be allowed to train doctors?" one doctor asked her, angrily.

Perhaps they didn't know that it was Elizabeth who invented what is called "the Sylvia stretcher". She had made it in an emergency when there was an accident involving a little girl she was taking to the hospital. The child's name was Sylvia and use of the stretcher probably saved her life. The stretchers were manufactured and sold, and the profits enabled Elizabeth to set up clinics and nurses training centers.

The group that did not snub her were the parents of children afflicted with infantile paralysis or crippled as a result of inadequate treatment. They brought their little ones to Elizabeth, and the children recovered and walked normally.

Elizabeth's method was proved over and over to be better than the old one of putting splints on the affected arms and legs to try to prevent the muscles from pulling them out of shape. That treatment was painful and did little good.

Because Elizabeth's patients walked after her treatment, the doctors decided that they couldn't have had infantile paralysis, after all, or they would still be crippled.

Doctors excused their mistreatment of Elizabeth by saying that she was cantankerous and that getting along with her was difficult.

"Perhaps I was impatient," Elizabeth admitted, "But it was hard to be calm when the life, health, and happiness of children were at stake!"

Doctors in the United States at first were unimpressed with her work, even when she relieved the most terrifying symptoms of infantile paralysis, sometimes overnight.

One doctor declared, "What is good about the Kenny method is not new, and what is new is not good!"

There were doctors who did not scoff. Dr. Phillip Lewin of Northwestern University, a recognized authority in the medical field said, "The Kenny treatment is one of the most outstanding advances in orthopedic surgery."

Sister Kenny lived and worked in the United States for ten years, but she often felt the need to check on the many Kenny clinics that had sprung up world-wide.

In February of 1950, the House of Representatives voted to allow her to enter and leave the United States whenever she wished without the need of passport, visa, or other official document. She was the only person they had ever given that privilege. It was a salute to her work, making it easier for her to continue it.

Development of the Salk vaccine has practically wiped out infantile paralysis in the United States, and the Kenny clinics have closed.

Sister Kenny's story belongs to history but it is still modern.

Another doctor, Miland E. Knapp, said of her, "She has knocked us so completely out of our complacent groove and thought . . . that some worthwhile advance is bound to result, both from her revolutionary ideas and the frantic efforts of her opponents to oppose them!"

There are hundreds of adults in the United States who owe their health and normal bodies to the care Sister Kenny or someone she trained gave to them as children.

Pioneers today may point to her example and say: "I will have the courage to try a new method. What is new may be good. It may even be better!"

4

AUSTRIA

by

JEANNE PIEPER

How many times have you read Peanuts and seen Schroeder bang out his favorite classical music on his piano or laughed with Lucy when she teased him about his annual birthday party for Beethoven?

When you can read about something in the Sunday comics, you know it has become a vital part of all levels of human life. Even if rock, jazz, or country music is your preference, you have probably at least heard the names of Austria's most renowned gift to the world, her musicians.

We celebrate Beethoven's birthday each year in one of the world's favorite comic strips, Peanuts. Mothers rock their babies to sleep humming a lullaby composed over a century ago by Brahms. Each Christmas we sing "Silent Night" with never a thought of that tiny village in Austria where the carol was composed in 1818.

Today almost every school and community has its own orchestra. Most music students' first faltering lessons include an adaptation of the works of one of the famous Austrian composers: Haydn, Mozart, Beethoven, Schubert, Brahms, Strauss, or one of the many others.

These artists lived and worked in Austria, that tiny Central European land of tall alps and the Danube river. At that time Austria was one of the German States. Now it is a separate country, as small as the state of Maine and less populous than the city of New York. But it is still the land of coffee houses, wine, music, and theaters . . . the city of constant anniversaries, festivals, and celebrations.

MUSIC

The first Austrian immigrants brought with them their love of music and the techniques and special beauty of the musical masters of their land. Not everyone would accept this gift however. The Quakers would not play music at all. The Puritans were only interested in hymns.

33

THE MORAVIAN BRETHERN

By 1741, a group of Central Europeans called the Moravian Brethern, many of whom were Austrians, had settled in Bethleham, Pennsylvania. They immediately began to create a musical life worthy of the Old World. They soon developed orchestras and vocal, instrumental, and chamber music groups to play the works of the Austrian composers. By 1815, Boston had formed a Handel and Haydn Society which began hosting classical music concerts.

At first, the performers were often pushed off-stage by rude shouts from the audience, demanding they play Yankee Doodle and other well-known folk songs, but slowly the "foreign" music won a place in the hearts of the listeners.

Wherever they went, the Austrian immigrants played their native music. Since the Austrians were more interested in blending into the new culture than preserving their old country ways, their musical heritage blended with them. They became conductors, singers, members of orchestras, and organizers of classical music concerts. The United States adopted their musical heroes! Some say that today there is more interest in the United States in Mozart than in the works of any composer, whatever nationality or era!

Austria contributed light music like the operetta and the waltz. The Trapp Family Singers spread Austrian folk songs throughout the United States. George Von Trapp, his Baroness, and their ten children became the most famous musical family in the nation. The play and movie, *The Sound of Music*, was based on the book written by Mrs. Von Trapp about her family. Most of us today know (and often try to sing, if only in the shower!) many of its delightful songs.

Another modern-day musical Austrian immigrant, Frederick Lowe, added the music of his past to the writing skill of his partner from the U.S., Alan Lerner, to give us popular musicals like Brigadoon, Gigi, Camelot, and My Fair Lady. Today Yankee Doodle may still be your favorite, but the gifts of Austria have given all of us a richer life with many more musical options.

PSYCHOLOGY AND SIGMUND FREUD

Besides humorously depicting Schroeder's devotion to his musical hero, Beethoven, the comic strip Peanuts often makes us chuckle over Charlie Brown's problems when Lucy decides to play psychiatrist.

We don't need to rush to the dictionary or the encyclopedia to understand what the comic strip is talking about! Humor probably more than anything else proves that an idea has become an important part of a culture.

A group of college students vacationing at Yosemite are roasting hot dogs (another Austrian invention!) over a campfire. One boy picks up his guitar and begins to sing a folk song:

> Oh Doctor Freud, Oh Doctor Freud,
> How we wish that you'd been differently employed!
> Now the set of circumstances
> Sure enhances the finances
> Of the followers of Dr. Sigmund Freud!

Soon all of them are singing, not realizing that all of their lives have been profoundly affected for the better by the Austrian of their song, Sigmund Freud.

Although Sigmund Freud only visited the United States once, his teaching made a tremendous impact on life in America. Psychoanalysis, Encounter Groups, teenage rap sessions, child raising techniques, the idea of helping rather than punishing criminals, interpretation of dreams, and everyday terms like inferiority complex, wishful thinking, and suppressed desire, all trace back to this intellectual revolutionary.

Freud's theories of the sub-conscious were as major a shift in thought as were the ideas of Copernicus (who theorized that the Sun, not the Earth, was the center of our universe) and Darwin, the evolutionist. Literature, Philosophy, Medicine, Psychology--even how to market and sell a product--there is scarcely a field that has not been influenced by Freud!

Only a few people in the United States became followers of Freud due to his lectures at Clark University (Worcester, Massachusetts) in 1909, and it was not until Hitler outlawed the teaching of Freud's theories, that psychiatry began to assume the importance it has today. Just as the Austrian immigrants taught their new homeland about their beloved music, it was Austrian immigrants who popularized Freud's teachings in the United States.

These learned men and women came by the hundreds during the Hitler years. They encouraged the new Freudian interpretations of drama, biography, and fiction. They wrote scores of books and scholarly papers; became directors of psychological institutes; worked with disturbed children; and gave advice to parents of normal children.

These immigrants were generally more interested in preserving and enlarging upon Freud's theories. The other people in the U.S. were more interested in their practical application. What emerged is a psychoanalysis (Freud's technique for finding out what is in your subconscious) that is so thoroughly Americanized that its effects on U.S. culture are no longer recognizable as a foreign contribution because the ideas of so many different people have been fused so perfectly.

Another part of daily life in the United States which is not thought of as a foreign contribution is the shopping center--large covered groupings of shops with attractive parklike malls. Yet over fifty of these commercial centers, including most of the early ones, were the brainchild of an Austrian immigrant, Victor Gruen.

When he immigrated to the U.S. in 1938, he spoke no English and had only eight dollars in his pocket. But he brought with him a sound architectural background from his home in Vienna. In scarcely a decade, his firm became one of the most influential elements in urban and suburban architecture.

Gruen was not particularly interested in the style or art of one building. He considered the use of the spaces he was creating. He wanted the stores he built to sell goods as well as display them.

Victor Gruen was concerned that the shopping experience be a pleasant and enjoyable one. He encouraged customers out of their cars and into his mall gardens to walk and visit among the shops. He had the vision and courage to try new ideas. Once, when watching the bulldozers break ground on his very first shopping center--which was to be the world's largest one at that time--he turned to his partner and said with a shudder, "My God, we've got a lot of nerve!" That nerve proved to be successful courage. The center sold $78,000,000 worth of goods the first year, more than double what the owners had expected.

Gruen's projects involved him with city planning. His centers needed expressways, parking garages, and efficient ways to move people from their cars to the shops. Many times he designed the suburbs surrounding a shopping center. In these, he included parks and schools, as well as houses. They were total communities where the recreational, medical, and employment needs of many of the residents could be met.

Victor Gruen wrote about his ideas, but mostly he put them into practice. He was a pioneer in environmental architecture. Today almost every suburb has its shopping center, its parklike mall, and its planned community residential tract. Many are copies of Victor Gruen's work--or expansions of his original ideas.

Once again, Austrian artistic sensitivity and idealism combined with the technology, courage, and efficiency of the United States to result in a new way of living for all of us!

SUPREME COURT . . . MOVIES

Many other illustrious Austrian immigrants cannot be forgotten easily. Three are: United States Supreme Court Justice, Felix Frankfurter; Manfred Sakel, father of the insulin shock treatment for the mentally ill; and sociologist, Paul Lazarsfield, whose many, many books have been avidly read by the general public as well as by scholars.

Sometimes referred to as California's greatest architect, Richard Neutra is customarily named among the few pioneers who have changed the architecture of the United States in the 20th century.

Psychologist Bruno Bettelheim is the author of many best-selling books on child care. He writes columns regularly for magazines and newspapers. Probably the best known Austrian name is that of John David Hertz, founder of Hertz Rent-A-Car.

The Austrian immigrants who have made their mark on the entertainment world are too numerous to list entirely. Some of the most well-known are opera's Rudolph Bing; conductor, Erick Leinsdorf; concert pianist, Rudolf Serkin; actor singers, Theodore Bikel and Maria and Maximilian Schell; stage and film star, Walter Slezak; and actresses Hedy Lamarr and Romy Schneider.

Austrian immigrants--contributing their many talents in diverse fields to help make the United States as it is today.

5

BELGIUM

by

JOYCE B. SCHWARTZ

Turn on your television set. Look at your school picture. Play an unbreakable phonograph record. Every time you do one of these things, you are enjoying a product made possible by an immigrant from Belgium to the United States. These Belgian immigrants rank high in importance to the United States, right along with Einstein (Germany) and Marconi (Italy).

Think also of the delectable Belgian Waffle. It too is a contribution from a Belgian immigrant.

A Belgian immigrant helped develop the electric streetcar that did much to determine the present shape of cities and towns. Yet another immigrant felt science should be something every one of us could understand and enjoy. He helped make that a possibility by writing a study relating history and science. Other immigrants were explorers, musicians, and writers. One is considered the Father of the Atlas Missile.

Who are these people who have given so much? And what do we know of the country where they were born and raised?

The cockpit of Europe. What country is that? Belguim, of course. Little Belgium, a corridor fought over and invaded by its neighbors century after century, an independent nation only since 1830, occupied by Germany in both World Wars. Belgium, little larger than the state of Maryland, a strip of territory you can cover in half an hour or less by plane--four or five hours by car. Belgium: a visually varied country from the flat lands of the North Sea--often called the "Coast with the Most"--to the green countryside, and on into the deep green, gold, and mauve of the Ardennes Mountains.

And not only Holland has dikes. They prevent flooding in the low-lying areas of Belgium also. Thickly populated, Belgium, as a map will show you, is bordered by the Netherlands, West Germany, Luxembourg, France, and the North Sea, on which it has a forty-two mile coastline. There are three languages commonly spoken in Belgium: French, German, and Flemish (a variation of Dutch). A large part of the populace speaks more than one of these languages.

39

Living as they do in the heart of Europe, Belgians have been sensitive to artistic influences. Through the centuries their artistic interests have enriched our lives in the fields of painting, music, and literature.

LEO HENDRIK BAEKELAND

Belgian immigrants to the United States have enriched us in other ways as well. When Dr. Leo Hendrik Baekeland discovered Bakelite, the first commercial synthetic resin (plastic), he launched an entirely new industry. His success led chemists to discover many other synthetic plastics, such as Lucite.

Dr. Baekeland received hundreds of scientific honors because he gave man something new. That something was Bakelite, "The King of Plastics." To the Bakelite Corporation, it was "the material of a thousand uses." For us, it is important because with its discovery, we were no longer solely dependent on nature for primary substances, such as stone, wood and metal, for manufacturing. Baekeland put into human hands the ability to create tough, primary materials through chemurgy. The science of Chemurgy, which he studied, makes plastics out of common items such as cottage cheese, starch, or sugar. Chemistry at work.

Born in Ghent in 1863, Leo Baekeland studied chemistry at the University of Ghent. His hobby was photography. In those days, photography was an activity that required much time. Long periods of idle waiting in a pitch-dark room were a nuisance to a young man with two jobs and a girl friend (his chemistry professor's daughter). He began looking for short cuts. The result was his development of a sensitized photographic paper.

Then, in 1887, four Belgian universities awarded the brilliant young chemist a post-graduate traveling fellowship. Two years later, when he was twenty-six, he married and traveled to the United States. He liked the country so well that he decided to remain. Still thinking about the photographic short cut he had found, he went to work for a photographic firm. Shortly afterward, he left to start his own business, the Neperal Chemical Company, in a small laboratory in Yonkers, New York. There he perfected his ideas and revolutionized the art of photography by inventing Velox, a paper which makes possible the quick printing of photographs in artificial light.

But professional photographers would not touch his innovation. Baekeland overcame that obstacle by ignoring the professionals and concentrating on the amateurs. Soon those amateurs were producing better pictures than the professionals, and George Eastman of Eastman Kodak decided to purchase the rights to this new paper.

Having hobbies can pay. There is a story that Baekeland, called to Rochester, New York, for an interview with Eastman, left home determined not to part with his secret for less than twenty-five thousand dollars, and almost fainted when he was offered a million. It is fact that in 1899 he received enough money to feel that he would be financially independent for life. He put it this way: "At thirty-five I found myself in comfortable financial circumstances, ready to devote myself to my favorite studies. Then truly began the happiest days of my life."

GUNKS?

His favorite studies concerned the unattractive plastic mixtures which organic chemists threw out because they formed a gummy mess that wouldn't crystallize or dissolve. Laboratory assistants cleaning these sticky messes out of flasks and tubes called them gunks.

It was these gunks that interested Baekeland. He began the happiest days of his life by producing one of these chemical failures. He was trying to discover the secret of a little red bug called *Laccifer Lacca* which, about a fortieth of an inch long and resembling an apple seed, produces lac from which shellac is made. It was important to Baekeland to learn how this small bug sucked the sap out of trees and converted it into an overcoat for itself.

Baekeland's idea was that the red bug's secret would provide a clue to the mysterious chemistry by which Nature makes resins--such as rosin, copal, and shellac--and the waxes of animal, vegetable, and mineral origin.

He combined two chemicals (phenol and formaldehyde) and got a gunk. But he wanted this gunk. He tried to control the reaction of the two substances. It didn't work. He tried to crystallize the gunk they formed. He failed. He tried every solvent he could think of, but the gunk wouldn't dissolve. When he tried heating the mass, hoping it would melt, it became harder and harder instead. Then, looking at the shapeless lump, he was inspired by his curiosity. Would that mass, he wondered, have value as a plastic?

He began to study the field of plastics, beginning with a study of glass, that man-made primary material whose inventor's name was never recorded. He discovered a report from Africa about a shortage of elephants in the jungle, especially those with tusks more than two and seven-sixteenths inches in diameter from which billiard balls were made. And an offer of $10,000 to anyone who could produce a substitute for ivory billiard balls. "What could he substitute for ivory to produce a billiard ball?" he wondered.

Baekeland studied and experimented. He realized how useful his gunky substance might be if only he could find a way to shape it.

Shape it he did. For after months of hard work, Baekeland discovered that he could mold the material into anything he wanted if he did so while it was still hot and soft.

Proudly the scientist invited a friend into his backyard laboratory. There he displayed a set of billiard balls which he had made out of the terrible stuff that had so annoyed chemists. One by one he dropped the balls on the floor, counting the rebounds. Then he dropped a set of ivory balls to prove that the balls he had developed were even springier than balls made of ivory. Next he pulled a phonograph record out of a cabinet, played it, then, laughing, tossed it on the floor. His scientist friend cried out, then stared in wonder when he realized the record had bounced but had not broken.

Imagine how thrilled Dr. Baekeland must have been. And although he had never patented his Velox paper because he thought lawsuits would be too expensive, he learned from that mistake. He protected his Bakelite process which he came out with in 1909 with four hundred patents. There were lawsuits in the courts for years. But when it was ruled that his rights to the process were basic, he approached those who had been suing him, told them not to try to figure out what they owed him, and asked that they join his company because, as he said, "This is a field that is going to require the brains of all of us."

The result was the Bakelite Corporation (which later became a subsidiary of Union Carbide Corporation) of which he was president until he retired in 1939. That company's rapid rise coincided with the quick growth of the automobile and electric industries. Baekelite is used to make everything from radio cases, to airplane propellers, to jewelry. Because it is a highly efficient insulating material, it has played an important role in the development of radio and other electrical communication tools of the 20th century.

GEORGE SARTON

Not all immigrants founded powerful corporations. Do you remember the story of the falling apple that knocked the idea of gravity into Sir Isaac Newton's head? The story is probably untrue, but none of us can forget that what goes up, comes down.

There was a young Belgian who thought science should be taught through history. In the days before World War I, as a young student in Belgium, George (Alfred Leon) Sarton decided to write a book about how science developed. He felt it would take only a few years but soon realized it was more than one person's lifework.

Born in Ghent in 1884, Sarton credited his father for some of his achievements because his father had insisted above all, on honesty, tolerance, and freedom. Also because his father had interfered very little with the development of his thoughts.

Sarton began his university studies in philosophy but soon abandoned them in disgust. He was more interested in the natural sciences. But the more he studied, the more drawn he became to the history and philosophy of science. *Isis*, a journal he began publishing in 1912, was devoted to that topic.

In the same year he began to collect notes for his *Introduction to the History of Science*. The work grew and grew. Dr. Sarton originally thought that a single book would be enough to cover the whole development of science. He was mistaken. The first 2,142 pages carried the story only to the end of the 13th century.

From the age of twenty-three, Dr. Sarton realized that the purpose of his life was largely determined. That purpose was to establish the history of science as an independent discipline, comparable to other scientific disciplines. Quite a road to choose. Especially when only 23 years old.

By this time, Dr. Sarton was married to Eleanor Mabel Elwes and had a daughter (Eleanor May, the poet and novelist May Sarton). But for all of his single-minded planning, his carefully begun historical studies were interrupted while he lived history instead. World War I erupted and Belgium was invaded. German officers made the Sarton home their headquarters. Dr. Sarton and his family left at once for England, and then moved to the United States.

Like so many other immigrants, Dr. Sarton and his family arrived in New York without money and without prospects. The next three years were difficult. But these difficult times ended when Sarton was chosen to be a research associate by the Carnegie Institution of Washington. From then on, he devoted a great deal of time to his studies. He lectured at many major universities, continued his writing, and for forty years edited the international review, *Isis*. He founded a second journal, *Osiris*, which published longer papers on the history and philosophy of science.

Later, a revised edition of his book, *The History of Science and the New Humanism*, was published. One reviewer said: "Books of this sort, in which an attempt is made to further the bringing together of what we know into a vision of life, are badly needed in our time."

It seems strange that Sarton is the man who is said to have abandoned the study of philosophy because he thought his real interest was in the natural sciences. Or perhaps he had been more deeply impressed by his earlier philosophical studies and his family's influence than he was aware.

But Sarton, like Baekeland, gave us something new, something important. His lifework led to a rethinking of the way science was taught. Courses began to be planned through the historical approach, picking out a few trends in science on which there was enough historical information to provide a continuous story. One of these showed that the scientific discovery that air had weight and pressure, led first to the development of vacuum pumps, and then to the invention of the barometer, which is used to measure atmospheric pressure, an important parameter in weather forecasting.

Sarton's basic idea that the historical story of science's growth is one of drama and importance to us all is the contribution for which he is most remembered. In today's jargon, he made science relevant.

There are many other important contributions by Belgian immigrants to the United States.

Father Louis Hennepin, a missionary, joined tha La Salle expedition bound for the source of the Mississippi. At one point Father Hennepin left La Salle and with a few companions discovered a long stretch of that great river. He was also the first European to sketch Niagara Falls. A book he wrote describing the Upper Mississippi Valley was the first travel book to fire European imaginations with stories of North America's great forests, wide plains, huge rivers, and colorfully-painted Indians.

Another missionary, Jesuit Father de Smet, made the final peace with the Indian chief Sitting Bull. He established many missions and was one of the outstanding pioneers of the 19th century American frontier.

FROM TROLLEY CARS TO MISSILES

It was the possibilities he sensed in electricity that made Charles J. Vandepoele a pioneer. An immigrant from Lichtervelde, in 1888 he invented the carbon brush which improved the efficiency of the electric generator. But more importantly, he demonstrated that electric transportation (trolley cars), operated either by street-level cables or overhead power, could work. Within a few years, electric streetcar systems that he had designed were installed in more than a dozen cities around the country.

Think of the shape of a starfish. The electric streetcar caused that shape in many towns and cities. Wherever the streetcars ran; parks, amusement centers, shopping areas, and houses spread out to a depth of three or four blocks. Lines radiating out of the old compact area caused the starfish population pattern. At distances far from the streetcar lines, the land remained undeveloped.

Times were right for those new urban transport vehicles. Then, as now, cities were bursting at the seams. Today, the possibility of inadequate gasoline supplies for the automobile may mean new growing pains for public transportation.

A much more rapid form of transportation owes much to Karel Bossart. Born in Antwerp in 1904, Bossart has been called the Father of the Atlas Intercontinental Ballistic Missile. He studied at Brussels University and at the Massachusetts Institute of Technology. As a project engineer for the study and development of a missile with a 5,000 mile range for Convair, Bossart managed to persuade that company to continue working on missiles, even after the Air Force lost interest. When the government decided to speedup work on missiles, Bossart and his team were ready. They designed and constructed the first intercontinental missile research vehicle in the world that could go faster than the speed of sound. This missile was the first successfully tested post-war supersonic rocket in the United States.

For many centuries the Belgians have been known not only for their technical skills but for their artistry in cooking and baking. Distinctive baking has been one of the leading family crafts handed down from generation to generation.

For hundreds of years, back to the 14th century, the Belgian Waffle, light, high, and crisp, has been a delicacy in Belgian homes and inns. The Van Belgian Waffle is said to go back to 1400 when the Van clan were gypsies. In those days, the women would set up fire pits on the church steps and sell their waffles.

Today, Pilou Horlander, a descendant of those Van waffle vendors, is still selling waffles. She is President of Van's Belgian Waffle, Incorporated, and has California shops in Redondo Beach and San Pedro.

"When I look back on my life," she says, "I think a woman is really something. Look what a woman can do if she takes advantage of what she has."

The petite, dynamic Mrs. Horlander is quick to point out that life in the United States has provided her with more complete personal happiness than she has known before. She goes about her life, that of being a wife, mother, and businesswoman, with confidence. She has seen hard times, but she has turned those hard times to her advantage, learning from them the ability to cope with life's difficulties.

The hard times she has been through stretch back to World War II when Belgium was invaded and she suffered from malnutrition because of food shortages.

Her experience with suffering also includes more than ten years in the Belgian Congo while that country traveled a long, bloody road to independence. There too, she discovered no magic shield to protect her from the violence surrounding her.

She treats the stability she has found in the United States like an unexpected treasure. "Americans are so protected," she says. "They don't realize how fortunate they are not to have lived under conditions outside their control."

Pilou's adjustment to conditions in her newly adopted country did not happen overnight. Working was the solution to her feeling of isolation. She needed a way to meet people, and the waffle shop and bakery idea was her solution. "I also wanted to provide something of quality from Europe that could be accepted in America," she explains.

After the 1964 New York World's Fair, which introduced the Belgian Waffle to the United States, Pilou started research and development work to adapt the waffle to the American market. She also felt that people in the U.S. were ready for the crepe (a thin pancake) and developed a dry mix from which both the waffle and the crepe could be made.

Her business began as a struggle with long hours and high expenses. Her husband, Doug, provided both financial and moral support. Then delighted customers spread the word, and her clientele and business grew.

The Van Belgian Waffle is said to be baked from the original family formula, which gives it an unusually crisp but tender texture. This formula is kept as a zealously guarded secret. It is said to contain special ingredients imported from Belgium which are not available in the United States. This waffle mix is a dry mix. The waffle itself is seven inches long, four inches wide, and an inch thick, a giant compared to the average American waffle. Traditionally, the waffles are made in

46

large-grooved waffle irons imported from Belgium.

Here is a recipe for one version of the Belgian Waffle, much like the restaurant version but using a liquid mix. You may use any waffle iron to prepare it.

1 3/4 Cup flour
1 Tblsp. sugar
1 Egg
1 1/2 Cups light beer
1/4 Cup oil
Vanilla extract to taste

Combine flour, sugar, egg, beer, oil, and vanilla in a mixing bowl and mix to a smooth paste. Allow to stand at room temperature at least two hours or overnight in the refrigerator. Grease waffle iron generously, warm it, and spread with a thin layer of batter. Bake until golden brown. Serve with sprinkled confectioner's sugar or top first with whipped cream then sprinkle with sugar. Makes about eight waffles.

There are many other Belgian contributions and contributors to the United States.

Maurice Maeterlinck wrote many books and poems with dreamy subjects and moods. He was concerned with the mystery of human life and the struggles people have within themselves. He also wrote studies on flowers and animals. Known for his mystical writing, he received the Nobel Prize for literature in 1911.

"It is surprisingly easy to persist in overlooking the simply obvious," Father Julius Arthur Nieuwland said when honored by the American Chemical Society. This unassuming, Belgian born, Indiana bred, scientist-priest graduated from the University of Notre Dame in 1899 and was a professor there from 1904 until his death in 1936. He discovered the chemical reaction which is essential in the production of neoprene, a synthetic rubber which was crucial to the United States during the terrible shortages of World War II.

47

Desire Defauw was born in Ghent. He entered the Ghent Conservatory when he was eight years old to study the violin, because, as he said, "I already know the piano." He became both a violinist and a conductor, with the NBC Symphony Orchestra and the Chicago Symphony Orchestra having been under his baton.

Another Belgian immigrant, Georges Simenon, is famous for his detective stories, especially the series about Inspector Maigret.

Beckoned by stimulating career opportunities and individual freedom, the talented Belgian immigrants have contributed much. The U.S. is certainly fortunate to have had the creative environment that attracted them. They too must have felt fortunate to have been welcomed to a land where they could see their ideas, innovations, and the new tools they forged, lead to the growth of their new country.

6

BULGARIA

by

VIRGINIA STEVENSON

The flow of immigrants from Bulgaria began during the second half of the 19th century. By 1918, there were Bulgarian colonies in some of the central and eastern states. Many of these steady, hardworking people found jobs on railroads, building lines that connected east and west.

Some became farmers in New Mexico and some went to Utah, Texas, Michigan, Montana, and Oklahoma, where they founded small businesses such as general stores. The general store, in former times, was the place where farmers met to gossip and exchange news.

Even though the total number of Bulgarian immigrants to the United States is not large, there have been a surprising number of learned people in the group. For example: Dr. Radoslav A. Tsanoff, Professor of Philosophy at Rice University in Houston, Texas for many years; Vangel K. Sugareff, who became a Professor of History at Texas A & M; George Dimitroff, who was in charge of the Harvard Observatory 1937-1942; and Professor Ivan Dosseff, who was on the faculty of Engineering at the University of Minnesota.

Stoyan Christowe wrote many stories and articles for leading magazines, as well as several books about his homeland.

Agop Agopoff, a New York sculptor, won several first prizes in the American Academy of Design. He created the well-known bust of Will Rogers. Rogers, from Claremore, Oklahoma, was a popular movie star, newspaper columnist, and humorist of the 1930's.

Assen Jordanoff made a name for himself as an outstanding expert in aeronautical engineering. He wrote many books on aviation. His books were bought in large numbers by the governments of the United States, England, Australia, and Russia.

One of the reasons for the founding of coffee houses, which were popular in the United States for many years, was to meet the tastes and habits of the Bulgarians who did not use intoxicating drinks the way some other groups did.

7

CANADA

by

J. H. JACK KIMBERLY

Vilhjalmur Stefansson. Arctic explorer. His life's work made him a legend in his own time. He disproved the theory that the Arctic would not support human life. He proved that a person can survive in the Arctic by living off the land--if he chooses to live as the Eskimo lives. He led a five-year-long expedition, living above the Arctic Circle the entire time. He found the Eskimo to be friendly and happy despite living in what seems to be a hostile environment. An Eskimo will laugh more in one month than a white man will in a whole year. If living in the Arctic is so tough, why are these people so happy? They are healthy and the road to happiness is through health.

Vilhjalmur Stefansson was explaining the nature of the moon's surface to a group of Eskimos. "How do you know this is to be true?" they asked. He explained that by looking through a telescope as long as a ship's mast, people could see the moon's surface. "Has the white man ever walked on the moon?" they asked. The answer was "No" because this was before the Apollo 11 mission in 1969. The Eskimos believe that their ancient ancestors walked on the moon. "How can the white man be so well informed, since he has not walked on the moon?" they countered. The Eskimos' ancestors, all truthful men, had walked on the moon and had seen everything. They came back and told about it. Why do these people believe their ancient ancestors walked on the moon? Is it possible that these people actually came from outer space and that this story has been handed down through the eons to the present generation--or is it just another mystery of the North?

The Eskimos believe in the spirit world--the spirits of the polar bear, the caribou, the seal--all animals. They believe that man's spirit is separate from his body. The spirit of the most recently dead relative will join the spirit of the next newborn baby. The spirit will act as a guardian angel for the life of the child. The spirit of the newborn is inexperienced--it needs the guidance of the older spirit to help it through life. Eskimos who convert to Christianity still keep many of their old beliefs and taboos. They love Sunday because it is a day of rest. They say the white man has given them one day a week to relax. They may break all the other nine of the Ten Commandments, but they will smile and say, "We are Christians, we don't work on Sunday."

MYSTERIOUS DISAPPEARANCE

Vilhjalmur Stefansson tells of many mysteries of the North. A Greenland colony, nine thousand Europeans, simply disappeared into thin air. There is evidence that they were farmers. In a single barn, stalls had been dug into the ground for as many as one hundred and four cows. By doing this, colonists were able to use the warmth in the soil to keep the animals from freezing to death during the cold Arctic winter. There is also evidence of horses, sheep, pigs, and fowl. The houses were small because there was a lack of timber for building and heating. The last recorded document found at the settlement was one written by Pope Alexander VI, in 1492. Where did these people go? The mystery remains. Did they melt into the Eskimo population and, like Vilhjalmur Stefansson, live in the Arctic as the Eskimos live? Could this account for the blond Eskimos discovered by Vilhjalmur Stefansson on Victoria Island? This too will remain a mystery.

It is interesting to note that men who spend time in the Arctic are always eager to return. There is a great fascination in a land that has a three-month-long night. The Eskimos store ample food for this long night. It is a time for rejoicing, feasting, dancing, visiting friends, and just having a good time.

Vilhjalmur Stefansson believed in the North. Food can be produced in abundance because the tundra soil is rich and fertile--so fertile that plants grow as much as an inch a day during the short growing season. The huge herds of caribou can be somewhat domesticated as the Laplanders have demonstrated in their polar regions of Russia and Finland. Coal has been found on Amund Ringnes Island, on Melville Island, at Peddie Point, on Lougheed Island, and on Banks Island.

Vilhjalmur Stefannson was a consultant for Pan American Airways in the planning of their polar flight route across the Arctic. During World War II, he was an adviser to the United States Government. His duties included training U.S. troops in Arctic survival. In 1947, he became Arctic consultant to the Northern Studies Program at Dartmouth College, which now owns his famous collection of books and materials on the Arctic. He wrote a number of interesting books on the Arctic, four of which are: *The Friendly Arctic, My Life with the Eskimo, Unsolved Mysteries of the Arctic,* and *Cancer, The Disease of Civilization.*

JAMES NAISMITH

Two peach baskets and a soccer ball were the humble beginnings of Basketball. At first it was played with nine men on each side, and the ball was called the Naismith Ball. Since then, Basketball, like the U.S., has grown into mind boggling proportions. Little did James Naismith know that his brain child would grow and grow until it encompassed the entire world, nor that professional basketball players would be paid millions of dollars each year to play the game.

More than twenty million people throughout the world play basketball today. The number grows each year. In the words of its creator, James Naismith: "It is easy to play, yet very difficult to play perfectly." One must be agile and quick thinking, have the old team spirit, and be in good physical condition to play basketball well. The popularity of the game grew quickly. A few people; a peach basket; and a game is underway.

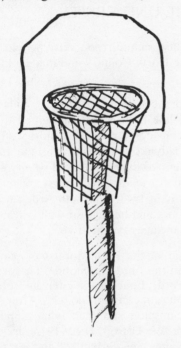

James Naismith took the game west to Denver, Colorado, where he enrolled as a medical student and graduated in 1898 with a degree in medicine. In 1916, he was stationed on the Mexican border as Chaplain of the First Kansas Infantry Regiment. He then served in France during the remainder of World War I.

He was a great believer in physical fitness, and wrote a number of books, including *The Basis for Clean Living.* He was also author of: *The Rules of Basketball,* a section on physical fitness in *The Modern High School,* and many magazine articles on physical fitness. He was Honorary President of the Basketball Coaches Association of America and Honorary Chairman and a life member of the Basketball Rules Committee. Naismith was often the guest of honor at basketball tournaments in the United States and Canada.

It is rare indeed that a man lives to see one of his creations gain world-wide recognition during his lifetime, but at Berlin, Germany, in 1936, Naismith attended the first basketball game played in Olympic competition.

James Naismith: Author, University Professor, Minister, Medical Doctor--a man of many talents. A salute goes to James Naismith, The Father of Basketball-an immigrant from Canada who gave the United States and the World--basketball.

FROM MAKE-UP TO THE UNIVERSITY

Canada is rich in natural resources. It is also rich in resourceful people. Here are only a few who have left their homes in the North Country and made a life and a name for themselves in the United States.

Elizabeth Arden. Businesswoman. A pioneer in ladies beauty aids. She produced a fluffy face cream and a cosmetic line that in time amounted to over three hundred items. Facial make-up was not considered proper by most women at that time. She gave the cosmetic industry a ladylike image and was the first to advertise ladies' make-up. Elizabeth Arden operated over a hundred beauty salons around the world. She was also one of the nation's leading race horse owners. Jet Pilot, a colt she raised, won the Kentucky Derby in 1947. Elizabeth Arden was the best advertisement for her beauty aids. She concealed her age so well that no one knew how old she was until her death in 1966, at the age of eighty-two.

James Couzens. The first general manager of the Ford Motor Company. In 1903, he invested twenty-five hundred dollars in the Ford automobile. He resigned in 1915, after a disagreement with Henry Ford. Four years later he sold his interests in the Ford Motor Company for twenty-nine million dollars. After being Chairman of the Detriot Street Railway Commission and then being appointed Police Commissioner, he was elected Mayor of Detroit (1919-1922) by large majorities. He was appointed to the United States Senate in 1922 and elected to full terms in 1924 and 1930. He donated twelve million dollars to the Childrens Fund of Michigan and two million dollars to the Childrens Hospital in Detroit.

Alfred Carl Fuller started as a door-to-door brush salesman. He started his own business and built it into a multimillion dollar corporation. He made special brushes at night and sold them door-to-door in the daytime. he believed in giving people value for their money. Other products were added to the brush line and backed by a reputable company. The next time a Fuller Brush Man comes to your door, you will know who Fuller was and how his business began and prospered. The Fuller Brush Man is an independent agent selling Fuller products on a commission basis--the more he sells, the more money he makes--and that's how Alfred Carl Fuller wanted it.

John Cantius Garand developed the M-1 rifle used so effectively by the United States Army during World War II. He was appointed a consulting engineer at the United States Armory in 1919. Fifteen years later he patented the M-1, a semiautomatic rifle that was light enough to be carried easily by soldiers. Garand received no royalties for the millions of these rifles manufactured because he signed his patents over to the government. He remained a consultant at the Springfield Armory until he retired in 1953. John Garand gave freely of his time and energy because of his patriotism for his adopted country.

S.I. (Samual Ichye) Hayakawa. His actions and personal courage became well known when he took over as Acting President of San Francisco State College in the midst of a student strike. With dedication and outspoken courage, he quelled the riots at San Francisco State College.

THE WORLD OF ENTERTAINMENT

The entertainment world is generously sprinkled with Canadian immigrants.

Guy Lombardo and his orchestra, The Royal Canadians, have been giving us beautiful music since 1924. This group has probably endured more successfully than any of the big bands--through the blues, country-western, jazz, bebop, swing, cha-cha-cha, calypso, and rock. People love to dance to Lombardo's music, the same soft danceable music he has played for half a century. At the 1975 New Years Eve party, 625 couples paid $210 each to spend the evening listening and dancing to Guy Lombardo's music at the Waldorf Astoria's Grand Ballroom. New Years Eve with The Royal Canadians has become a tradition in the United States. Their famous "Auld Lang Syne" has rung the New Year in since 1929. The Royal Canadians has been around longer than any of the big bands and enjoyed success on radio and television and in films. They have been playing "The Sweetest Music This Side of Heaven" for more than fifty years.

Mary Pickford. Actress. Her youthful, innocent beauty, her tiny figure, and her golden hair endeared her to the public and earned her the title, "America's Sweetheart." She won the Academy Award for Best Actress in 1929 for her performance in Coquette. After starring in many famous films, she retired in 1932.

Walter Huston. Actor. He had many hits in vaudeville. His performance in Dodsworth won him the New York Film Critics' Award. He became well known in films throughout the years. His performance in The Treasure of Sierra Madre won him the Academy Award for Best Supporting Actor in 1948. His son John has become an accomplished director.

Marie Dressler. Actress. At the age of fourteen she left home and joined a theatrical company touring the United States. She appeared in Mack Sennett films and became a well-known star through the years. She reached the peak of her career after reaching the age of sixty when she became a number one box office performer. Marie Dressler starred in many films and in 1931, she won the Academy Award for her role in Min and Bill, which co-starred Wallace Beery in 1931.

Mack Sennett. Actor and director. He was the originator of slapstick comedy. He produced the first feature-length comedy. He then opened his own studio, The Keystone Company. One of his best known creations was The Keystone Cops, crazy police who ran helter-skelter across the screen. People laughed until tears ran down their cheeks. The first pie-in-the-face was a custard pie flung into the face of Ben Turpin under Sennett's direction. Mack Sennett's studio turned out over a thousand comedy films. He gave us millions of laughs for many years. The Keystone Cops and Charlie Chaplin comedies may still be seen from time to time on television.

Lorne Greene. Actor. He is best known for his role as Ben Cartwright of Bonanza fame. This show, for fourteen years, brought wholesome, exciting entertainment to children of all ages.

Monte Hall. This well known master of ceremonies on the long running Let's Make A Deal is reputed to have been kissed by more women than any other man in the world.

Rich Little. Actor, impressionist, and comedian. His impersonations of well-known actresses, actors, and public figures have endeared him to the public. His portrayal of former President Nixon is one of his best impersonations.

Rod Cameron. Actor. He has starred in many films and is best known for his strong he-man roles in Western movies.

Gezelle McKenzie. Singer and actress. She has thrilled millions of Americans with her beautiful voice. She has starred in films and television and always puts on an entertaining show.

One of the most talented songwriters and singers of this generation is Paul Anka. He and his music are familiar all over the world as well as in his native land of Canada.

There are many, many, more great entertainers, too numerous to mention here. A salute goes to all these fine entertainers--immigrants from Canada.

SPORTS

John Longdon. Jockey, horseman, and multimillionaire. As a boy, he fell in love with pictures of race horses and through hard work and dedication became one of the world's greatest jockeys. The horses he rode won over $24,000,000 in purses. He won 6032 races during his career. He rode in 32,406 races and at one time or another won every major race in the country at least once. In 1943, he won the jewel of racing, The Triple Crown, with Count Fleet, considered by Johnny to be one of the greatest horses of all time. On April 4, 1966, he rode his last race in competition, winning the San Juan Capistrano Stakes with George Royal--a great way to end a brilliant riding career. John Longdon then turned his talents to training race horses. With Majestic Prince, he came very close to winning racing's Triple Crown as a trainer. Majestic Prince took the Kentucky Derby and The Preakness, but ran second to Arts And Letters in The Belmont. Johnny Longdon sums up his feelings about his adopted country--the land of opportunity: "I was never afraid of hard work. This is the best country in the world. There are so many opportunities. People don't seem to take advantage of them. You might not be the best but you can be among the best."

BUSINESS

Cyrus Steven Eaton. Financier and Industrialist. After being graduated from McMaster University in Canada, he returned to Cleveland, Ohio, where he had earlier worked as a clerk for John D. Rockefeller. He acquired interests in various power companies and banks, and formed the Republic Steel Company which grew to be the third largest steel company in the United States. His skills and talents have been displayed throughout the years in his work as director/chairman of the board for a number of companies (including Republic Steel). To honor his birthplace, Pugwash, Nova Scotia (known to local residents as Dogbath), he organized the Pugwash Conference, a meeting of scholars and intellectuals from around the world who gather in order to help improve international relations.

James Jerome Hill. Railroad magnate. He and three Canadian partners bought the St. Paul & Pacific Railroad which had been in receivership for five years. He reorganized and rebuilt it into the St. Paul, Minneapolis, and Manitoba Railway Company and became its president. A few years later, he brought together several small railroads which extended all the way to Seattle, Washington. Hill's personal supervision of the company's operation made it the most profitable and successful of all the transcontinental systems. He and his associate, the powerful J. P. Morgan, acquired a large interest in the Northern Pacific Railway and the Chicago, Burlington, & Quincy Line. Hill had mining interests including the Mesabi iron ore development in Minnesota. A great organizer, he began as a clerk in a store and worked there for four years. He then went on to become one of the richest men in the United States.

Willaim Sowden Sims. Commander of the United States fleet in European waters during World War I. He wrote a book on navigation that was used for years by the Navy and Merchant Marine. He was Naval Attache at Paris and Leningrad

(1897-1900) and when he returned to sea duty, he became convinced of the inferiorty of the U.S. Navy, despite its victories in the Spanish American War. He met Captain Percy Scott of the British Royal Navy. Scott had developed a new continuous-aim fire technique for ships fighting a sea battle. Sims was convinced that this new method should be adopted by the United States Navy and he wrote several letters to the Navy Department urging improvements in naval gunnery. His letters being ignored, he then wrote directly to President Theodore Roosevelt. Sims was brought to Washington and served as naval aide to the President (1908-1909). His efforts brought about many changes and improvements in naval ship design and battle procedures. He is credited with being the most powerful and influential officer in the history of the United States Navy. In 1920, he wrote *The Victory at Sea* with Burton J. Hendrick, winning the Pulitzer Prize for history.

CHEMISTRY

Herbert Henry Dow. Chemist and industrialist. The Father of Creative Chemistry. Through his tireless efforts, he did more than any other man to make the United States independent of other countries for a supply of chemicals. Herbert Dow's life was not easy. Despite many failures and adversities, he persevered until he achieved success. Because of his youthful appearance when he was in his early twenties, he wore a big mustache so that investors would feel that he had the maturity and ability which would be needed to make a profit with their investments.

Prior to his entry into the chemical field, most chemicals were imported from Europe and sold on the market at exorbitant prices. He invented an electrolytic process to extract many chemicals from brine (salt water). He developed the first process to extract iodine from ocean water. He mass-produced many chemicals such as bromide, chlorine, and synthetic indigo at a fraction of the cost of their European counterparts. He added bleaching powder, insecticides, pharamaceuticals, and other chemicals to his line of products.

With his special electrolytic process, he extracted magnesium from brine, alloyed it with steel, and chose the trademark Dowmetal. He patented over one hundred chemical formulas. He received one of the highest honors in the field, The Perkin Medal For Chemical Achievement.

Failure was not in Dow's make-up. The word "can't" did not exist in his world. When an experiment did not work, he would analyze the problem, try to determine just why it had failed, and start all over again. He made a number of unsuccessful attempts at business before making it with the Dow Chemical Company, which became one of the giants in the industry. Dow chemicals are widely used in oil refining. Herbert Dow succeeded by hard work, a deep-rooted belief in himself, and a refusal to accept defeat.

Joseph Medill. Editor and publisher. He is credited with the reorganization of the old Whig party which had lost its effectiveness because its members were fighting among themselves. He renamed it the Republican Party and succeeded in bringing the warring factions together to spearhead the election of Abraham Lincoln. He was elected Mayor of Chicago after he acquired the controlling interest in the Chicago Tribune.

The Medill School of Journalism was established at Northwestern University in his memory.

BONES AND HEALTH

Daniel David Palmer. Founder of Chiropractic. He was born on a farm and apparently had little formal education. Not much is known of his early life. He became interested in Osteopathy after the death of his wife.

He believed that if bones of the skeleton, in particular the back vertebrae, were out of line, pressure would be exerted on the spinal column, and that this could bring on nervous tension. Eventually the strain of any bone being out of line would drain the body of energy and resistance. The body would then become more susceptible to disease. By realigning the displaced bone, the body would regain its strength and heal itself.

Daniel Palmer combined two Greek words: "cheir" meaning hand and "praktikos" meaning practical. He blended these two words into Chiropractic--"done by hand."

At one time he went to jail for six months for practicing medicine without a license. Undaunted by the jail term, he started the Palmer School of Chiropractic. He wrote three books including a textbook on Chiropractic which attacked practitioners of medicine for not accepting his ideas. After his death, his sons, Bartlett and David Daniel, took over the school, and it flourished despite opposition from the medical profession.

Today, tens of thousands of Chiropractors are licensed in the United States, Canada, and around the world. Although the equipment and methods are greatly improved, the basic formula is much the same: "Find the cause and the body will heal itself."

Once again a man and his beliefs had triumphed over adversities, and a new profession was born.

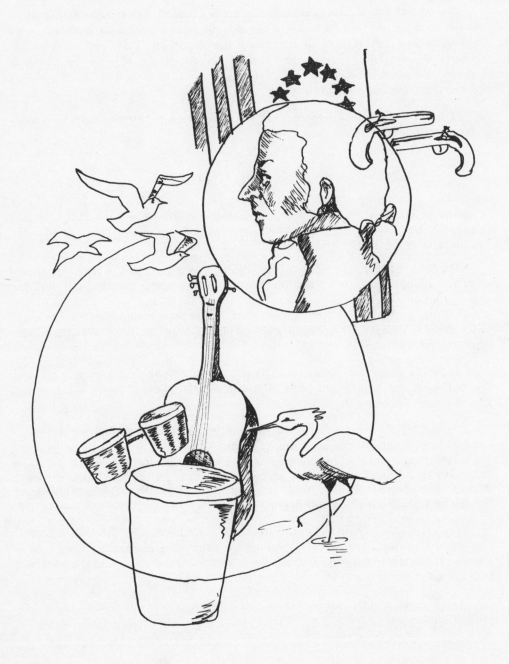

8

THE CARIBBEAN

by

HOWARD L. CLEVELAND

Sweeping in a gentle arc southeast from Puerto Rico, there lies a thousand kilometer string of islands whose group names, Leeward and Windward, are derived from the winds that for centuries have borne sailing ships around the world. Lee, meaning shelter, is the direction toward which the wind blows. Windward is the direction from which the wind comes.

During the 15th through 19th centuries, trading vessels plied the Caribbean in great numbers, and the population of these islands grew rapidly. At least nine million African slaves were brought to the West Indies and to what is now the United States during this period. While most Caribbeans today have African ancestors, many trace their roots back to Europe and Asia.

Some of the early Caribbeans were gentry who went there to carve out plantations but the majority of those who voluntarily migrated to these islands where indentured. They were poor in their homeland and agreed to ship out to some Caribbean island on the promise--often not kept--of a land grant in exchange for three or four years of labor.

ALEXANDER HAMILTON

In what was then the Danish West Indies, a small leeward island called Nevis became the adopted home of one James Hamilton and his common law wife, Rachel Fawcette Lavien. On January 11, 1755 (or 1757--historians differ on the year) there was born to this couple a son whose later hand in the birth of the United States was of incalculable proportions.

Alexander Hamilton went to the Colonies when he was 17 to enroll in Kings College, New York City. He interrupted his education in 1776, before graduating, to direct his energies to the Revolution. Before he was 21, he had written two important pamphlets urging independence for the Colonies. He joined the Continental Army under General George Washington and eventually became an aide-de-camp on Washington's staff with the rank of lieutenant colonel.

Following the war, he became a lawyer after a short but intensive apprenticeship, and soon became one of the most distinguished attorneys in New York. It seems natural that in the course of events Hamilton would later become a member of the New York Legislature and a delegate to the Constitutional Convention which met in Philadelphia from May to September of 1787.

Although a conservative in both politics and economics, he was not burdened with prejudice or loyalty to any one state or region in the Colonies--probably because of his foreign birth. Although Hamilton believed that the Constitutional Convention was a "mere waste of time" producing "motley and feeble" measures, he also believed that the Constitution was the best to be obtained under the circumstances so he supported the final draft.

His view on the separation of powers was stated simply:

> Give all power to the many and they will oppress the few. Give all power to the few, they will oppress the many. Both therefore ought to have power, that each may defend itself against the other.

In an effort to obtain New York's ratification of the Constitution, Hamilton wrote a series of 85 essays in collaboration with John Jay and James Madison. The authorship of individual essays was kept a secret but Hamilton probably wrote about two-thirds of them. They were published in the New York newspapers and later reproduced in book form (1788) under the title of *The Federalist.*

President Washington chose Alexander Hamilton for the most important Cabinet post--Secretary of the Treasury. The war had been costly and the new nation was heavily in debt. In assessing Hamilton's qualifications it is worth noting his early employment. When he was 11, he began working in a counting house--a trading firm on the island of St. Croix. By the time he was 15, he headed the firm!

While serving on the Cabinet, Hamilton formulated three important fiscal policies: The Funding Bill (interest-bearing bonds), the Assumption Bill (the Federal Government taking over the states' debts), and the Bank of the United States (a private bank with semipublic functions--patterned after the Bank of England). He also recommended excise taxes and tariff protections--still issues of disagreement to this day.

Political parties developed largely because of differences between Thomas Jefferson and Hamilton. John Adams and Hamilton are credited with being the leaders of the nation's first political party, the Federalist Party. Jefferson became leader of the Democratic Republicans which later became the Democratic Party.

After retirement from public ofice in 1795, Hamilton resumed his law practice in New York. He remained one of President Washington's closest advisers, preparing two drafts of Washington's Farewell Address (1796), Washington choosing the first to prepare his speech.

During John Adams' tenure in office, his Cabinet often sought the counsel of Hamilton. When Adams ran for re-election in 1800 against Jefferson and Aaron Burr, he did not get the support of Hamilton and was defeated. The election for President produced a tie between Burr and Jefferson and the decision had to be made by the House of Representatives. Hamilton vigorously supported Jefferson in the House and he infuriated Burr by labeling him and "unfit and dangerous man" Jefferson was chosen and became the third President of the United States.

The smoldering Burr-Hamilton relations flared anew in 1804 during Burr's bid to become governor of New York. Hamilton attacked Burr's candidacy. Burr retaliated, charging that Hamilton had assaulted his honor, and challenged him to a duel.

At dawn on the morning of July 11, 1804, the two statesmen settled their differences on the banks of the Hudson River at Weehauken, New Jersey. There remains considerable doubt that Hamilton intended to fire at Burr. Burr's shot found its mark and Alexander Hamilton--one of the men who shaped the course of the United States--died the following day before reaching his 50th birthday.

JAMES AUDUDBON

The War for Independence was over. New states were being admitted to the Union. The frontier was somewhere--everywhere west of the Mississippi. This was the era of the American Experience and it produced one of the earliest (if not the first) authentic American artists. American, because his subjects (the wildlife of the wilderness) and technique (part folk, part scientist, part fine art) were the product of that experience.

John James Audubon was born April 26, 1785, on the Caribbean island of Santo Domingo (now Haiti) to a Creole mother and Jean Audubon; a retired French naval officer, prosperous merchant, plantation owner, and slave trader who had fought on the side of the Colonies in the Revolution.

Soon after the birth of Jean Jacques (John James), upheavals on Santo Domingo made it no longer profitable for his father to remain. In 1789, he returned to France with his two illegitimate children. His wife, Anne, who had waited patiently at home in France while Jean sought his fortune, accepted and loved the children.

Although young John James was given ample educational opportunities, including having tutors for music, drawing, and fencing, he often avoided school to wander in the woods where he would hunt, fish, and collect curiosities of the fields.

Following a rebellion in Santo Domingo, John's father suffered serious business losses and finally in despair, sent his 18 year old son to the United States to live on a farm he owned near Philadelphia. He hoped that John would find himself, under the guidance of an old Quaker friend.

Audubon rejected the restraints his father's friend attempted to place on him. Instead of farming, he preferred to hunt and fish and to sketch birds--the one

pursuit to which he was beginning to devote more and more time. His innovative genius led him to insert wires into the bodies of dead birds, allowing him to freeze them in in-flight poses for his sketches.

Returning to France for a brief visit in 1805, Audubon formed a partnership with one Ferdinand Rozier for the purpose of mining lead on the farm near Philadelphia. But that business venture (and others in Kentucky) failed, mainly because Audubon could not resist the lure of the woodland.

Neither could he resist the charms of Miss Lucy Bakewell and although her father reckoned Audubon's financial prospects to be very poor, they were married with his consent. Soon thereafter, Audubon formed another partnership with

Lucy's brother Thomas to operate a steam powered grist (grain) and lumber mill at Henderson, Kentucky. Thomas Bakewell had this to say about his brother-in-law:

> He was an admirable marksman, an expert swimmer, a clever rider, possessed great activity, prodigious strength, and was notable for the elegance of his figure and the beauty of his features, and he aided nature by a careful attendance to his dress. Besides other accomplishments, he was musical, a good fencer, danced well, had some acquaintance with legerdemain (magic tricks), worked in hair and could plait willow baskets.

The mill enterprise bankrupted the following year with Audubon salvaging only his hunting rifle, the clothes on his back, and his precious drawings. Taking his family, he migrated across the Kentucky slopes, down the Ohio River, and through the marshes of the Mississippi River. Audubon's unrelenting search for unfamiliar birds, in order to record them on his sketch pad, eventually took them to New Orleans. Along the way he supported his family by painting portraits and tutoring. Then Lucy obtained a position as a governess, and when she opened a school for girls, she supported her husband while he sought to have his drawings published.

She encouraged her husband but refused to follow him in his wanderings, not wanting to subject her children to additional hardships and poverty. In 1826, unable to interest any publishers in Philadelphia in his drawings, Audubon made a fateful decision. He managed to gather enough money for passage to Great Britian and there his genius was recognized.

With subscriptions flowing in from Liverpool, Edinburgh, and London, *The Birds of America* first appeared in folio size in 1827. Audubon had given the world the first great collection of North American birds drawn in their natural habitats.

After producing a five-volume work entitled, *Ornithological Biography*, he returned permanently to the United States and started work on *The Viviparous Quadrepeds of North America*. This work, consisting of 30 plates and three volumes of text, was completed by his sons and a collaborator, John Bachman, after his death in 1851.

Audubon was the earliest and the most influential American conservationist. His great curiosity about bird life led him to devise a means of attaching an identification tag to them--which is today known as banding.

The Audubon Society was named in his honor by George Bird Grinnell in 1886 and was incorporated in New York in 1905 as the National Association of Audubon Societies, later shortened to the National Audubon Society.

Goals of the Society include the conservation of soil, water, plants, and wildlife, with particular interest directed to wildlife. The Society has been active in supporting the passage of laws to protect birds. New York enacted legislation to prohibit the sale of feathers of migratory birds (1911), and a Federal Migratory Bird Treaty Act (1918) prohibits killing or capturing most non-game species.

Notable immigrants from the Carribean have largely chosen the arts for a career. In recent years professional sports, especially baseball and horse racing, has attracted many talented performers.

THE WORLD OF ENTERTAINMENT

A list from the field of entertainment would include musician, singer, actor, and producer Desi Arnaz, who was born in Santiago, Cuba. Another multi-talented personality is Jose Ferrer. Born in Santurce, Puerto Rico, he became a first-class producer, director, and actor. The late Frank Silvera, from Kingston, Jamaica, also excelled in these areas. Actress Rita Moreno began life in Humacao, Puerto Rico; dancer Pearl Primus hales from Trinidad, British West Indies; and actor Henry Wilcoxon's birthplace was Dominica, British West Indies.

9

CENTRAL AND SOUTH AMERICA

by

LILLIAN H. POST

Although there have been fewer immigrants from Central and South America than from Europe and Asia, they do account for over 700,000 pieces of the United States mosaic.

These immigrants brought with them the spectrum of all talents and abilities known to man. They have blended their cultures smoothly with the culture of their adopted country. Their contributions have increased the lovely Latin American spice in the United States.

That which we call Latin America (from Mexico southward where the native language spoken is Spanish or Portuguese) was explored and settled by immigrants from Europe, Asia and Africa during the time the eastern part of the United States was being explored and settled. Because the route to the upper part of North America was shorter and more direct, and because the flight from religious persecution in England forced immediate settlement rather than exploration, North America was settled by permanent colonists first. Spain and Portugal, on the other hand, were seeking riches as well as land, so they sailed the southern routes across the ocean to Mexico and Central and South America. There they found the great Aztec civilization in Mexico, the Indian civilizations in Central America, and the fabulously rich civilization of the Incas in Peru.

In order to hold each new territory while they searched for more gold, precious jewels and metals, every ship that carried booty to Europe returned with adventurous settlers and the families of the explorers. These people for the most part spoke Spanish. Therefore, with the exception of Brazil, the native tongue of the South and Central American countries became Spanish.

Brazil, the largest country in South America, is located in the northeastern section of the continent. Since it was explored and settled by the Portuguese, its native language became Portuguese. While Brazil had no rich Indian civilizations to conquer, its rich, lush, farm lands attracted many families from Portugal. Soon the country was divided into large plantations, called haciendas. Because Brazil bordered the Atlantic Ocean and was directly across from Africa, it was easy to import slaves to work on these haciendas.

The equator passes through the northern part of South America. As one moves southward from the equatorial regions with their hot climate, the temperatures become cooler. The seasons below the equator are at a different time of the year than the same seasons in North America. For example: Christmas time in Minnesota means severe cold and snow while Christmas time in Argentina means bathing suits and sunshine. However, the industries and crops are basically the same for both the North and South Temperate Zones. As a result, people have moved from one area to another within the Latin American countries, rather than immigrate to the United States in large numbers.

These countries supply the necessary raw materials to the United States and the world for the manufacture of products we all use each day. For instance, the steel plants of our nation import the elements essential to steel-making from Latin America. Venezuela sends us iron ore, oil and cacao. Columbia sends textiles and coffee. Brazil gave us the first large orange and Chile sends us copper. Guiana gives us a girls' best friend--diamonds; Peru sent us the pepper tree and tomatoes (not bad together!). The first bananas we had were grown in Costa Rica. Ecuador sent us tobacco and Argentina brought us that dynamic dance, The Tango.

THE PANAMA CANAL

Panama's greatest contribution to the United States and to the entire world, was the Treaty of 1903, which gave the right to build the Panama Canal. It took seven years to build this short cut; and it is an experience of pride in engineering ability to travel through the series of locks. The tropical growth on both sides of the man-made locks appears impenetrable as your ship slowly covers the seven to eight hour voyage between the Caribbean Sea and the Pacific Ocean. Each of the six lock chambers holds your ship steady as the water either rushes in to elevate your position, or drains to lower it. Eleven thousand Panamanians work for the Canal Company and provide this marvelous short cut for the imports and exports of countries around the world.

The beauty and the culture of the Latin American countries and their peoples have greatly enriched all of our lives. Columbus reached the coast of Venezuela on his third voyage in 1498. He wrote of this discovery: "In this blessed land I found the mildest climate ... trees very green ... and people ... of a very lovely stature and many wear pieces of gold around their necks and some have pearls wound around their arms." We still import gold and pearls from this blessed land.

The late President of the United States, John F. Kennedy, once said, "The people of the United States have much to learn from Brazil's rich historical and cultural heritage; and I am happy to note the creation of a new Brazilian-United States Institute here in Washington to facilitate greater cultural and educational contacts between our two countries."

It could be said that of all the facets of Brazilian culture, perhaps the most forceful ever to penetrate into people's homes has been the music of Antonio Carlos Jobim's "Bossa Nova," popularized by Charlie Byrd, the noted guitarist.

Probably the most prolific music writer and lyricist who ever lived was Heiter Villa-Lobos, who had 780 works published. He said, "Musical creation constitutes a biological need for me; I compose, because I have to." Born in Rio de Janeiro in 1887, he conducted twenty-three different orchestras in the United States, and in equally as many other countries. Composer and cellist, he will never be forgotten.

In the early 1930's, the voice of a little Peruvian Indian girl startled and delighted those around her. That girl's musical talents have since become a source of amazement and joy to the whole world. Born in 1927 in a small village 12,000 feet up the side of the Andes Mountains, Emperatriz Chavarri taught herself to sing. Her voice covers a range of four octaves. She sings from the do in low baritone (a man's singing range) to the do in high soprano (a woman's high singing range). Her mother was a Peruvian Indian and her father was half Peruvian and half Spanish. They were very poor. The Bishop of the Catholic church in Lima heard about their daughter's unusual voice and arranged for Emperatriz and her family to move to Lima. There, she attended a Catholic school for girls. When she grew older, she sang on the Peruvian National Broadcasting Company radio station. As a professional singer, she chose the name Yma Sumac.

It was not long until the world heard about Miss Sumac's unusual talent; and she was invited to the United States for a concert tour. She performed at the Hollywood Bowl and in Carnegie Hall. She made many recordings and performed in the 1954 movie The Secret of the Incas. Yma Sumac became a citizen of the United States in 1955.

The revival of the woodcut (pictures cut in blocks of wood and transferred to paper by covering the surface with ink) has been credited to Antonio Frasconi, a native of Argentina. He was born in Buenos Aires in 1919, and later moved with his family to Montevideo, the capital of Uruguay. When he was very young, he loved drawing and spent many hours gradually developing his artistic skills. However, his family did not approve of this, calling it a waste of time; and they encouraged him to study something more important. Nevertheless, he continued with his hobby, attending art school at night while he worked in his family's restaurant during the day. Then at the age of twenty, in Uruguay, he held his first art show with an exhibition of his drawings.

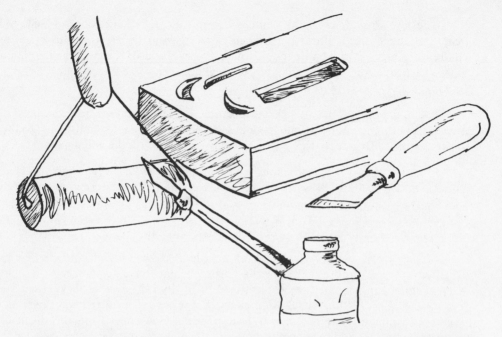

After this time, he began to experiment with wood carving and became completely fascinated with that art form. He has had more than sixty "one-man shows" in the United States, Europe, and Latin America--and three major exhibits in United States' museums. In 1963, one of his designs was chosen for a United States postage stamp that had a printing of 120 million. Additionally, he has designed and illustrated; children and adult books, magazine covers, Christmas cards, calendars, record album covers, and book jackets.

Frasconi came to New York in 1945, and since that time has translated everyday subjects of the land into woodcuts. From the vineyards of Central California to the markets of New York City, Antonio Frasconi has become known as an artist of the people.

Another immigrant whose contributions to the U.S. will always be remembered is the sculptor from Venezuela, Marisol.

Perhaps the greatest example of transition from one vocation to another during a lifetime is illustrated by Juan Arzube. Born in Guayaquil, Ecuador in 1918, Juan began his education with the Christian Brothers School. At the age of nine, he was sent to England to attend school. In 1932, he returned to Ecuador and earned his Bachelor of Arts degree at the college in Guayaquil. Meantime, he had decided that he wanted to be an engineer. He studied at the Rensselaer Polytechnic Institute in Troy, New York, where he received a degree in civil engineering. His first job was supervising the construction of a hospital as a specialist in health and sanitation.

Juan decided to move to Los Angeles, California, where he thought there would be greater opportunity to do the work he wanted. In Los Angeles, he taught English, translated English lessons into Spanish for a correspondence school, and studied radio techniques. He played the lead role for the CBS Romance of the Rancho series.

One day he participated in a Catholic retreat at Malibu, California, and it was at that time--when he was twenty-seven years old--that he decided the Church would be his vocation. He enrolled in St. John's Seminary in 1948 and was ordained a priest in 1954. He became one of the three auxiliary Catholic Bishops in Los Angeles, with his official title being Most Reverend Bishop Juan Arzube.

That tennis great, Pancho Seguro, left Ecuador to compete as an amateur in tournaments throughout the United States. He has since become a professional and a great teacher and coach--as many of his successful students can attest.

The Pittsburgh Pirates baseball team has reached into Central America for many of its prominent players. Manny Sanguillen, one of baseball's finest catchers, emigrated from Panama, as did second baseman Rennie Stennett and outfielder Omar Moreno. Outfielder Tony Armas hails from Venezuela, and both infielder Frank Taveras and outfielder Miguel Dilone emigrated from the Dominican Republic.

The music of Guiomar Novaes and Sergio Mendez of Brazil, and Claudio Arrau of Chile, has added new dimensions to piano artistry. Many hours of listening pleasure has been provided by the music of composer Lalo Schifrin, and by popular singer Dick Haymes of Argentina. The stage and screen has benefited from the directing abilities of Leopoldo Torre-Nilsson of Argentina and Alberto Cavalcanti of Brazil. We all have enjoyed watching that suave actor Fernando Lamas of Argentina and admired the beauty and charm of Jennifer O'Neill from Brazil, as she has so vividly portrayed the heroine in many films. Actresses Martita Hunt and Olivia Hussey, and the multi-talented writer of novels, short stories and poetry, Jorge Borges, all emigrated from Argentina. Other great writers who have given countless hours of fascinating reading to students and scholars include Pablo Neruda from Chile, and Euclides de Cunha from Peru.

The first machine to fully automate shoemaking, the Consolidated Hand Method Lasting Machine, brought a huge increase in production and a huge decrease in the price of shoes. It was developed by Jan Ernst Matzeliger from Guiana.

One of the stars of The Flying Nun television series is Alejandro Rey, from Argentina. I can still feel the humor of him being taken in by the "Flying Nun" in every episode.

INTERESTING ANIMALS

The torrid climate of Central America and the northern part of South America has created lush jungle lands, wherein exotic birds and animals live. Many of our homes are enlivened by the songs and conversations of canaries, parrots, and myna birds. Monkeys have moved from the jungles to the zoos, and finally into small cages in private homes, in many parts of the country.

The cold mountainous region of Peru is the home of a small, furry animal that has become a household pet, as well as an added attraction to our school classrooms. We know it as the "Guinea Pig." This small animal, measuring about six inches in length and weighing several pounds when full grown, lives in the wilds of the mountains of Peru. It belongs to the family of rodents and is properly called a "Cavy." The babies are born with eyes open, all of their teeth, and completely covered with their coats of fur. They run around the first day, and although they drink their mother's milk, they eat solids such as vegetables and leaves immediately. Their high-pitched squeak sounds much like the sounds made by a pig.

The Indians who live in the mountainous regions of Peru, catch these little wild animals in traps and keep them in their homes where they are allowed to run around on the floor and eat crumbs.

When the conquistadors came to Peru, they took Guinea Pigs back to Spain. Traders carried them up and down the coast of Europe and they became household pets from Spain to England. They were sold in the market places in England for a Guinea (rate of exchange such as our dollar). One could hear the vendors calling out their wares, "Buy one pig for a Guinea," and that is where they got the name "Guinea Pig."

As we look back on the history of the United States, and evaluate each facet of its culture, thanks should be given to all of Latin America and its people for their many contributions to American cultural enrichment.

10

CHINA

by

JOAN S. FOLLENDORE

Upon his arrival in the United States, one immigrant's last name "Su-Sing" sounded like "Johnson" so it was Americanized to Johnson S.S. Chow was his first name in China, where the last name is placed first.

This famous artist of the Far East, brought his gift to America, where he also gained fame and respect as a specialist in his field in the U.S. also. In Soochow, he started painting at the age of eight. His father was an artist and taught him the classical discipline of the Chinese school of painting. He learned to express the Taoist and Confucian blending of philosophical ideals.

The Taoist believes in the harmonious combination of heaven, earth, and nature, rather than conquering nature. The artist's personality is expressed through his depiction of nature, in other words, trying to identify himself with nature.

The Confucianist believes in humanitarianism, including the display of eight virtures: loyalty, honoring elders, kindness, love for fellow man, trustworthiness or sincerity, righteousness, harmony in nature, and peace. These are what Professor Chow has taught hundreds of people in his adopted country since immigrating. Before that, over one thousand students in Hong Kong studied under this philosopher of nature.

As a boy, he studied many of nature's children; flowers, trees, birds, and fishes, to name a few. He would sit and observe the miracles of nature in his father's garden. He counted every petal, each color in a flower; and he studied how different parts of a tree react to a heavy rain. He observed, listened to, and carefully analyzed everything in nature.

Professor Chow's artistic skill and talent is indeed a credit to the Southern Chinese school of painting, which stresses soft, subtle, and elegant lines, as opposed to the more powerful and vigorous northern style. Using a Chinese brush and water colors made from natural elements (rather than from chemicals) on rice paper, Professor Chow brings life out of images, inspiring calmness and tranquility.

Luke Tao, President of the C.S.A. at the University of California, Los Angeles, has said: "On behalf of all members of Chinese Students Association, I extend my gratitude to have the honor of your coming to our campus. We all feel fortunate of having you to promote the vast knowledge of traditional Chinese painting and to introduce this concept to American students."

In Chinese homes around the world, four disciplines (pastimes) for children are established to help form their character, not because they may need them for a future profession. These four are: music, chess, calligraphy (the art of handwriting forms), and painting. In America sometimes only one or two of these are stressed.

Amelia (Americanized from Hsi-ling) Chow was one of these fortunate Chinese children. Her mother, Mrs. Johnson Chow, whose maiden name is Loo Shing-Ro, is herself an excellent artist. She taught her daughter the style in which she specializes, called Kung-pi. It varies from Professor Chow's free style, Hsieh-i, in that it uses meticulous line and coloring. Amelia, now a graduate student, paints in both styles because her parents taught her from the time she could first hold a brush.

These three family members have had many exhibits together. Entering the "Family Room" of one of these showings gives one a warm feeling and a beautiful gift to the eyes.

CINEMATOGRAPHY

"James Wong Howe is the very best cinematographer," say the people in his business; and if a person is respected like that by his own peers--he has really made it. James Howe came from China at the age of five, over 70 years ago! He became an assistant cameraman at eighteen. During his filming of more than 140 movies, he has had only one argument with a director! Howe opened a Chinese restaurant at one time; but his two Academy Awards convinced him that cinematography was the right field for him.

In 1883, Richard Wing's grandfather, Chow Gong Wing, began selling noodles for five cents a bowl in Hanford, California. At that time, Hanford was a huge camp of 15,000 railroad laborers who had been left without jobs when a railroad track was completed. This town of Hanford has much the same population today as it did in the 19th century when Chow Gong Wing arrived after a nine-month voyage on a sailing vessel from China. He operated a restaurant in Hanford and became a famous chef, introducing dishes that have become everyday entrees in Chinese restaurants all over America. Gourmets still go to Hanford for the unique Chinese cuisine created by Chow Gong Wing's grandson, Richard Wing, with the help of twenty-two members of the Wing family. As Richard Wing says, "A chef has a sacred duty to help sustain, maintain, restore, and revitalize the body."

Another accomplished Chinese immigrant is Ieoh Ming Pei, who designed the John F. Kennedy Memorial Library in Boston. Jacqueline Kennedy chose Pei because he wanted the structure to be thought-provoking, rather than awe-inspiring, and to be something people would use--a living memorial.

One outstanding person who did much to raise the standards of the Chinese in the United States was Ng Ho Cheow. He established the first Chinese newspaper in Los Angeles, and later the first one in San Francisco where he also established a publishing firm. He also founded schools so that the Chinese could learn to read and write both Chinese and English. This revived some of the Chinese cultural heritage, as well as giving the Chinese a new insight into American life and how to cope with it. Later Ng Ho Cheow became the first Chinese to be inducted into the California Hall of Fame.

Dr. Min Chueh Chang was the co-discoverer of the pill. I guess you might expect an immigrant from the most populous country in the world to be concerned with birth control. Many other Chinese immigrants have made contributions in the fields of medicine, science, art, architecture, and opera. Among them have been several Pulitzer Prize winners.

Everyday ambassadors of good will from China to the United States are the Panda Bears that were a gift from China to President Richard Nixon when he was in Peking, in 1972. They are only found in the Himalaya Mountains in southwest China, and parts of Tibet, but now these rare and popular animals also can be found in the Washington, D.C. Zoo.

Both Japanese and Korean karate are offshoots of the Chinese Tai Chi Chuan and the popular martial art called Kung Fu. Like everything else which goes from one country to another, it has been modified somewhat to fit the national temperament and physical characteristics of the people in different countries. Tai Chi Chuan was originally a basic health and longevity exercise in about 1,000 A.D.; then Kung Fu developed for self-protection; followed by karate.

While chop suey and chowmein surely weren't Chinese food, spaghetti was. About a hundred years ago, a U.S. ship sailed into the harbor at Canton, China. The skipper and a couple of his officers stopped at a restaurant for a meal. The cook didn't want to prepare food for these "foreign devils" as Caucasians were called in China, so he just took a little of this and a little of that, warmed it together, and called it Chop Suey. The Americans liked it so much they brought the cook to the United States and set him up in a restaurant. People in the U.S. have had Chop Suey and Chow Mein ever since. Many people think spaghetti came from Italy, and it's true it came to the U.S from there, but the Italians got it from China when Marco Polo was the first to return from crossing Asia by land.

Tea as a beverage was invented in China over two thousand years ago and introduced to England in the 16th century; and from there to its colonies in the New World.

The Chinese believe the New Year begins when new life comes out of the soil. This generally occurs during the first fifteen days of February. It does seem logical to begin the year when new life begins. This is an especially happy time for the Chinese, when they have new clothes, pay off their debts, visit friends, eat well, and exchange gifts. Sounds like Christmas!

Since the time some 2500 years ago when Confucius inaugurated the family system of mutual support and assistance, the Chinese have been industrious workers, relentlessly pursuing economic gains for themselves and their families. This is a form of built-in social security wherein the families take care of each other, and it is one of the reasons why Chinese tend to live in areas known as Chinatowns. You will find very few Chinese ever applying for welfare. They take care of their own. Another reason the Chinese stick together comes from the meaning of "China" to the Chinese. In Chinese it is known as Jung Gwo, meaning "central country." All other countries are but satellites. The United States is known as Mei Gwo.

Of all the names the Chinese have given other countries, that for the U.S. is most flattering. Mei Gwo means beautiful country. But it was not always truly beautiful to the Chinese immigrants. In the 1850s, many Chinese came to make money in the Gold Rush. Only a few of them did. Gold had attracted people from all over the world. Dozens of towns sprang up and the thousands of new inhabitants needed food and services, which were Chinese specialties.

RAILROAD BUILDING

Other Chinese immigrants were employed as railroad construction workers and contributed immensely to the first transcontinental railroad. The segment from San Francisco, California, to Promontary point, Utah, was constructed largely by Chinese labor.

How could America get along without railroads and its freight service even today? Donner Pass is the highest pass in the Sierras. Quite a few people died right there trying to cross over this peak, before the railroad came into being. Imagine the job of building a railroad through the desert areas of Nevada, where the temperature goes over 100 degrees in the summer, and is well below freezing in winter. It's amazing they could do it under conditions like that.

In 1867, labor was very scarce in California. The Central Pacific (which later became the Southern Pacific), in its endeavor to build eastward from the West Coast, found itself competing for workers in areas where most people were homesteaders, miners, or gold seekers. They began hiring Chinese track laborers, who were eager for employment. They proved themselves to be peaceable, patient, and industrious. Before the first transcontinental rail line was completed, the Central Pacific had as many as 12,000 Chinese laborers on the payroll. They made up about 80% of the work force. They made it possible to complete the western end of the transcontinental railroad, giving the United States many years head start in developing the vast unsettled areas of the west.

Some Chinese-Americans were transported to other parts of the country and used as strike-breakers. These actions led to the establishment of laws to protect labor workers. In many states in the late 19th century, only U.S. citizens could own property. Therefore, Oriental immigrants had to wait until they had a child so that they could buy property in the child's name.

Audrey and Jayne Meadows, two actresses who are familiar to all from television, are sisters who were born in Wu Chang. And Keye Luke is the Chinese character actor who has appeared in so many movies everywhere.

From the time when the expression "Not a Chinaman's chance" (referring to the many difficulties the Chinese had a hundred years ago) originated, to the time the United States became truly "Mei Gwo" to the Chinese, there was a series of steps of which all of us can be justly proud. The Chinese immigrants persevered like other early American citizens and everyone has benefitted from that. They performed honorably and beneficially to a beautiful country.

11

CZECHOSLOVAKIA

by

MABLE CORINNE PARRISH

Czechoslovakia--shaped like a wrinkled, squashy, comfortable Santa Claus boot--is one of the smaller mother/father nations. In fact, Czechoslovakia is so small it could be slipped into the state of Florida with room to spare. Yet Czechoslovakia has contributed literally hundreds of famous immigrants who have helped make the United States great.

In April of 1735, the first group of Czechoslovakian refugees arrived in Savannah, Georgia, aboard their tiny sailing vessel The Two Brothers. The second handful--twenty-five men, women, and children--arrived in February of 1736.

These small bands of Czechs brought with them their joy and zest for life. They also brought with them their traditions--traditions that are often thought of as having originated in the United States.

The two groups first traveled to North Carolina, where they found a land exactly to their liking. Then they began to separate--traveling to the north and to the east. Wherever they went, they established orchestras and bands, large church choirs, Easter sunrise services, the Christmas Star, and their Christmas Eve feasts. They even contributed their paper-thin ginger snaps! Traditions--brought to us from Czechoslovakia.

Following the first influx of Czech refugees (who fled their beloved homeland to avoid persecution), wave after wave of Czechoslovakians immigrated to the United States. Most of them arrived by way of England and France, then scattered like leaves of autumn across the U.S. cultural scene. Their names are legion! We find them listed in every anthology of composers, musicians, writers, teachers, or scientists.

Rene Wellek ranks as one of the highest contemporary scholars of the history of literary criticism. He taught at Iowa University and--after 1946--at Yale. His textbooks have been a basis of study in every major university in the U.S.

His impressive knowledge of European, English, and American literature is manifested in his massive and monumental work--*A History of Modern Literary*

Criticism (five volumes!). In addition to being well versed in contemporary literature, he demonstrated his knowledge of very early literature as well when he wrote and published *Bohemia in English Literature.* These volumes are a comprehensive analysis of every well-known piece of American and English literature and are invaluable textbooks.

Among the many Czechoslovakian writers, we find the names of Franz Werfel, Hans Natonek, and Franz Weiskopf.

The last named, Franz Weiskopf, wrote only in his native language until he learned English in the United States. He has since written books in Czechoslovakian, German, and English. (Three different languages! And some of us find it difficult two write in *one* language!).

One thing stands out in our study of the contributions of Czechoslovakian immigrants: although they all love their adopted country, they have never ceased to love their homeland.

For example: Egon Hostovsky--A noted Czechoslovakian novelist who settled in New York and became a United States citizen. He held classes and taught the basics of writing, while writing only in his native language! He is regarded as the world's most important contemporary Czechoslovakian writer. Yes, he writes and speaks and teaches in English; and all the while his books, written in Czech, must be translated!

GEORGE PLACZEK

As is true of every country, the list of Czechoslovakian contributors to the making of the U.S. could go on and on. Included among the names of Czechoslovakian scientists, we find that of George Placzek.

Easygoing, almost untidy in appearance, George Placzek was a warm-hearted intellectual of unusual refinement--a truly cosmopolitan European.

He traveled all over the world and made friends wherever he went. As a result, there was hardly a language he could not speak faultlessly and articulately. It is said that he could shift abruptly from one language to another without faltering and with great fluency in each.

After working on the atomic projects in England and Canada, he finally joined his many friends in Los Alamos, New Mexico. That was where his exceptional linguistic skills--together with his extensive technical knowledge--came to the fore and had a far-reaching effect on the perfection and the success of the first atomic bomb. With his ability to speak and translate practically every language spoken among the two to three thousand scientists gathered from all over the world, his talents were in great demand!

Like many of those who worked at Los Alamos, Placzek turned his attention to peacetime work after World War II. He became a member of the Institute for Advanced Scientific Study and had his mind set on a professorship. However, his death cut short a promising career that would surely have given much to the young men and women entering the field of science. Sadly, he was really known only among his contemporaries.

Czechoslovakia! A small, boot-shaped country surrounded by Austria, Hungary, Russia, and Germany. Its immigrants have shared their traditions and their scientific knowledge and have trailed their contributions across the United States!

12

DENMARK

by

MABLE CORINNE PARRISH

The Danes--together with the Norwegians and Swedes--were the early Scandinavians who traveled by way of Greenland and Iceland to Vinland, their name for North America. They came as explorers and adventurers--not as conquerors. Their only weapons were handknives and swords and were no match for the bows and arrows and other weapons used by the Indians. Thus, they were driven out of the continent of North America and had no real chance to settle or colonize.

We have no way of knowing just how far they may have traveled into the interior of North America; but we do know that many of them died during these travels and were among the first non-Indians to be buried in North America. Denmark, like other nations, has since contributed literally hundreds of men and women who have helped make the United States the great nation it is today.

One of the world's greatest authorities on the atom and nuclear research, Niels Bohr, is often called "Denmark's Grand Old Man of Science." After being graduated from the University of Copenhagen, he went to England to do research work under two of that country's greatest scientists. Although much was already known about the atom, there were still perplexing details regarding the motions and orbits of the tiny electrons that make up the atom. It was Bohr's explanation of the light/energy principle that won him the Nobel Prize in physics in 1922.

After leaving England, he returned to his beloved Denmark; and was head of research at the University of Copenhagen when Denmark was overrun by the Nazis. In protest of their high-handed ways, he shut down the University's atomic research department! It naturally followed that he was in serious trouble! Thus, in the fall of 1943, Bohr was smuggled aboard a fishing boat and taken secretly to Sweden. From there he was flown to England, hidden in the bomb bay of an airplane. He managed to take with him all of his priceless and precious atomic research data.

From England, he flew to the United States, joining some two to three thousand of his colleagues in Los Alamos, New Mexico. It was this group of scientists that perfected the atomic bomb; and Niels Bohr was in the packed auditorium on that fateful day when it was announced that the bomb had been dropped and that the war was at last over.

We cannot help sympathizing with those scientists for their desire to celebrate the completion of what they had started. They shouted, stamped, and whistled--much as did the men at mission control center in Houston, when Neil Armstrong stepped on the moon. At last, Mission Accomplished!

However, every man there regretted what the bomb had done to innocent human beings. And--like many of the other scientists then at Los Alamos--Niels Bohr has since confined his scientific research to peacetime uses of nuclear power. Right now, of course, they are trying to solve the world's energy crisis problem.

Victor Borge--born in Denmark in 1909--began the study of music at the age of five. At the age of thirteen he gave his first concert.

Victor Borge is famous as one of our century's foremost comedians, while being also an accomplished musician; and he is noted for his combination of these two skills.

He writes his own script and composes music, even playing the lead when it is required! He was on tour in Sweden in 1938 when Denmark was invaded by the Germans, so, instead of returning home, he immigrated to the United States. During his entire first year in the U.S., he spent his time in various motion picture houses--viewing as many as three or four movies a day! In this way, he learned both to understand and to speak the English language.

Borge has guested on almost every conceivable TV program. He has given his own shows; and has toured the world, giving of himself and making us all a gift of his own special brand of talent and humor.

Victor Borge--comedian and humanitarian. He has been the national chairman of CARE; was chosen the Funniest Man in Music in 1951 and Comedian of the Year in 1954; and in 1958 won the award he cherished above all the others he has earned; The TV Father of the Year award.

Victor Borge--an immigrant, an American, and a beloved and talented clown!

Laurence Gronlund, a graduate of Copenhagen University, immigrated to the United States at the age of 23. He already spoke flawless English, and was able to obtain a position teaching German at a high school in Milwaukee, Wisconsin. While there, he studied law at the University of Wisconsin. It was while studying law that he took up the banner against corruption in politics.

After only a short time in the legal profession, he gave up the practice of law to devote his whole attention to this new interest. He began writing, and the first of his books--*The Coming Revolution*--showed his desire to effect change.

90

Obsessed with his pet subject--socialism--he traveled from coast to coast, lecturing. He opposed everything that held back the advancement of the working man. He resented the growth of great, octopus-like industries like railroads, lumber, and shipbuilding.

His views didn't mellow until Congress passed the Anti-Trust Act of 1890--which was supposed to prevent the growth of these developing corporations. It was then that Gronlund abandoned his theory of revolution in favor of government leadership. He discontinued lecturing on socialism and confined his efforts to working within the democratic system. (This is shown by the publication of his book *New Ecomony: A Peaceable Solution of the Social Problem*. He had great hopes the Anti-Trust Act would 'work'.)

He joined the staff of the New York Evening Journal and remained there until his death--working for the advancement of all classes of labor.

There are many kinds of artists. Some paint in oils or pastels or do charcoal drawings. Some are musicians. some create a statue from a slab of marble. Jens Jensen was none of these. Jens Jensen created beauty· by arranging plants and flowers and growing things.

Carl Sandburg--biographer and writer--called Jensen "one of the ten most useful men in Chicago." Born in Denmark, he immigrated to the United States in 1884 and became one of the nation's greatest landscape architects. His chief labor of love was the remaking of the entire Chicago park system!

And whether or not one agrees with Carl Sandburg, when we view the magnificent stretches of that city's parks, we must agree and admit that Jensen added greatly to the beauty of that part of the U.S.

It is October; the year, 1918. World War I is taking its toll in human lives. German U-boats (submarines) and destroyers are terrorizing the sea. Then, miraculously, the Kaiser's subs are being destroyed in their nests! His cruisers are vanishing into thin air! And--just as miraculously--the war is over!

One of the men partly responsible for the abrupt ending of World War I (the "War to End Wars"!) was a little-known Danish immigrant by the name of Signius Wilhelm Paul Knudsen, better known as William S. Knudsen.

William Knudsen, mechanic, arrived in New York at the age of 20. He brought from Denmark his keen mind, his mechanical ability, two strong hands, and his inherent Viking boatbuilding know-how!

At the outbreak of World War I, he was working for the Henry Ford Corporation. When the auto industry was asked to convert from automobiles to shipbuilding, Knudsen was put in charge of building Eagle Boats--known as Ford's

"Tin Lizzies of the Sea." (Not such a far cry from the old Viking Dragon Ships.) Under Knudsen's command, the Eagle Boats were turned out on the assembly line--the first time assembly line construction was used in the manufacture of marine equipment.

The Eagle Boats--together with Mosquito Boats (small boats made of wood)--silently and quickly maneuvered in and out of German submarine bases and destroyer ports. Undetected, they effectively crippled the German fleet, pouncing and disappearing at will.

The German High Command gave orders to make one last offensive attack; but the German soldiers and sailors--already sick of a war they could not win--knew the command to attack was only one of retaliation with no hope of success. They therefore went aboard their own ships and submarines and anchored them to the piers and docks! When the command was given to attack, there was no way they could move out! They were moored fast. Any captain or commander who tried to stop the men from carrying out their purpose was slain. That ended the offensive and--in effect--the war!

A mechanic from Denmark! To quote a Bible scripture, "Who knows whether thou art come to the kingdom for such a time as this!" (Esther 4:14)

After the war, in 1922, Knudsen went to work for General Motors Corporation. With his ability and determination, it was inevitable that he eventually become head of that corporation. When World War II broke out, he was appointed Director of Production for the United States War Department.

Truly, Signius Wilhelm Paul Knudsen--William S. Knudsen--mechanic genius from Denmark, was a Man of the Hour!

Jacob August Riis had no formal education. He was taught by parents and private tutors. At the age of 21, he immigrated to the United States and floated from job to job. In 1887, he was on the staff of the New York Tribune; but it wasn't until he landed a job as reporter for the New York Evening Sun that he found his true calling. The editor gave him the job of political reporter, and Riis began delving into the degrading conditions that then prevailed in the New York slums.

He traveled through the ghettos at all hours of the day and night, photographing the worst sights he could find: ragged, hungry, lice-infested children; rat--and insect--filled tenements; and down and out men and women, forced to scavenge for food. His stories and photographs were front page features in newspapers across the nation.

In 1890, he published *How the Other Half Lives*. His true articles and pictures shocked the nation and did more than any other one thing to rouse a previously unfeeling public into demanding that the worst of the shameful slum conditions be cleaned up.

Jacob Riis had many foes--landlords and corrupt politicians. But he also had powerful supporters. One of the most faithful of these was the head of the New York City Police Board--a future United States President: Theodore Roosevelt. It was Roosevelt who stood between Riis and those who would have his head! It was also Roosevelt who saw to it that Riis had access to police files and journals and case histories.

Jacob Riis continued his crusade against poverty and disease--photographing and writing. In 1892, he published his two books--*Children of the Poor* and *Children of the Tenements*; both fully illustrated with his own special photographs. His steady stream of words and pictures are classic examples of how men and women can effect change without violence.

Added to his work for children, Riis was instrumental in founding the Jacob A. Riis Neighborhood House, a "slum house," in the infamous Mulberry Bend District. At "the house," literally hundreds of men and women found the help needed to return from nothingness to meaningful and useful lives. Many of those who were helped remained at Neighborhood House to help others.

Riis' autobiography was published in 1901--*The Making of an American*. This man's autobiography should really have been entitled, "The Man who Helped in the Making of America!"

In addition to the illustrious immigrants from Denmark, much of the craftsmanship for which Denmark is famous has traveled across the ocean and made its contributions.

BEAUTIFUL HANDIWORK

Her industries have grown by leaps and bounds, yet Denmark still maintains the high quality of handiwork for which she has been famous for the last two centuries. Products well and artistically done are still the ideals of the Danish craftsman. Every piece of porcelain, silverware, jewelry, and furniture shipped to the U.S. bears witness to this statement.

Denmark's porcelain industry was founded in 1775 and was called the Royal Copenhagen Manufactory. The trademark chosen, three wavy lines, is still used on the company's products. The three small lines represent the three divisions of Denmark: The Sound, the Great Belt, and the Little Belt. But we need not look for the three wavy lines to know and recognize Danish porcelain! The satiny smoothness of the product is enough to identify it--just as the smooth texture and outstanding simplicity of her furniture tells us it was manufactured in Denmark!

Danish silverware, porcelain, jewelry, and furniture are simple, distinctive and beautiful. Each piece is a fine example of the application of the theory that art principles can be used in making lovely things for everyday use.

Ah, yes! No discussion of Danish exports would be complete without at least a mention of Danish pastries! The creation (and distribution) of these incomparable delicacies is in itself an art that has done more for the advancement of the American weight problem than almost any other one thing! Every bakery across the U.S. features rich, luscious cakes whose recipes originated in Denmark's kitchens.

So--all things considered--Denmark has given as much as any other one country: her people, her art, her music, her distinctive cuisine, and her beauty. Truly, Denmark has helped in the building and creation of the United States.

13

ENGLAND

by

ELIZABETH M. BIRKS

England is a land steeped in tradition, with a history recorded as far back as the days of the Roman Empire. The island geography of England gave birth to the largest commercial navy of its time. Men set sail to begin a commerce between two continents, returning with stories of the wonderful New World being full of promise. A charter was obtained from King James the First to form a trading company, under which any newly discovered land would belong to the Crown, and any disputes would be settled by the English Courts. Huge sums of money were raised to enable the first group of immigrants to settle in the New World; but the settlers were to be disappointed in the promises they had heard of a "land of plenty." They lived for over two years, scraping a living from the land when their provisions were gone. Their original contact with the Indians had been unfruitful, but during a truce, an Englishman, John Rolfe, married an Indian maiden, Pocahontas. As a wedding gift, his father-in-law gave him the pick of the Indian tobacco crop, which grew like weeds. Rolfe sent it to England, whereupon orders were sent by the London Company. The discovery of the value of tobacco was made by an Englishman, thus starting the export of fine Virginia tobacco--the best in the world.

The Pilgrims were religious dissenters, trying to worship Christ without interference from the Church of England. In order to survive their first winter, they learned about American vegetables, traded beaver pelts for corn with the Indians, and shot wild turkey. This set the menu for Thanksgiving Day feasts, enjoyed by millions each year. Three main cultures emerged from these English settlements: the planter society of the South, the more socially conscious people of New England, and the varied Middle Colonies which were agricultural as well as commercial. Each of these cultures started to create big cities.

Hereford cattle were imported from England, starting an excellent beef trade. The western regions of the New World gave birth to a flourishing fur trade which had a financial center in London. It was the Mountain Man in American history who started the development of the natural resources of western America which continues to this day. It was the courage and resourcefulness of the American pioneer that made it worthwhile for the English to invest their money in a then new but growing nation. The United States was buying and borrowing too much; and President Andrew Jackson tried to stabilize the banking system. He encouraged people to exchange goods on the security of land, instead of buying goods from England with gold, in order to keep gold in the U.S. It was in this way that England became involved with the financing of ranches, railroads, and countless other interests. Time and events have seen the results of this investment opportunity, with the United States consequently becoming the richest country in the world. The many years since Independence have seen many nations following the example of English immigrants and investors in having faith in the future of the United States.

Looking back, we can appreciate this contribution, which in itself is a cornerstone in American history. However, it is more intriguing to look back to individual contributions made by innumerable men and women from England, who not only gave their efforts, but most importantly their language. To mention but a few may whet the taste to search for more.

CHARLIE CHAPLIN

Charlie the Clown, who everyone knows as sporting shabby clothes and a black toothbrush mustache, was born in London on the 16th of April, 1889. He was christened Charles Spencer Chaplin. His parents were music hall artistes. They were extremely poor, and any money his father earned was spent on drink, with the result that young Charlie was taught to dance and sing practically before he could walk. His mother boasted of his talent at the age of two, but it wasn't until he was five that 'he made his first professional debut when his mother suddenly became ill and his father pushed him on stage as a replacement. In his panic, he sang the only song he could remember again and again until he was dragged off the stage.

His parents in their great poverty drifted apart, his father dying of resulting weakness, and his mother being forced to give up the stage and her children due to her constant ill-health. Charlie and his brother were sent to an orphanage until his mother was well enough to care for them. When he was seven, he joined a touring music hall act, The Eight Lancashire Lads, which lasted a year. The next two years were spent at school and comprised all of his formal schooling. His mother's mind was failing and one day he returned home to find she had been taken away. He spent months on the streets of London fending for himself, and in his wanderings worked his way back on the stage, taking small parts in the music hall, and gradually getting bigger parts in plays such as Peter Pan. At the age of 24, when the company was at the end of a very successful tour of the United States, Charlie was signed up by the then expanding U.S. film industry. He left for California and the movies. He appeared on the screen for the first time in 1914, a solemn little figure, jauntily swinging his cane, wearing a shabby tail coat, a scruffy derby hat, enormous boots, baggy pants and an absurd toothbrush mustache. His face nervously twitching but held high, with large black rings around his eyes, he sauntered along as though he owned the place. This comic character, which Chaplin invented, did have a history. It was a caricature of a pompous, fat town councilman who lived on the island of Jersey. This man had amused Charlie, when he had directed the parades during a fete, and continually got in front of the camera. Many of Chaplin's studies were taken from his life on the London streets. The big feet were naturally funny; the bowler hat, which just perched on his head, assumed a variety of comic positions, giving a sense of ridicule; his baggy trousers displayed a lost sense of respectability; and the whirl of his cane gave him a professional air. His character was difficult to define. He was continually eluding his audience--suggesting that he was something else--mimicking. The policeman could hardly arrest him for he would have been arresting himself.

The Keystone Company offered him a contract. All the films were silent, and the studio was a vast open stage with the sun deflected on to it by muslin. Several films were made at the same time, thus causing confusion. Much of the material was slapstick comedy as for example, the Keystone Cops--the helmeted fools who never got their man. Chaplin found it difficult to settle in, as he did not like violence and he had been used to a much more subtle performance. In his first film, Making a Living, which took only a week to produce, he wore a frockcoat, top hat, walrus mustache and eyeglass. He was a minor success. His next film, Kid Auto Races at Venice, established his reputation. With other Keystone comedians, he was sent to a children's auto race track at the seaside resort of Venice, California, and told to improvise a film. In his comic outfit, he spent his afternoon dashing out onto the track, getting in the way of the dummy camera which was supposed to be filming the races, while the real one was filming him. It was the first time he used the splay-footed, shuffling walk which broke into a dignified sprint when chased by the Keystone Police and the cameramen. Delighted by his success, he wore the same costume and make-up in every film for the next twenty-five years.

During 1914, Chaplin performed in thirty-five films, twenty-two of which he directed himself. When Chaplin left Keystone at the end of the year and joined the Essanay Company in Chicago, he only made fourteen films in as many months at a salary of $1250 a week, a more substantial sum that the $150 he had received from Keystone. He was signed up by Mutual for $10,000 a week at the age of twenty-seven. This sudden wealth had no great affect on him then or for the rest of his life.

In 1921, after eight years in the U.S. he paid a sentimental visit to England. He was warmly welcomed, and was not only hailed in London, but throughout Europe. He was very flattered by this response and referred to his visit in his book *My Trip Abroad.*

He was an intellectual giant who not only produced, directed, and starred in his films, but also wrote and conducted the music. The "little tramp" figure was the best known in the world, paving a way for future British comics such as Bob Hope and Laurel and Hardy.

SAMUEL GOMPERS

Like many who emigrated from England, Samuel Gompers was born in London in 1850, of poor parents. He was the son of a Dutch cigar maker. His working life started with a job as a shoemaker's apprentice. It was not long before he joined his father to become a full-time member of the working class; and at the age of ten, he found himself earning the princely sum of one shilling a week (about five cents). Although they were working, conditions were so bad that his father decided to immigrate to the United States, taking along his family. They arrived in 1863 to work at their craft of cigarmaking; and found themselves in a wretched slum, similar to the one they had left. Factory life was enjoyable to Gompers, but he joined a group of friends to try to shorten the working hours and to get higher pay. Their requests to the management were refused, which gave them no alternative but to strike. Since Gompers was the leader, he was put on a blacklist and prevented from working.

The European political climate was such that the United States became a place for radical agitators. These were men who were wanted for political crimes or who were discontented with their native political situations and sought the freedom of the U.S. Gompers became inspired by the writings of Karl Marx, who himself had never left Europe. He also wanted to change the appalling conditions in the factories. He believed that the class conflict between the working classes and the factory owners was going to be infinitely greater as industry grew. The so-called middle classes would be a jumping station for the few that got richer, or the others that went down. However, as the working class swelled, their lives would become worse, and in their desperation, they would rebel and try to seize what the owners had gained from the results of their labor.

The output of manufactured goods in the U.S. doubled from 1870 to 1890. Railroads connected the Atlantic and Pacific coasts; the telephone and electric light were becoming part of daily life; but the wages and conditions of the workers did not change. Gompers became impatient to rectify this and met, and was influenced by, Carl Laurell and Adolph Strasser, two European immigrants well versed in socialistic ideas. They asked Gompers to infiltrate Socialist meetings to learn about all they said and wrote, but not to join. They persuaded Gompers that in the effort to oppose capitalism, he should organize the workers with common interests and complaints, into groups or trade unions. The unions then as a group would be able to confront their employers with demands for shorter hours, increased wages, security, better working conditions, and less supervision. The unions if turned down by their employers would be able to call a strike. However, Gompers and his friends were not the first to call strikes. Earlier, the New York bakers had refused to make bread due to low wages. The confused leadership of the Noble and Holy Order of Knights of Labor (the Knights) and their neglect to unionize led Gompers to challenge them. The Knights was an organization which hoped to check capitalism by forming a coalition of middle-class reformers, craft unions, and the masses of semiskilled and unskilled workers. This organization was conducted in secrecy so that their members would not become blacklisted for being agitators. It was as a member, that Gompers tried to develop a separate program to replace the Knights as the dominant labor oragnization. His immediate example was taken from the British Trades Union Congress, where skilled workers were grouped by craft into geographic, or shop locals. They in turn were bound to a national union of the craft, led by men who were elected and who had full control over the member locals. Strikes were national, not local, and strike funds were paid to members and their families for sickness and loss of income during unemployment, and on death.

Gompers inexhaustable efforts enabled this scheme to be extremely successful. He was a brilliant public speaker and an unusual man, having two sides to his character: an inflated ego, but on the other hand, an unfailing and tireless energy to help his fellow workers. Both of these characteristics helped contribute to the secret of his success. His attachment for the men he worked with and for, encouraged his passion for organization. However, with large numbers of immigrants arriving from Europe who were mostly unskilled and used to lower standards of living and thus less eager to rebel, the threat of devastating strikes was weaker. In ensuing years, the economic crisis provoked widespread strikes with great historical significance.

Gompers, along with other union leaders, was disturbed by the indifference of the Knights to their more effective new ideas; so a meeting was called to form a federation similar to the British one. Gompers represented the cigarmakers, and finally the Federation of Organized Trades and Labor Unions of the United States and Canada was established. Endangered by the threat of this new Federation, the Knights joined the Federation in a series of strikes and were considered to be still the most powerful labor organization. Dramatically the Federation, in competition, announced a plan to press for a national eight-hour-week. Gompers took a leading part at a rally in Union Square. Reluctantly the Knights joined in, and a general strike took place. However, in a resulting clash two days later, four men were killed. In protest, a bomb exploded while a meeting was taking place the next day in Chicago's Haymarket Square. All unions were condemned as a result, and were thought to be anti-establishment. At a conference two weeks later, an agreement was reached between the Knights and the Federates. As a result, Gompers was elected president of the then formed American Federation of Labor (AFL).

Through forty years of leadership, Gompers watched the AFL membership rise from 140,000 to 4,000,000. It was not an easy job as he only had limited power. He died having achieved what he wanted most of life, which was to provide the workers with better conditions, shorter hours and greater wages, and also the organization to demand them.

THOMAS COLE

Thomas Cole, who was born in the industrial district of Lancashire, England, became a painter and the Father of American Landscape. He had seven sisters and being the only boy immersed himself in reading books, one of which was on the United States. He became passionately interested in going to the U.S. and talked and thought of nothing else. However, his parents were extremely poor and the chance of it actually happening seemed impossible. His father owned a small lumber mill which failed; and when he started another factory, Thomas was sent away to school. Times were hard; and when his father failed again, he was removed from school and apprenticed to a calico designer. He became fascinated by making engravings on wood blocks to print patterns on calico, but in his spare time he played the flute and dreamed of going to the U.S. To his great surprise, his father one day announced that they were going to immigrate, so in his eighteenth year, he and his family sailed for Philadelphia.

His father opened a dry goods store and Thomas found a job as a wood engraver. Unfortunately, his father had no better luck than when he was in England--his business failed within the year--so he moved the family to Ohio. However, Thomas stayed on in Philadelphia as he was still working for the wood engraver. He made friends with a young law student, sharing lodgings; and they visited the West Indies together. Their ship was waylaid by pirates who searched it from stem to stern, brandishing their swords. They reluctantly withdrew when they could not find any loot, however, they insisted on shaking hands with everyone before they left. This left an impression on Cole's mind for his future work.

Thomas was overwhelmed by the beauty of the islands as he wandered around exploring the towering cliffs, the bright blue ocean, and the mountains covered with exotic flowers. It was there that he started to paint, though little did he know how successful he would be later. He rejoined his family in Ohio, where his father now had a wallpaper manufacturing business. For a couple of years he helped by designing the patterns, during which time a German portrait painter, named Stein, kindly lent him a book on painting. Cole read it eagerly and began to paint a few landscapes using homemade brushes and paint scrounged from a chair factory. He then tried portrait painting, using his family as models, with some success. This gave him the incentive to pack his belongings and tour the surrounding towns trying to earn his living by painting portraits. Luck was against him, another traveling portrait painter having preceded him, so he returned home. His father moved to Pittsburgh to start yet another factory, but Thomas stayed on in Ohio, convinced that he could become a successful painter. His next attempt was a number of religious paintings, but unfortunately they were destroyed by vandals. Disheartened but not discouraged, and used to the constant uprootings, he yet again joined his parents. His mother, believing in his talents, encouraged him to continue, but his father urged him to take a more reliable job.

After a great amount of self-conflict, he decided that he must be a painter. In order to achieve his aim, he decided to go to Philadelphia. Though he did not have the money for lessons, he would be able to visit the Academy of Fine Arts and study the landscapes there. Setting out on foot, with no overcoat, but with a heavy fringed tablecloth that his mother had given him to keep warm, he reached Philadelphia and found a tiny attic where he started painting landscapes. His paintings were of remembered scenes of the West Indies, and of the countryside in Pennsylvania and Ohio. To increase his income, he found a job decorating household wares, but every spare moment was spent in the Academy studying landscapes of great European painters. Lack of friends and loneliness made him once again rejoin his parents, who were then in New York.

At long last his luck changed. He was allowed to put some of his paintings in a shop window. They were sold for forty dollars--to him it was a great fortune. One of his paintings was bought by George Bruen. Bruen was a wealthy man and realizing Thomas' talent persuaded him to visit the Hudson River Valley, one of the most beautiful panoramic spots in the U.S. He financed the trip to enable Thomas to see with his own eyes the marvellous mountain peaks, the rivers, and deep forests. Thomas tramped around making sketches and notes of all he saw, and on his return painted numerous landscapes which were bought by three artists--John Trumbell, William Dunlop, and Asher Durand. They consequently became firm friends. They admired Cole's paintings, saying that they showed a quality they had been trying to achieve all their lives.

From then on, Thomas Cole's fame was assured. His works were sought after by prominent collectors. In 1820, he went to London to meet some of the top English painters such as John Constable and William Turner. He then travelled to Italy feasting his eyes on historical paintings to return home to paint his own. He died at the age of forty-seven, but not before he was established as the Father of American Landscape. His work inspired future American artists to depict the beautiful country they lived in, pioneering a truly national school of painters.

It is hard to believe when living in the 20th century, that there was a time in the U.S. when hospitals were practically non-existent and doctors few and far between.

WILLIAM MAYO

William Worrall Mayo, who was born in 1819, set out with independence and dedication to alter the course of medicine. His father died when he was seven; and he was brought up in a family of distinguished physicians. His mother lived near Manchester, an industrial district, during a time when all the spinners and weavers were out of work. It was a time of rioting, when there was little food to quell the unrest. These events made an impression on Mayo which left him with a lifelong desire to help the underdog, though he was himself not brought up in poverty. Nearly three-fourths of the English children at that time had no education; but Mayo went to a grammar school where he studied Latin, Greek, literature and science and mathematics. He was also inspired by a chemistry teacher, John Dalton, and never lost his avid interest for chemistry.

Although Oxford and Cambridge Universities were the places to study medicine, William began his studies in Manchester; and continued them in hospitals in London and Glasgow. However, he was an independent and impatient man and did not stay long enough in any one hospital to obtain a license to practice. This meant years of work, and a longer time to secure a hospital appointment. The appeal and adventure of going to the U.S. was so great that at the age of twenty-five, he set off across the Atlantic.

He had no trouble in finding work in New York City as an instructor of Chemistry in Bellevue Hospital Medical College. The conditions were appalling--infectious diseases were rampant, particularly yellow fever, cholera, typhus, typhoid fever, jail fever, and ship fever. It was not long before Mayo left for more open country, thoroughly disheartened by his experience. He decided to settle in Lafayette, Indiana, and with a partner, Alphonso Roath, set up premises as a tailor. He lasted a year and decided to return to medicine, taking his degree as a doctor of medicine, though a degree at that time was not necessary to practice medicine. Cholera was sweeping the country, creating panic and a demand for more doctors. Mayo successfully treated his patients but realized how little the new science of chemistry contributed to Medicine. There were few scientific procedures, or instruments of precision to help diagnosis, let alone a stethoscope--even the thermometer had not yet been invented. Surgery was confined to the amputation of a crushed leg or the removal of a cancerous sore. Because of this, he decided to work as a pharmacist as well as attending to the needs of his patients.

At the age of thirty-two, he married Louise Wright. She not only gave him two sons who were to follow in his footsteps, but she also gave him unfailing help in his work. He continued to research into chemistry, advocating that the chemical analysis of a patient's urine could give some indication to the cause of his ill health. However, he was also called to outlying districts to attend his patients. So, packing his saddlebags with medical and surgical supplies, he rode off on his horse

104

to not only deal with aches and pains, but with malaria, typhoid and scarlet fever; and became a victim of malaria himself.

He went to the University of Missouri to work as an assistant to the Professor of Anatomy and was granted an additional degree. He then applied to become a surgeon in the Civil War, desiring the experience in the field. The pay was also far more substantial than members of his profession generally earned.

After the war, he moved to Rochester, a grain depot for most of southern Minnesota. He took part with great enthusiasm in all the community life, providing the city with its first library and, as a member of the school board, initiating the building of a new school. He waged battles for a system of sewers, a gas works, and an electric light plant. However, he did not neglect his medical practice, and designed his own examining table of wood which was covered with a thin mattress and had a detachable board that could be fitted at the end when a longer surface was needed. It is still that type of table, with a few modifications, that is used in the Mayo Clinic today. He also realized that the recording of cases provided a valuable source for the statistical study of disease, a custom not practiced by his fellow doctors. In performing autopsies, he checked his diagnoses by studying these specimens under a microscope in his laboratory in a corner of his office, still maintaining his ideas on the value of chemical analysis.

He was still a general practitioner, but he desperately wanted to become a surgeon. So he went to New York for several months to study, and then returned to Rochester to practice all he had learned. Meanwhile, his two sons, Will and Charlie, went away to medical school, after which they returned to Rochester to help their father.

Late in 1883, a tornado hit Rochester, resulting in devastation. Houses were flattened and many people killed. William Mayo organized a temporary hospital, and realizing that he needed nurses to tend the patients' needs, he asked the teaching Sisters of St. Francis to help. Before this tragedy, the mother of the Sisters of St. Francis had been asked by her bishop to open a hospital in Rochester. She told Mayo that if he took charge of the hospital, they would finance it. The hospital was built to William Mayo's and his sons' specifications, laying the foundation stones of what was to be the famous Mayo Clinic. Before long, the institution was self-supporting even though it was without the support of the local community. They only had the bare necessities, having to wait to buy blankets with the money they would earn.

The Mayo's spent much time travelling, visiting other hospitals to study the techniques of their surgeons. As there were three of them, this did not hinder their work. Gradually their reputation spread and doctors sent their patients to them, or summoned them to their patients' homes. They persuaded well-established surgeons and physicians to come to work with them at Rochester, and formed a formidable team which was to gain worldwide recognition. They always had at least fifteen fellowship men working at the Institute of Experimental Medicine. Their library held a collection of the most important books for research and statistics. The new clinic cost at least three million dollars. These factors made Rochester one of the centers of medicine. The Mayos' contribution was enormous, and though their biggest contribution to actual medicine was surgery, their reputation for the development of teamwork and education in medicine is very evident today.

THE BEATLES

Penny Lane, Yellow Submarine, and It's Been a Hard Day's Night are songs that are sung all over the world, by young and old, and are nearly as famous as the four young men who hit the world, with their enchanting music--The Beatles. Originally there were five Beatles: John, Paul, George, Pete Best, and Stu Sutcliffe. Stu Sutcliffe died tragically from a brain tumor, and Pete Best (drums) was replaced by Ringo, who was so named for all the rings he wore on his fingers.

They were discovered in a club in Liverpool, England--a poor, tough town, very much influenced by the wit and sense of humour of the Irish, who sought jobs there. The northern clubs were well established and music was taken very seriously. Returning seamen brought back records from the United States so English and U.S. music was closely entwined. Rock and Roll, which exploded after World War II, the Blues, and Country and Western were all familiar to the Beatles, but it was Rock and Roll that had the greatest influence on their music. The magical quality of ther music drew hoardes of fans. Paul and John started to compose their own music, and it was not long before Brian Epstein discovered them. He became their agent and launched them into their international career.

Success and popularity preceded them to the United States. Millions of people flocked to hear their concerts during their tour of the U.S. There was mass hysteria as fans besieged them, adulated them, and began to copy their dress and long hair styles. The apparent simplicity and innocence of their songs was deceptive. There was a freshness to their songs which set the feet of the young and old tapping. They started a new concept in music, improvising primitive songs into poetical and trancelike melodies. Their long hair and strange wit intrigued people and started a whole new wave of pop music which turned out to be a multi-million dollar commercial industry.

Of course to list the English contributions of people living today would fill a book but here are a few names of English celebrities who have contributed their talents in the U.S.

From the world of music and ballet came Leopold Stokowski a composer and Margot Fonteyn, a prima ballerina who was born in Reigate and who has with

Alicia Markova from London, done much to inspire and entertain audiences. From the world of pop, Mick Jagger, Cat Stevens, and Elton John are names that all the young of today recognize. The record stands are full of their original music that they have not only composed but recorded and sung. Tommy Steele, born ten years earlier, performed his musical talents before pop music was an everyday occurance.

RADIO & TV

From the world of radio and TV: performer and producer, David Frost, who spends much of his time commuting back and forth between England and the U.S. to put on his chat shows. Top directors and producers such as Ken Russell, Alfred Hitchcock, David Lean, and David Warner have all been lured to Hollywood to produce films of great interest. They have encouraged their counterparts to come over from England to act. Here again the list of famous actors and actresses is immense. The following are a few that have had starring roles, some winning Oscars in doing so: Dawn Adams, Julie Andrews, Richard Attenborough, Claire Bloom, Joan Collins, Peter Cushing, Diana Dors, Shirley Eaton, Peter Finch, John Gielgud, Cary Grant, Joan Greenwood, Alec Guiness, Anthony Quayle, Ralph Richardson, Paul Scofield, Peter Sellers, Robert Shaw, Maggie Smith, Elizabeth Taylor, Peter Ustinov, Glenda Jackson, Peter Lawford, Margaret Leighton, James Mason, Roger Moore, Robert Morley, Laurence Olivier, and Michael Caine, Tom Courtnay, Michael Crawford, Albert Finney, James Fox, Susan Hampshire, David Henning, Anthony Newley, Terence Stamp, Michael York and Susannah York--not forgetting the Mills family--Hayley, John and Juliet; and Lynn, Michael and Vanessa Redgrave.

These contributions are a small example of those made by the daring and inventive English who left their country bringing a culture and language to the U.S. There are many others but all of them have helped create a free country forming a firm foundation for the children to come.

14

FRANCE

by

NEDRA WOOLF

We have become so accustomed to seeing the total tapestry we call the United states of America, we fail to see the individual threads. The threads that appear again and again in the allover design are the red, white, and blue ones of the French. The people and countries are so interwoven in every area that it seems natural that the national colors of the United States and France are the same.

The pattern began with French fishermen casting their lines and nets off the coast of Newfoundland. How long ago were they fishing in these waters? It is difficult to tell but when Jacques Cartier discovered the Gulf of St. Lawrence in the 16th century he was surprised to find a French fishing boat hauling in its catch. They told him they had been coming there for many years.

Jacques Cartier, pushed and pulled by the hope of finding a quick Northwest water passage to the East Indies, sailed westward. Cartier pushed on and discovered the St. Lawrence River, which would open the way for more and more discoveries. There followed Pere Jacques Marquette, a missionary dedicated to converting the natives in the New World. Priest he was but also he was deeply interested in opening up new territory for the glory of God and France. Accompanied by a small group of men, Pere Marquette went deeper and deeper into unknown territory. He was the first white man to travel the entire length of the great Mississippi river.

Twice, France's actions shaped the destiny of the United States. The first time was when she helped the thirteen colonies win their independence and the second time was when she offered us the opportunity to buy the Louisiana territory. This purchase opened up the West for the young Republic. However, the contributions of French immigrants that came here were outstanding.

THE HUGUENOTS

The first real wave of French immigrants swept up on our shores were the Huguenots (French Protestants). In the late 17th century, the ruling powers of

109

France decided they would no longer allow any religion but Roman Catholicism to be practised. The Huguenots were given the choice of converting or leaving the country. Most of them were very well off as they were the merchants, manufacturers, artisans, and wine producers of France. It was difficult to go, and leave their homes, farms, and businesses. They felt that perhaps this madness would soon pass. On the contrary, it grew worse; all rights were taken away, the Protestants' churches were closed. Convert or die by torture became the order of the day. This included every Huguenot in the land, seven years of age and up. Those that could, escaped to other countries. Some of them fled to Holland.

In the Dutch town of Leyden, some of the Huguenots met a group of Puritans who had come from England to the more liberal atmosphere of Holland. There they were making plans to go to the New World, where they could live in religious freedom. When the Mayflower sailed to establish the colony of Plymouth, there were Huguenots aboard. On the passenger list was "Wm. Mullins, his wyfe, his sone Joseph and young Priscilla." The name actually was Guillaume Molines but the Puritans couldn't pronounce it let alone spell it and it became Mullins. It was this Priscilla Molines who became the wife of John Alden and provided the inspiration for Longfellow's famous tale, "The Courtship of Miles Standish."

The inhumane persecution continued and more and more Huguenots fled France, many of them immigrating to America, such as the little French boy, Apollos Rivoire. Apollos' parents, unable to escape themselves, managed to get him out of France to his uncle in England. In a few years, his uncle arranged passage for him, hoping he would have a better chance in the colonies.

The thirteen year old boy sailed into Boston Harbor in 1716. He stood on the upper deck of the ship, glad to see land after three months at sea. He looked in wonder at the mass of docks, shipyards, and warehouses which rimmed the harbor. The smells, color, activity, the many ships anchored there were exciting. The young French boy was also frightened. How would he do in this strange land so far from all his family? What kind of man had he been apprenticed to? Would he be kind? What of his master's family? After all, he thought, I have to live with him for ten years. Will I become a welcome part of the family? He knew he would be fed and clothed and taught how to become a silversmith but also he would be under his master's complete authority. All these thoughts pounded away at the young boy as he looked out upon the busy harbor of Boston.

Fortunately for Appolos he had been apprenticed to Mr. Coney, one of the most respected silversmiths in Boston and a considerate man. There was much silver to work with as silver was considered to be one of the safest investments. There were no banks at that time, and those who could saved all types of silver coins. They would then take their silver coins to a silversmith to be melted down and made into plates, cups, candle holders, and other household items. This practice eventually resulted in most of the available silver being used up, and Boston decided to issue paper money. Mr. Coney was hired to engrave the plates for that first paper money in America.

The Huguenot immigrants quickly adjusted to Yankee ways and Americanized their names. Apollos Rivoire, by the time he finished his apprenticeship, called himself Paul Revere.

REVOLUTIONARY WAR HEROES

In France, the Rivoire family died out, but Apollos was destined to be the founder of a famous American family and to start the Revere Copper and Brass Company. His son, Paul Revere, would become familiar to every schoolboy for the next two hundred years. He was one of the founders of the Sons of Liberty and a leader of the Boston Tea Party. Even today, the echo of that famous cry, "The British are Coming!" calls up the thrill, the fear, and the excitement of our forefathers on that night so long ago.

The Huguenots very soon became part of whatever community they settled in. One field they neither entered nor were interested in was that of politics. That is, they were not political in the 17th or the early 18th century when the greatest number of Huguenots came to this country. However, by the time of the American Revolution, their children and grandchildren were very much involved. In addition to Paul Revere who we already have met, there was James Boudoins, leader of the Council in the Massachusetts House of Representatives. He nursed and kept alive the infant independence until it grew strong enough to go it alone. It was Henry Laurens who went to France and convinced Rochambeau and other French officers to help the Revolutionary forces. Laurens also managed to arrange a personal audience with the French king, obtaining the royal approval. This saved months of negotiations and allowed help to reach the Colonies as soon as possible.

John Jay, another Huguenot, was one of the strongest influences in working out a good peace treaty. He got the boundries of the new United States extended to the Mississippi River and the undisputed recognition of their independence. Jay saw to it that the French did not dictate any of the terms. The Americans were grateful for the help France had given, but they had fought too hard, too bitterly, and too long to allow themselves to be dictated to by any foreign power.

The terms that John Jay obtained were attributed to "Yankee shrewdness" which, the Americans congratulated themselves, was more than a match for "French Subtlety." This Yankee shrewdness of John Jay's came from his Huguenot background, didn't it?

We can't leave the Huguenots tucked snugly in the history books without mentioning Peter Minuit who made one of the all time real estate deals. He bought

Manhattan Island from the Indians for twenty-four dollars. On this island now stands a large section of New York City where the cost of land is figured by the square foot. And what about Peter Faneuil who gave Boston, Faneuil Hall, usually called the "cradle of liberty." It was in this hall that men gathered to protest the many English injustices. From there, first came the whisper, then the shout for independence.

LAFAYETTE

In this fight for independence, individual Frenchmen came to help. The young Marquis de Lafayette volunteered his assistance in every way.

One of the great passions that moved the French during the latter part of the 18th century was a hatred and distrust of England. When the news of the revolt of the English colonies reached France, this excited the 19 year old marquis. He thought how great it would be to join the revolutionary forces and help give England a good sound beating. What an adventure this would be, Lafayette thought. He was an officer in the French army but he hadn't seen active service and what fun to see action and against the English!

The Marquis had lost both parents and was sole heir to a fortune so large he had no idea just how rich he was. He bought and completely equipped a ship and

112

gathered a group of French officers at his own expense. They sailed, all eager to offer their services to the Revolutionary army.

The elegant Marquis de Lafayette was 5' 9" tall, slender, with reddish hair, blue-gray eyes and a sharp backward-sloped forehead. He carried himself as the aristocrat he was with a family tradition of chivalry. The Lafayettes had always been brave. They had been among those that had searched for the Holy Grail. They had been defenders of virtue and innocence, slayers of dragons. One of them had ridden by the side of Joan of Arc. These tales, one must agree, had become rather exaggerated through the years, but they had been part of Lafayette's childhood, and he had made these tales his.

Lafayette and his fellow officers were anxious to reach Philadelphia where the Continental Congress was in session. They were impatient and eager to get into the fighting and were looking forward to a warm welcome.

Unfortunately, sometime before Lafayette's arrival in Philadelphia, Frenchmen had been arriving with commissions of general, major general, and other high-ranking titles. These had been obtained from Mr. Deane, the American agent in France. Mr. Deane had neither the authority to hand out military rank nor did he prove to have good judgement in picking men. Those that arrived had proven not only incompetent but had demanded tremendous sums in payment for their services.

When Lafayette and his men arrived, Congress groaned at the thought of having to deal with more incompetents. Instead of the warm welcome they had expected, the Frenchmen were shocked at the icy cold reception.

Lafayette was so angry at this type of behavior that he sat down and immediately dashed off a letter to Congress. One line rang out of the pages, catching the ear of every member of Congress. "I have the right," the Marquis wrote, "to ask two favors at your hands: The one to serve without pay, at my own expense, and the other that I be allowed to serve first as a volunteer."

Congress was only too happy to give Lafayette what he asked and made him a major general. This title Congress thought of as an honorary title. Not Lafayette. He took it very seriously and asked to be sent to the battlefields immediately.

Congress received another angry letter, this time from Washington. He wrote, asking, how absurd could they be, giving a major-generalship to a boy hardly old enough to be a lieutenant? Nevertheless the French boy reported for duty to General George Washington.

A few days later, Washington invited the young officer to attend a review of the troops. Lafayette could not hide his shock. "Mon Dieu! Is this the army to defeat the English?" he thought in despair as 11,000 ragged, often barefooted, men without a complete uniform among them passed before him. Washington seeing Lafayette's reaction, told him he realized how this must look to an officer fresh from the French army.

"I am here, sir," Lafayette replied controlling his disappointment, "to learn, not to teach."

Washington found himself beginning to like this young aristocrat who seemed to be more than he appeared. As the weeks passed, a friendship grew between these two that was to last through both of their lifetimes. Lafayette who had come for adventure and a lick at the English was beginning to understand why the Colonists were fighting. He grew to love and respect George Washington and began to grasp the meaning of the word Independence.

VALLEY FORGE

Then came the winter at Valley Forge. Washington had picked this location well. It had rich farmland which would provide his men with plenty of food. This was true, but the farmers refused to accept continental paper money, believing it had no worth, but was all Washington had. The farmers smuggled their produce into Philadelphia where they sold it to the British for gold.

Clothing was even more difficult to obtain. It had to be brought in by ships, which had trouble getting through the English blockade. Through the bitterly cold winter, the men had neither enough food or clothing. Surprisingly, the elegant marquis, used to every type of luxury, never complained as he endured the hardships at Valley Forge. He found it exciting meeting and knowing different types of men. He tried very hard to learn American ways and speech. He wanted very much to become Americanized.

To those at Valley Forge, that winter it seemed as though they had been forgotten by their country, even the whole world. Then came the news that France had declared war on England and had signed a formal treaty with the Colonies.

The men at Valley Forge hoped again and victory seemed possible. But in Boston, when the first of the French ships arrived in the harbor, the Bostonians' feelings were mixed and confused. They knew how desperately help was needed. On the other hand, it was not too long ago that many of them had fought against the French as British citizens. Many of the Bostonians were sons and grandsons of Huguenots who had fled the terrors and atrocities in France. They knew first hand of the inhuman treatment their forefathers had suffered. How, they asked themselves, does one greet such recent enemies, suddenly our allies? The strange currents of politics were as confusing then as they remain to this day.

The arrival of the French turned the tide and independence was won.

Lafayette saw enough action to satisfy even him. He proved to be a brave and clever soldier, living up to the Lafayette family tradition. He wrote back to his friends in France, trying to explain this strange but exciting idea that had infected these Americans, this malady called Independence which enabled these ill-equipped, badly and inadequately fed and clothed, unsoldierly men to fight on in the face of unbelievable obstacles.

It must have infected Lafayette also. In just a few years, he would take an active part in the French Revolution and in the government of the new French Republic.

For his services to the United States he was given citizenship by an act of Congress.

The French revolution sent many French men and women of noble blood to the U.S. They brought with them the elegance of the French aristocracy, the fine art of cooking, dancing, style, all the niceties they had enjoyed at home. From France came the solid, hardworking, energetic, talented Huguenot and the refinement and polish of the aristocrat. It does appear that we received the best of both worlds.

STEPHEN GIRARD

1812, and we were again at war, and again a Frenchman appeared to help. Money again: the U.S. Treasury tottered on the edge of bankruptcy, and Stephen Girard arranged an eight-million dollar loan issue, which put the U.S. Treasury back in business.

Girard: merchant, financier, philanthropist, had been born in Bordeaux, France. He was not a very handsome man. Blind in one eye from birth, he was possessed with a driving ambition. He sailed out of Bordeaux at the age of fourteen as a cabin boy and never went back. In a few years, he was a shipmaster and shortly after that, a merchant. He picked Philadelphia to settle in and at one time he had eighteen ships sailing between Europe and Asia and the United States.

He bought the building and assets of the first U.S. Bank when Congress refused to renew the bank's charter. When the war of 1812 ended, he helped start the second United States Bank.

He became well known in the commercial and financial life of the country. No matter how busy he was, he always managed to have time to do things for his adopted town, Philadelphia.

In 1793, an epidemic of the dreaded and highly contagious yellow fever hit Philadelphia and the death toll grew higher each day. Stephen Girard acted as superintendent at the yellow fever hospital. He worked around the clock, nursing and caring for the patients personally. He had no medical background, but a great compassion and need to help people. He kept up this pace for sixty days, refusing to stop until the emergency was over.

He moved to a farm when he grew older, one located in South Philadelphia. He read everything he could find about farming as he knew nothing about it. His books on farming sat very comfortably next to Voltaire, one of his favorite French writers.

"To rest is to rust," was one of his frequent sayings; and one of his best liked sayings was, "If I thought I was going to die tomorrow, I should plant a tree nevertheless today."

He left most of his great fortune to establish Girard College, a free school which he wrote in his will was to be for white male orphan children. In 1968, according to a Supreme Court ruling, the school began to admit black orphan boys.

Someone, once said of Stephen Girard: "...there is something grand in the onward steps of the poor cabin boy, maimed in sight...a stranger in his speech, unhappy in his married life, overcoming disadvantages...building a great estate to enrich his adopted city...the fatherless and the dependent."

So it goes on and on. There is that great big lady holding a torch, that stands on a tiny island in New York Harbor--the Statue of Liberty. It was built and given to U.S. by the French. It was on this very same island, many years ago, that one of the earliest Huguenots, Isaac Bedloe grazed his cattle.

How about the French engineer, L'Enfant, who made the plans for the new national capital and established the eagle as the symbol of America. Then there is Rene Jules Dubos, bacteriologist, who gave us the first antibiotic commercially produced. He influenced studies that eventually led to the discovery of streptomycin. And there is Alexis Carrel, the first American to receive the Nobel Prize in the field of physiology or medicine. This was for his work in successfully suturing blood vessels and transplanting organs. He received honors from all over the world. He is the author of many books, one of the best known being *Man the Unknown*. He even wrote a book with Charles Lindbergh, the famous flyer.

In the field of art, there were many, but one that comes to mind eagerly is Augustus St. Gaudens. He was the sculptor of the Adams Memorial outside of Washington, D.C., which is considered the finest of its kind ever produced by an American sculptor. Another unusual Frenchman was Raymond Loewy, an industrial designer. It has been said he invented this profession. That may or may not be, but he did change the American industrial look. Among his many innovations was the redesigning and streamlining of the locomotives and the cars of the Pennsylvania Railroad. He redesigned the interiors of the trains, even to the non-spill coffee cups for the dining cars.

There are the Du Ponts. The first of the Du Ponts to come to the United States was a printer and publisher. He and his family had to leave France because of his views. He wanted freedom of the press, reforms in labor laws, and an end to the oppression of people. When the Du Ponts arrived here, they started a company to make gunpowder; and today the Du Pont Company is one of the great chemical companies of the world.

It was a Frenchman's idea that enabled the Wright bothers to come up with their first airplane. Octave Chanute came to this country at the age of six. He was a civil engineer for most of his life and it wasn't until he was in his sixties that he became interested in aeronautics. He came up with the idea of flexible wing control surfaces, which is basic to all airplane design. The Wright brothers motorized a basic Chanute biplane; and made their historic flight.

And still they come, still contributing in the theatre, films, science, music, and sports.

Men like Jacques Cousteau, marine explorer. He has taken us into the beauty and excitement of the wonderful underwater world. His son Phillippe now accompanies him on the trips of exploration all over the world. During the times they find themselves landlocked, California is their home base. Jacques Cousteau's other son, Jean Michel stays ashore working at his profession as as architect.

MUSIC AND MOVIES

In music, ranging from classical to pop, there are many. Roger Wagner, famous director of the Roger Wagner Chorale was born in the small town of LePuy, France. Some years ago, Dr. Wagner was a member of the French Olympic team and was a finalist in the Decathlon. An athlete becoming an outstanding musician, you ask? To a Frenchman nothing is impossible! Perhaps that is why the French have always melded into the United States so well.

Darius Milhand and Pierre Monteux are conductors of great symphony orchestras; Michael Potnaref, composer, who wrote the musical score for the movie Lipstick; and Sylvie Varton and Regine, young pop singers, all have the U.S. as their address.

Flipping the pages of a Who's Who in the film industry we find names like Jean Renoir, internationally famous film maker and son of the famous French artist, Pierre Auguste Renoir; Louis Malle, who recently won an Oscar for the most outstanding foreign film; and Just Jaeckin, another film maker, all making their homes in the United States.

We also see the names of Robert Florey, film director and Jean Louis, costume designer and famous clothes designer. What of the actors and actresses

117

that have added so much to our entertainment: Charles Boyer, Claudette Colbert, Yvette Mimeux, Leslie Caron, Louis Jourdan, Catherine Deneuve, and Monique Vooren?

In the arts? Francoise Gilot, well known artist and for some time associated with Picasso. She now lives and works in La Jolla and is married to the famous Dr. Jonas Salk of the Salk Institute.

Another famous Frenchman is at the Salk Institute, Dr. Roger Guillemin, scientist, head of research at the institute.

Then there is the internationally famous writer, Anais Nain, who also called the United States her home. Her books have had a great upward surge recently and are being read by the young and reread by her contemporaries.

On the other side of the coin we see that a recent Gold Medal winner at the Olympics in skiing, Jean Claude Killy now lives in the U.S. as does the well known tennis star, Francoise Durr.

It is impossible to read any history of the United States, past or present, without falling over French men and women.

It is difficult to sum up the French immigrants' contribution in one neat phrase. That they added exciting ingredients to the melting pot is certain. The term "melting pot" was first used by a Frenchman, Jean de Crevecoeur, to describe the different types of people that went to make up the United States.

The announcement that Michelin, the French company famous for its tires and guide books, had been chosen to produce New York City's official Bicentennial guide book raised questions in some minds. However, it was a Frenchman who originally bought Manhattan Island, and it seems to me, in the course of natural events, shouldn't the French be the ones to tell its history and points of interest?

C'est la vie!!!

$E = MC^2$

15

GERMANY

by

MARILYN D. HALL

Encounter is the way people realize what they are able to give one another. The theme of Germans in the United States has been one of shared experiences. It has been a people-to-people exchange; and both nations have a feeling of gratitude towards each other. Many of the achievements of the modern world would not have been realized if it had not been for this remarkable blending of these two nations.

As we look back, we see an enormous list of names of people who would not have been able to realize their potential, exercise their imagination, or develop their inventions had it not been for the ties that bound these two nations. People like Werner von Braun, who showed us how much the United States had to offer in the field of rocket technology; the famous architect Ludwig Mies Van Der Rohe; brilliant scientist Albert Einstein who became a professor at Princeton University; and Johann Roebling, an engineer whose dream materialized in the U.S. as the world famous Brooklyn Bridge.

From the very beginning, the history of the United States has been influenced by the contributions of the German people who brought with them their own qualities of leadership, ingenuity, and imagination. Many men of the Revolutionary Army who fought at Valley Forge were German.

The main wave of German immigrants (nearly one and a half million) to the United States was between 1881 and 1890. In a period of one hundred years, over six million Germans immigrated to the United States, more than from any other nation. Attracted to the United States by cheap public land and, later, free homesteads, the German immigrants came in droves. One incentive was the Homestead Act, passed by Congress in May, 1862. This provided that any person over twenty-one, who was the head of a family--and either a citizen, or an alien who intended to become a citizen--could obtain the title to 160 acres of public land if he lived on the land for five years and improved it. Or, a settler could pay $1.25 an acre in place of the residence requirement.

We have heard much about oppressed people eager to escape their troubled homeland and settle in the colonies owned by Great Britain in the New World. We know mostly about the Pilgrims, the Puritans from Great Britain, and the Huguenots from France. But there was also William Penn, who established a Quaker colony in 1681 called Pennsylvania. He was the man who brought the first German settlers over to live in the New World. They sailed on the Concord, the German Mayflower, and when they arrived, set up a community of thirteen families called Germantown, which is today part of Philadelphia. In the years that followed, many hundreds of Germans arrived and settled in Pennsylvania. Others, more adventurous, journeyed westward across the continent.

In the 1800's the French Emperor Napolean had invaded and taken over much of Germany, making it impossible for many farmers and artisans to continue to make a living. They immigrated to the United States where possibilities for economic expansion were great. There were many movements in Germany to overthrow feudalism. Feudalism is a political and economic system where a person holds land as long as he pays homage and allegiance, usually in the form of military service. In 1848, an attempt was made in Germany to unify thirty-eight states which were under the rule of petty princes. It failed; and thousands of intellectuals, politicians, and revolutionary leaders fled to the United States; thus, workers and creative people crossed the Atlantic toward hope and the promise of better lives.

THEIR NEW HOME

Much of the German immigration went west along the Erie Canal to the Great Lakes and then to the prairies. Cincinnati has included prominent Germans in its population since the beginning of the 19th century. Martin Baum, a successful businessman, was mayor of Cincinnati. The first German paper was a weekly, *Die Ohio Cronic*. By 1840, the German immigrants were well established in that Ohio River town. Many owned vineyards or were engaged in trade and industry such as the jewelry business and the manufacture of stoves and musical instruments. By the middle of the 1840's, the German element in Ohio was in full bloom in Columbus, Dayton and Toledo. The Toledo Express was published in 1856 by three brothers, Guido, Emil and Joseph Marx.

The German immigrants felt particularly at home in Wisconsin also, because the soil, climate, and products were familiar and reminded them of whence they came. There among the heavily wooded areas, they found a home away from home. Milwaukee was known as "the German Athens" and became the cultural center for the German mind and intellect. Beer gardens, singing societies, a German-English academy, a Free Thinkers club--all flourished in Milwaukee.

In the 1830's the Germans settled and peopled the banks of the Missouri River. Eventually, there were German communities throughout the United States. The immigrants had such occupations as: food processing, brewing, steel making, electrical engineering, railroading, and printing. Along with their skills, they brought many customs. The Christmas ritual of religious services combined with exchanging gifts around the holiday tree is of German origin. So too is the celebration of New Year's. The Germans introduced the kindergarten, or children's play school. They also promoted the concept of a state-endowed university patterned after the German universities.

Freedom of religion was anything but taken for granted in most of the nations of Europe. Because of religious persecution, William Penn in 1682 traveled through the Rhineland, inviting Mennonites and other Protestant sects to settle his new colony. In the New World, these congregations kept to themselves in tightly-knit isolated settlements. Many of the descendants of these first settlers still live on these centuries-old lands and follow the same customs and traditions. They are not allowed, for example, to contract civil marriages, baptize children, swear oaths, take vengeance, use force of any kind, or participate in wars. These are the Hutterites who wear the costume of the 19th century and, even though they are German-Americans, are known as the Pennsylvania Dutch.

The first German-American exchanges in scientific fields began in 1766 when Benjamin Franklin (of kite-flying fame) visited the Royal Society of Sciences in Gottingen. During the 20th century, a great number of foreign students traveled to the United States to learn about the American achievements in the field of applied science, publicized at the World Fairs in Chicago and in St. Louis. Werner Heisenberg won the Nobel Peace Prize in 1932 and taught at the University of Chicago. By the outbreak of World War II, many of the prominent German scientists had fled to the United States. Albert Einstein was a brilliant German whose theory of relativity was condemned by the Third Reich. When he immigrated to the United States, Germany lost its lead in scientific research; and with his help, the U.S. became a leader in the field.

In the field of psychology, the entire school of Gestalt psychology moved from Berlin to the United States when its founders (Wertheimer, Kohler, and Koffka) immigrated as a group. The same thing happened in sociology when Max Horkheimer and Theodore W. Adorno moved from Frankfurt to Columbia University.

AIRBORNE

The conquest of sky and space was a venture in which both Germans and Americans have made major contributions. From the mythological Greek, Icarus, and his dream of flying, to Leonardo da Vinci's first bird-like flight contraption; to be airborne has always been one of man's preoccupations and devout wishes. In the year 1891 in Germany, Otto Lilienthal was airborne for all of 82 feet. His glider bird was the first successful flying machine made with a rigid wing structure; and to his research, the Wright brothers added a gas driven motor and accomplished the first motorized free flight. This event took place at Kitty Hawk, North Carolina, on December 7, 1903. It was a posthumous triumph for the German glider flight pioneer. Orville and Wilbur Wright in turn helped German aviation get off the ground by founding the first German flying school and aircraft factory in Johannisthall, near Berlin. After World War I and, heyday of the Red Baron (about whom Snoopy wistfully dreams), an air bridge between the two continents was established.

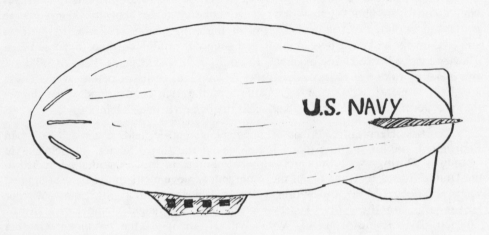

In 1927, Lindbergh was the first man to fly across the Atlantic Ocean alone, and that same year Chamberlain and Levine made the first direct flight from New York to Berlin. The first transatlantic flight from East to West (against the wind) was piloted by the Germans von Hunefeld and Kohl and the Irishman Fitzmaurice in April 1928 from Berlin's Templehof Airport. They were enthusiastically greeted by New York, as was the Graf Zeppelin dirigible, a hydrogen inflated airship. The inventor of this lighter-than-air craft, Count Ferdinand von Zeppelin, was in America during the Civil War as an observer, and made his first balloon ascent in the U.S. The most famous dirigible was the Hindenberg, which opened up a passenger route across the Atlantic in 1936. The era of the Zeppelin was cut short when the Hindenberg, coming from Germany, crashed in a fiery ball while landing at Lakehurst, New Jersey, on May 6, 1937.

During the next twenty-five years, people became used to the age of modern flight which culminated in jumbo jets; and man's imagination turned to space flight. Even the early days of rocketry were associated with German names, particularly Werner von Braun's, whose research in liquid propellant rockets was the basis for the U.S. space program. Working along with William Pickering and James Van Allen, von Braun was responsible for the United States' first space achievement: Explorer One, a pencil-shaped, 31-pound spacecraft that orbited around the world in 1958. A cooperative research project resulted in the solar probe Helios which was built in Munich and launched from Cape Canaveral, now called Cape Kennedy. It came closer to the sun than any other previous spacecraft.

Music is the art which most easily communicates without the use of words. The first instrumental group in the United States which one could call an orchestra was put together in Boston in 1798 by Gottlieb Grautner, an immigrant from Germany who had played in Haydn's orchestra in London. Grautner formed a Philharmonic Society and a Handel-Haydn Society in Boston. Many of the first conductors in the U.S. were from Germany, the "land of classical music."

German conductors have left their brilliant mark on symphony orchestras in the United States. Fritz Reiner conducted the Chicago Symphony Orchestra until Georg Solti took over in 1969. Many other composers such as Paul Hindemith, and interpreters like Bruno Walter were driven into exile to the U.S. by Hitler. The great Wagnerian soprano Helen Traubel outraged her mentors by singing in night clubs. The works of Lukas Foss, a conductor, composer, and pianist, display a wealth of melodies which have been used in jazz as well as classical music.

The first two decades of the 19th century saw the growth of physical education in the United States. There was close cooperation between American educators such as Horace Mann and George Bancroft and the German immigrants Friedrich Ludwig Jahn, Carl Beck, Carl Follen, and Franz Lieber. Jahn (1778-1852), called the Father of Gymnastics, saw the physical and moral value of gymnastics. He developed his own theory based on the question: "What good is the soundest mind in a feeble body?" He designed the parallel bars, the horse, the rings, and the horizontal bars. During the Napoleonic Wars, many of his students immigrated to the United States and brought with them his ideas. Carl Beck and George Bancroft founded the Round Hill School in Northhampton, Massachusetts, equipping it with the first gymnasium in the United States to use Jahn's equipment. Many of the refugees from Germany founded the first athletic clubs in Cincinnati, 1848, and in Brooklyn, 1850. Baseball and football fans are grateful for the contributions of the sons of German immigrants, such as Lou Gehrig, Honus Wagner, Babe Ruth, and George Stuhldreyer.

One thing was very noticeable about the way the people in the New World got their work done--they used their minds to find simple useful ways of dealing with problems of everyday life. They used new and often bold ideas in addition to whatever materials were available. This was the beginning of what would be called the Industrial Age in the United States. Many European inventions were improved on or completed in the United States. Philipp Reis' work (1861) on the telephone was successfully completed in 1876 by Alexander Graham Bell. Heinrich Goebel thought up the idea of the incandescent lamp, but it was Thomas Edison who made it possible for many of them to be manufactured for industrial use. Ferdinand Braun's work in electro-physics laid the foundation for the development of television in the United States. The ingredients were: German and American minds, United States resources and money, mutual desires for progress and cooperation between men and nations. The result was: great advances in technology and a better life style.

THE ARTS

Revolutionary ideas in dance started in the early 1900's in America and spread to Europe. These new ideas, such as dancers wearing scarves and robes which would flow as they moved, were enthusiastically received and adopted in Germany. As American dancers such as Isadora Duncan and Ruth St. Denis appeared in Germany and were warmly welcomed, German dancers such as Mary Wigman and Hanya Holm came to the United States to live and work. In the 1930's in Germany, the Third Reich was cutting short the development of modern dance. German dancers were anxious to be near the ever-growing centers of dance innovation, the largest of which was New York City. Now a major ballet company, the Stuttgart Ballet Company, is putting Germany back in the dance world--and they perform in the U.S. frequently.

A decisive factor in American art in the 19th century was the creative exchange between German artists who received their inspiration from the American countryside and history. The famous painting "Washington Crossing the Delaware" was painted by the German Emanual Leutze. This idealistic portrait of the General and his officers standing in the small boat would indicate that the artist had little awareness of the seaworthiness of such a vessel. For years American school children have given the painting the irreverent sub-title "Sit Down, General, You're Rocking the Boat." Leutze used the Rhine River as a model for the Delaware River. Studying art in Philadelphia, he finally settled in New York. He received much of his inspiration from the rugged scenery of the Rocky Mountains; and Congress commissioned him to paint a mural for the U.S. Capitol entitled "Westward the Course of Empire Takes Its Way."

Albert Bierstadt (1830-1892) was born in Germany and immigrated to the United States when he was two years old. His work can best be characterized as "romantic realism." Bierstadt was a road surveyor in 1858 and spent the summer sketching the United States countryside in its unspoiled state. His paintings reflect the national spirit at the time the West was won.

In the last sixty years, it has been realized by the artists of Europe that

126

people in the United States are more open-minded and ready to accept some unusual things in the world of art than many Eurpoeans. When a huge European art show was presented in the U.S. in 1913, there followed a tremendous excited response from New York, Boston, and Chicago, the centers of American art. Old World art styles gave way to new "abstract expressionism"--that is an emotion conveyed by reducing a figure to its bare esstentials. Several leaders of the New York school of "abstract expressionism" were Jackson Pollack, Franz Kline, and Willem de Kooning. American art now swung through Europe, finding new acceptance in the German Federal Republic. Each country added to the other's ideas and courage in trying new forms, shared the knowledge, and encouraged continued growth and acceptance.

After 1933, a whole wave of German artists immigrated to the United States. Among the first to arrive was Josef Albers. He was an American artist born in Germany whose whole artistic preoccupation was focused on a concept he called "Homage to the Square." His paintings consisted of a series of superimposed squares, that is, one inside another with varying tones of color--somewhat like a nest of boxes. He preferred using house paint and ink, and created prints by means of computer-activated machinery. His theories of color have been set forth in his book, *Interaction of Color*. There were also among the painters George Grosz, whose pen and ink drawings showed the condition of Germany before World War II; and Hans Richter, Max Ernst, and Max Beckmann. Max Ernst painted of secret fantasies--of pencilled forests and surrealistic landscapes. He had a far-out sense of humor, one of his paintings being entitled "The Horse, He's Sick." Ernst fled to the United States in 1941 where he married the American art patron, Peggy Guggenheim. His painting can be summed up as a statement against the boring art of trivia. The impact of these German artists has changed the concept of art and given it a new freedom.

Beckmann painted about the deep despair of the state of modern civilization. His painting "The Dream" is a mocking nightmare portrayal of the chaos after World War I. His disquieting figures show his impressions of the true nature of modern man and the hopelessness of war. Beckmann spent the final three years of his career in the United States.

U.S. architects in the 19th century had already found fresh and independent approaches to functional structure. The famous German architect, Walter Gropius, had already startled the world by creating a new architecture of the future. After he left Germany in 1937, to head the Harvard Graduate School of Design's architectural department, he left his imprint on many of the buildings in the United States. His most famous building is the Pan Am Building in New York. Another architect, Ludwig Mies Van Der Rohe, left his unmistakable stamp on the present day skylines of Chicago and New York. The Seagram Building was built during four years between 1954 and 1958 and was jointly designed by Mies Van Der Rohe and Philip Johnson.

Perhaps one of the most famous German cartoonists was Thomas Nast. He began his career at the age of fifteen working for four dollars a week. We can thank him for the creation of Santa Claus. He based the jolly, white-bearded figure on Pelze-Nicol (fur-clad Nicholas), a folk figure of his native Bavaria. He also created the political symbol that represents the Republicans. In connection with the political symbol that represents the Republicans. In connection with the political preoccupation of people in the U.S., he invented the authority figure known as Uncle Sam. Many World War I recruiting posters have this figure with white chin beard and a stovepipe hat, pointing a finger; and a caption saying "Uncle Sam Wants You." Nast's keen eye and fertile imagination along with his comical approach make him one of the most famous cartoonists in the United States. In fact, he is considered the parton saint of cartoonists.

In the area of the press, there was a landmark incident that affects our personal freedom. The German immigrant Peter Zenger began the *New York Weekly Journal* in 1733. It was not a completely free publication, as the state government kept a close watch on all publications, carefully scrutinizing what was written to see if there were statements considered dangerous to the government. Making such statments was called "seditious libel" and was punishable by jail. Zenger's paper was full of scathing attacks on the then-Governor of New York, William Cosby. Cosby charged Zenger with seditious libel (even though Zenger was poorly educated and the accusations were written by Zenger's backers). Zenger was arrested on November 17, 1734, and imprisoned. After nine months in prison, Zenger came to trial in the Supreme Court of New York. His backers hired a brilliant and famous Philadelphia lawyer by the name of Andrew Hamilton. Hamilton admitted that Zenger had printed the so-called libel, but that the issue before the court was the truth or falsity of the printed material; that if it could be proven true, Zenger was not guilty. The jury accepted Hamilton's eloquent plea and found Zenger not guilty. The law that truth was a defense in a libel suit (not recognized until 1805) was the first victory for freedom of the press in the Colonies.

ON STAGE

In the 19th century, Germans in the United States learned about each other from literature and newspapers. But with the emergence of the motion picture, the cultural exchange resulted in brilliant contributions to the motion picture industry. During the 1920's and 1930's, the Germans went to Hollywood in droves. Here are just a few of the many directors and stars. Ernst Lubitsch, whose romantic light touch gave us great sophisticated comedies like To Be Or Not To Be. Billy Wilder, co-author and director of the gothic comedy-melodrama Sunset Boulevard. Fritz Lang. Otto Preminger who directed Exodus and was a pioneer in bringing formerly forbidden themes to the screen such as drug addiction in The Man With the

Golden Arm. Josef Von Sternberg, famed as the mentor and interpreter of the Dietrich mystique. Luise Rainer who starred in The Good Earth and won an Academy Award for her performance. Emil Jannings, one of the greatest stars of silent movies. Hedy Lamar, the sultry star of Ecstasy and the American film classic Algiers. Erich von Stroheim, a great director of silent films and later a fine actor. The romantic actor Paul Henreid. Character actor Walter Slezak. The legendary Marlene Dietrich, whose beautiful legs were responsible for the term "cheesecake." The contemporary director of such film hits as The Graduate and Who's Afraid of Virginia Woolf, Mike Nichols. Stage and screen actress Betsy von Furstenberg. These and many others helped to turn the nickelodeon into the art form it became. It can truthfully be said that Hollywood owes its reputation to the German talent that helped to shape it.

By the start of the 20th century, many large cities in the United States maintained full time foreign-language opera companies. One of these was the Irving Place Theatre in downtown New York, operated by Heinrich Conried, who later became the general manager of the Metropolitan Opera, and brought Enrico Caruso to the United States. Germany's loss was America's gain as some of the most distinguished names in theatrical history graced the marquees of Broadway starting in the 1930's. Audiences were privileged to enjoy the performances of Mady Christian, Elisabeth Bergner, and Helmut Dantine, as well as productions by artists of the eminence of Max Reinhardt who left the stamp of his genius on cinema, opera, and the legitimate stage. The German writer Franz Werfel collaborated with American playwright S.N. Behrman on the stage adaptation of the former's story, Jacobowsky and the Colonel, featuring Oskar Karlweis and Louis Calhern in the title roles.

Many German authors were fascinated with the larger-than-life heroes of the American West. German author Karl May specialized in romantic novels of the American West and its swashbuckling heroes. After the World War II, many German authors such as Heinrich Boll, Thomas Mann, Gunter Grass, and Ewe Johnson were widely read in the United States. These, and many other authors who were forced into exile in the U.S., left their mark on U.S. Literature. Herman Hesse became the poet laureate of the young people of the 1960's. Lion Feuchtwanger, Erich Maria Remarque, and Bertolt Brecht were deeply influenced by their American experience and reflected their feeling in their works.

"The richest man in America" when he died in 1848 was John Jacob Astor. His name is still a household word as the ultimate status symbol. Most of his money was made through investments in Manhattan real estate, though he began as a humble German immigrant, owning a small shop in New York City. He bequeathed great sums to establish community facilities such as the Astor Library, now a part of the New York Public Library.

President John Kennedy spoke of the interesting cultural impact that the immigrant brought to America. "To the influence of the German immigrants in particular--although all minority groups contributed--we owe the mellowing of the austere puritan imprint of our daily life. The Germans clung to the concept of the 'continental Sunday' as a day not only of church-going but also of relaxation, of picnics, of visiting, of quiet camraderie in beer gardens, while listening to music of a band." In a way, the Germans gave us life style values that we hold and cherish to this day.

16

GREECE

by

JEANNE PIEPER

Pretend you cannot hear--and have never heard one word--and then close your eyes for a few minutes. Now you are also blind! How will you learn words and what they mean? How will you say what you feel and what is inside your head without words and a way to talk? Does it feel awful...something like being locked in a dark, soundproof closet?

An immigrant from Greece, Michael Anagnos, was a Director of the Perkins Institute for the Blind in Boston which helped children who were like this to communicate. They learned how each letter of the alphabet felt when it was drawn on their hands. Eventually they discovered how to put these letters together to spell out words. Imagine! They had to learn to spell before they could know what a word meant!

Among the many things Anagnos did was to start a kindergarten for blind children. It was the largest and best equipped such school in the country, if not the world. Probably his most famous student was Helen Keller. She was so brilliant, she learned a number of languages, wrote books, and lectured around the world, even though she could not see or hear! Who knows what would have become of her without the work of the Perkins Institute to which Michael Anagnos devoted so many years of his life. At his funeral, the Governor of Massachusetts spoke these words of praise: "The name of Michael Anagnos belongs to Greece, the fame of him belongs to the United States, but his services belong to humanity."

Poems were written in his honor, newspapers wrote editorials in tribute to him, countless letters of condolence and respect poured in from admirers around the world. One blind graduate of his school wrote: "I have always wished for literary ability, but never so much as now, when I desire to express what Mr. Anagnos has been to one graduate of the school. Then multiply that by every life which his life has touched, and you have the result of his influence in the world!"

EDUCATIONAL ADVANCES

Michael Anagnos immigrated to the United States from Greece when he was thirty years old to become the assistant of the then Director of the Institute, Dr. Samuel Howe. Upon Dr. Howe's death, Anagnos was the logical successor, although some wondered if a man who was not a native of the U.S. could manage to get the financial support that he would need to continue the school. The inspirational work of Michael Anagnos soon overcame any doubts they had!

Immediately every branch of the Institute began to respond to his energy and wisdom. He far excelled Dr. Howe as a fund raiser, quickly accumulating one million dollars worth of contributions. He started a printing department to make books for the blind. He gathered a museum of stuffed objects to use in teaching the blind and the deaf, and founded a reference library on blindness and the blind, in Boston. He continued, while improving on, the methods of education that Dr. Howe and his predecessors had discovered.

Today, handicapped people are demanding--and achieving--their rightful place in society. As we learn to fear their differences less, we learn to accept their limitations more; and they have more opportunities to enjoy useful, fulfilling lives. Much thanks can go to Michael Anagnos, who devoted his life almost one hundred years ago to helping blind people learn how to care for themselves.

John Zachos was another Greek who immigrated to the United States because of Dr. Howe. Although Dr. Howe was not from Greece himself, he was very interested in the country, even fighting in the Greek Revolution of 1828. Zachos was the son of a Greek General killed in that war, and Dr. Howe became his guardian.

John Zachos' life was a full and useful one. He was a medic in the Civil War, a Unitarian Minister, and an authority on elocution (the art of public speaking).

One of his chief contributions to the United States was his work as a teacher. After the Civil War, the slaves were free but there was much debate about whether they could be taught to read. Most of the slaves had been kept ignorant on purpose and had no schooling of any kind. Some people did not realize that the slaves' lack of abilities was due to not having been taught. They thought that Negroes were uneducated because they were not smart enough to learn abstract ideas; but could only learn to do the physical work they had been formerly trained to do.

John Zachos wrote a book in 1874 called *A Phonic Primer and Reader*. It was designed to be used in night school classes for the freed slaves. He proved that Negroes could be educated. That was a brave thing for a man to do in the 1860's, even in the North. Today, adult night school and the idea that race has no bearing on a man's intelligence and ability to learn are accepted parts of our society. John

Zachos helped these ideas become part of the United States' culture by his work over a century ago.

A contemporary Greek immigrant, Dr. Helen Astin, is following in John Zacho's footsteps at U.C.L.A.--only her emphasis is on education for women. As vice president of the Higher Education Research Institute, she is devoting much of her time to discovering how women are treated in the fields of education and career development and the ways women can advance their status in the modern world.

Dr. Austin immigrated to the United States as a foreign student in 1951 and her husband, who she found in the U.S., is also involved in educational research. She wrote many books and became a member of the National Research Council Board of Human Resource Data and Analysis.

The changes such as those we see happening in society around us are rarely spontaneous events, but rather they are the work of many women (and men!) who have the courage to explore and implement new frontiers.

BLENDS OF OLD AND NEW

Greece is one of the oldest countries of the world. Many other modern events, besides educational advances, can be traced back to this birthplace of civilization. Little did the Ancient Greeks dream that one day people would be watching via sattelite TV a girl in a white dress light the torch to signal the beginning of the Olympics just as it was done almost 3000 years ago in Greece. Nor did their playwrights and poets ever imagine that men would step out of a capsule named after their god Apollo, and walk on the moon; or that 20th century children would watch Hercules on television!

From ancient time, Greeks have been interested in plays and entertainment, and much of our theater today can be traced to them. Three Greek brothers who brought this interest with them to the United States when they immigrated eventually became movie theater tycoons. In 1945, the Skouras brothers owned 750 movie houses in the United States and 450 more throughout the world. One brother, Spyros, became president of Twentieth Century Fox.

These three immigrants, Charles, George, and Spyros, had the old Greek idea that the theater should be a community center with responsibilities to its audience and to the country. So, during World War II, they turned their theaters into neighborhood patriotic centers. They hired an advertising man--another Greek immigrant--to hold rallies at their theaters so the people could learn what they could do to help win the war. They made special patriotic films and even started a weekly radio program called This is Our Cause. Their theaters were the first businesses (other than banks) that were allowed to sell war bonds.

Soon all the other theaters followed their lead. Once again, "foreigners" had started natives of the U.S. moving on behalf of the country that belonged to both of them. The nation's champion war bond salesman, who personally sold over five and a half million dollars woth of "E" war bonds, was also an immigrant from Greece. His prize was to christen a Liberty Ship and on September 7, 1944, he swung his hand and let the bottle of champagne break against the bow of the S.S. Michael Anagnos, named after his countryman who had helped so many of the blind.

SPONGES

The Greeks who have immigrated to the "New World" still always feel a special tie to their "Old World" heroes--both real and mythical--who were running the civilized world long before the western world was on a map. One of their ancient businesses, the gathering and selling of sponges, is today almost exclusively done by Greeks, either in their own country or in Tarpon Springs, Florida.

When an American banker, John Cheyney, discovered the sponge business in 1890 in Florida (then consisting primarily of a few natives form the West Indies), he decided this was a business worth developing. He talked to John Cocoris, a Greek employee in a sponge warehouse in New York where imported Mediterranean sponges were stored.

Cocoris told Cheyney that Greeks had been diving for sponges since the time of Homer, long before the birth of Christ. Because a diver needed to hold his breath for a long time to be of any use underwater and because deep water exerted a tremendous pressure upon the unprotected body, it was a very dangerous job which left most sponge divers dead or invalids before they reached the age of 30. However, since 1870, the more progressive Greek sponge divers had started using scientific methods such as: watertight rubber suits and glass helmets with air hoses attached to them. This allowed them to stay under water for as much as five to six hours.

This was enough for the banker, who immediately imported Greek equipment and divers, and within a few years, Tarpon Springs became the major source of United States sponges with the town being occupied almost entirely by Greek-Americans. Although the most efficient scuba diving gear was not developed until World War II, this Tarpon Springs venture could be considered as the forerunner of underwater diving in the United States.

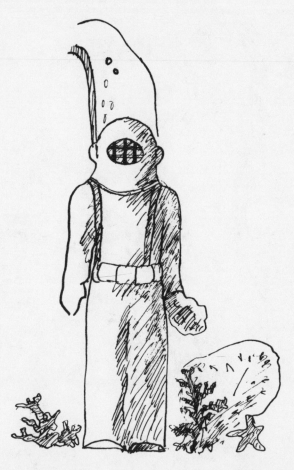

There are many other Greek immigrants whose names you may recognize: the late Dimitri Metropolis, musical director of the New York Philharmonic; and actresses Irene Papas and Melina Mercouri, to mention just a few. Immigrants from Greece, both the famous and the not-so-famous, have blended their old world heritage with new world ways to help shape the United States into what it is today.

秋
收
冬

17

HONG KONG

by

JOAN S. FOLLENDORE

Hong Kong is the most popular duty-free port in the world, attracting one million shoppers every month. It is a lovely little island filled with prosperous, hard-working Chinese, in western-style dress; and surrounded by ancient sampans (houseboats, sometimes called junks), filled with families who live their entire lives on them. Some never set foot on dry land, they are born and die on the sea.

From Hong Kong, the U.S. receives literally tons of clothing for every size and shape. Their handwork is remarkable in sewing and decorating garments. They make everything by hand, and so fast, from leather goods to chess sets and jade and ivory sculpture. We treasure these gifts from the only place we could receive them--Hong Kong.

Although Hong Kong's population is 98% Chinese, it is a British colony, and therefore considered a separate entity regarding immigration to America.

Nancy Kwan, the incredibly beautiful movie star, who Americans have grown to love, was born in Hong Kong, as was Wendy Barrie some years earlier.

Another of Hong Kong's contributions to the United States is the *Oceania*, the world's largest floating restaurant, which harbors in our fiftieth state, Hawaii. It was built in Hong Kong, and was not converted from a passenger vessel. It is patterned after the famous floating restaurants of Hong Kong. The banquet and party rooms seat 1000; and 2000 can be accommodated throughout the ship.

Overall length is 280 feet, beam approximately 60 feet, and draft 16 feet. The ocean-going tug *Fugi Maru* brought the Oceania to Honolulu in 43 days. During the tow, the Oceania was forced to change direction three times to avoid potentially disastrous Pacific hurricanes. She traveled 5200 miles at an average of 5.5 knots when the seas were calm, arriving August 29, 1972.

The Chinese dragon is probably the most familiar symbol to Americans, but few know the real significance of this strange beast. The dragon is the primary animal of the four sacred, supernatural beasts and symbolizes power, vigilance and protection. The noble unicorn stands for perfect good. The long-lived phoenix is an omen for good government. It is the bird found on the roofs of most Chinese shrines and palaces. The enduring tortoise, the only beast still existing today, brought forth literature and philosophy.

Dragons can swim, fly, crawl, and climb. They have wings, claws, beaks, hooves, tails, and fangs. Dragons can be visible and invisible as they please. They can make themselves small as a silkworm or fill the heavens. In winter dragons live in watery depths, but in spring they rise up to spend summer in the clouds.

There are four main types of dragons. Celestial dragons guard the mansions of the gods. Spiritual ones make the winds blow and bring rain to nourish the land. Dragons of the earth fix the courses of streams and rivers. But bobtailed dragons create whirlwinds that can destroy whole towns and cities.

The ancient Chinese often prayed to the dragon. The dragon was thought to rule the East, influence the coming of spring, control rain and symbolize the renewal of life. The emblem of the entire Ch'ing Dynasty was the dragon, as well as being the emblem for countless emperors through the ages.

It was believed that eclipses were caused by a dragon swallowing the sun or moon, and the townsfolk would beat gongs and drums, rattle sticks, and blow horns to drive him away. Indeed, it is recorded that in 2435 B.C. the Archer Lord delivered the moon from a dragon by shooting arrows into the sky. Later his wife wound up on the moon and her face can still be seen there.

Tales tell us of wisemen riding dragons beyond the sea and returning with art, letters and material blessings. A trip on a dragon was the hope of every little boy and girl, and of their parents, too.

18

HUNGARY

by

JEANNE PIEPER

Who do you think is more powerful? The President of the United States of the editor of a major newspaper?

Your answer will depend upon how you define the word "power." However, in 1973, President Richard M. Nixon was forced to resign his office. It was the work of a newspaper, *The Washington Post*, that uncovered and researched the Watergate scandal that eventually led to the President's downfall.

Almost any large newspaper has its claim to fame: some dishonest politician it has sent to jail or some business it has exposed that was defrauding consumers. Right now there is probably an enterprising reporter at your own local newspaper who is working on gathering facts to improve life in his community.

These writers and editors may think that they are inventing the way to make their newspaper a successful public servant, but they are just following in the footsteps of a Hungarian immigrant, Joseph Pulitzer, the founder of modern American journalism.

Before him, newspapers were read primarily by the wealthy. He changed that by cutting the price of his paper in half (from four cents to two cents per copy). He insisted on lively, exciting writing that would be easy and interesting to read. "The American people want something that will arrest their attention, enlist their sympathy, arouse their indignation, stimulate their imagination, convince their reason, awaken their conscience," Pulitzer told one of his writers almost one hundred years ago. An editor today would find it hard to improve upon this advice!

Pulitzer knew that most people are very busy, so he made his writers explain things in as few words as possible. They were to put the most important items first so that the reader would still know what happened even if he only had time to read the first few paragraphs.

Most importantly, everything they wrote was to be accurate and well researched. Once Pulitzer read in a popular book of his day that Marc Antony did not deliver an oration at Caesar's funeral. Knowing that Shakespeare had written differently, and wanting to find out the truth, he sent his staff to interview scholars all over the world. Since they were unable to locate anybody who had attended, or had any firsthand or secondhand knowledge of Caesar's funeral (more than eighteen centuries earlier!), they could not write the story!

Accuracy and public service were so important to Joseph Pulitzer that he left a two and a half million dollar fund to the School of Journalism at Columbia University to encourage those standards in books and newspapers. Awards from this fund are still given today, and a Pulitzer Prize is one of the highest honors a writer can earn.

Another Hungarian immigrant is listed in history books as the founder of an important American industry. He was in an entirely different field and lived many years earlier, during the gold rush on the opposite side of the United States from where Pulitzer lived. Agoston Haraszthy is responsible for starting the California wine industry. Today, California produces almost all the wine in the United States, and the United States has become the sixth largest wine producer in the world.

When Haraszthy brought his family in a wagon train to California, he looked for other ways than gold to find his fortune. He visited the missions, and immediately noticed the vineyards around them. These grape fields were more than just lush greenery to him.

Haraszthy immediately saw the future of the grape industry in California and the money it would bring him! He sent away for plant cuttings from many of the most popular kinds of grapes in the important vineyards in Europe. One of these was the grape that started the huge California raisin industry.

This bold adventurer soon became the State Grape Commissioner and studied the European methods that would improve the quality of California wines. Because he brought in vines that would grow almost anywhere in California, the industry spread all over the state. Within twenty years, there were over 130 million individual plants bearing grapes! By 1971, California was producing over 333 million gallons of wine a year, all thanks to the foresight of this Hungarian wine connoisseur and pioneer.

Today, the vineyards he started over one hundred years ago are still called Buena Vista--the name he gave them--and they still use some of his original equipment.

Only eighty years after Haraszthy started to create his legacy (around the time of World War II), a group of Hungarian immigrants who were scientists played a major part in harnessing atomic power.

The most important of these Hungarian-born atomic scientists were Eugene Wigner, Edward Teller, Leo Szilard and John von Neumann.

Each made his own special contribution. At first, they all worked on the development of the atomic bomb. Later, Edward Teller worked on the hydrogen bomb and on ways to use this new type of power to help rather than destroy mankind. John von Neumann (often called the world's smartest man by his fellow scientists who admired his calculator-type brain) was one of the five members of the Atomic Energy Commission when it was first set up. His forceful leadership enabled the United States to come up with Intercontinental Ballistic Missiles within a few months of the discovery that the Russians already had them.

These Hungarian scientists knew that the Germans were working on solving the problems of atomic power. They were extremely afraid that the Germans might discover a way to use atomic power in the war before the United States could. Because they had seen firsthand what would happen if Hitler were to rule the world, they knew how important it was to discover a way to stop him.

In the United States, scientists were working on exploring the atom. But most of these scientists were only engaged in theoretical research in universities, often with little money and without the government being aware of the importance of their work. Also, before the Japanese bombed Pearl Harbor, many people in the United States--even government officials--did not realize that their nation and way of life could actually be threatened.

But the Hungarian scientists who had immigrated to the United States knew better. They insisted that new discoveries be kept secret, so that they would not fall into the hands of an enemy. This attitude towards secrecy was a new idea to many people in the U.S.

In January 1939, Leo Szilard became one of the first scientists to stake his reputation on his belief that the new atomic information could be applied to a bomb. By March of that year, he and his colleagues at Columbia University had completed a laboratory experiment that proved to them that the liberation of atomic energy was possible in their lifetime.

"That night I knew the world was headed for sorrow," Szilard later related. But he felt certain it would also be headed for sorrow if Hitler were to succeed with his plans. To him, there were two questions of utmost importance. Where was the United States in the race to make the bomb? And did they have time to win that race?

The Hungarian scientists, and the many brilliant men working with them, knew they had to obtain government support for their project. They finally managed to have a letter delivered personally to President Roosevelt who gave them money from Army and Navy funds to help buy materials for their experiments. But it was only six thousand dollars in a race against time! Only six thousand to make the discoveries that would change the whole nature of modern warfare between nations!

It was not until the summer of 1942 that the Army Corps of Engineers under General Leslie Groves took over the coordination of the project. Finally things began to happen quickly.

Although their ideas were still only theory--nothing had been proven--General Groves was impressed enough with the work of the scientists to order full speed ahead! Yet Groves himself admitted more than twenty years later that he never estimated that the bomb had more than a 60% chance of working!

United States industry, money, and know-how were put into this top-priority project. In the end, the bomb was used against the Japanese, not the Germans. It ended the war on the eastern front after the war in Europe had already drawn to a close! It was then that the scientists discovered that the Germans had not been as close to discovering and using the atomic bomb as they had thought.

The invention of the bomb in the United States was the result of "foreigners" adopting their new land as home and of native Americans treating those immigrants as worthwhile, intelligent equals they could trust. The fascinating story of the making of the atomic bomb is told in an absorbing fashion in *Manhatten Project* by Stephane Groueff.

INTERESTING PARALLELS

The modern day newspaper profession, the California wine industry, and atomic research--these three subjects could not be further apart, yet all were major contributions of Hungarian immigrants. Strange as it may seem, all of these immigrants had much in common.

All were adventurous men. A scientist by his very nature seeks the new and the unknown. Haraszthy, the wine maker, was a character right out of a movie of the Old West. He left his first home in the U.S. after falling into debt in Wisconsin, and set out for California. He lost his fortune again in California, and took his family to Nicaragua, in Central America, where he later died.

Pulitzer, the newspaper publisher, left home at the age of seventeen to join the army, any army! He was rejected by the Austrians, the French, and the British because he was thin and awkward and had very poor eyesight. Finally he was accepted, to fight in the Civil War on the side of the North.

All three men would do anything. Every experience was a new challenge; whether it was a job as a deck hand on a ferry boat or as a gravedigger (some of the first jobs of the to-be millionaire, Pulitzer) or an opportunity to invest in banks, restaurants, or land (like Haraszthy).

They were egotistical, stubborn, opinionated, aggressive, and self-confident in the face of the many obstacles that would have stopped weaker, less determined people. All of them were soon involved in politics in their new land. Pulitzer and Haraszthy won legislative offices and the Hungarian scientists were primarily responsible for the government supporting atomic research.

They al' had a dream--an impossible dream perhaps--that they made come true by unbelievable effort. Pulitzer wanted his voice heard, to reform the many abuses he saw in society. He was a perfectionist and an idealist--forever unsatisfied with his own labors and the work of those about him. In spite of poor eyesight, he worked 18, 20, even 24 hours a day, which caused him to spend the last twenty-four years of his life blind and subject to nervous fits.

Haraszthy's dream was money, power, and adventure. For this he risked his fortune time and time again until he eventually disappeared, leaving only his clothes and his horse at the side of a Nicaraguan river. Some say he committed suicide. Others claim he fell into the river and was eaten by crocodiles.

The Hungarian scientists drove themselves mercilessly to keep Hitler from overtaking the world. Later, men like Teller crossed the nation trying to convince people of the danger of an armed and powerful Russia. Teller was such an egotistical maverick--so divorced from the friendship of his fellow workers--that when he tried to persuade the scientists at Los Alamos, New Mexico to stay after the war and continue their research, they threw garbage at him; and no one would listen to his plans.

Bold, arrogant, intelligent dreamers, yet perfectionists who did not know, nor were willing to learn, the meaning of "no" and "I can't." These, and others like them, deeply affected the world in which they lived, and left a legacy that influences our world today. Only they, and those closest to them, really know the price they had to pay in their personel lives. Most likely they were only happy on the verge of an accomplishment; and then they immediately pushed on to ever-demanding new challenges. Driven people rarely rest until they die!

There are, and have been, many driven men and women in the world. These Hungarian immigrants worked and fought so that their dreams would live and last, as have so many of their fellow countrymen. Hungarian immigrants have profoundly influenced our world today by being leaders in other areas of scientific endeavor.

Albert Szent-Gyorgyi received the Nobel Prize for medicine in 1937 for his isolation of ascorbic acid. This made it possible to then synthesize vitamin C. He also explored the chemistry of muscles, isolating actin, a protein found in muscle fiber; and he did cancer research.

George Von Bekesy received the Nobel Prize for medicine and physiology in 1961 for his findings concerning the inner ear. One of the foremost investigators of how we hear--and how we receive messages through our other senses as well--Von Bekesy greatly influenced the theory of hearing.

SOLAR ENERGY

A remarkable woman, Maria Telkes, will be praised for generations to come for her work toward developing solar power. She designed solar water distilleries for use on life rafts; solar generators; and solar heating equipment for houses. She invented a means for storage of solar heat, ways to make electricity from the sun, and solar stills to convert salt water into pure water.

Theodore von Karman laid the foundation for jets to be used in commercial aviation. Director of the jet propulsion research program at Caltech (California Institute of Technology), his ideas influenced the design of the first airplane to break the sound barrier, the Bell X-1. Chairman of NATO's aeronautical advisory group from 1951 until his death in 1963, von Karman was considered one of the chief organizers of the fantastic technological revolution in the field of aviation after World War II.

The inventor of the long-playing phonograph record, Peter Goldmark, also developed a device which may become as common as the telephone is now, in homes of the future. Under his direction, the EVR (Electronic Video Recording) was created. This is a method of recording the picture and sound of any TV program and storing it for playback later at one's convenience on any standard TV set.

Another Hungarian immigrant who is rapidly becoming famous is Gabor Balazs. He has invented a device which is revolutionizing techniques for fighting skyscraper fires. To him, the Towering Inferno was not just a movie, but a real example of what can happen when a fire breaks out in a high-rise building. While in a hospital, recovering from an accident, he put his mind in gear and coupled his engineering training with his practical experience, added a dash of creativity, and came up with ideas which he has since been turning into reality.

One of his devices, the size of a shotgun shell, is placed in window panes on each floor of a multi-storied building. When activated by the fireman on the ground below (or in some cases, automatically from the heat), it explodes, blowing out the glass. The fire rushes towards the outside and the fresh oxygen supply. Firemen can then easily enter the room, and pressure cannot build up that might cause the whole floor of the building to explode. Two of the many noteworthy buildings which will be much safer, thanks to Balazs, are the Sierra Towers in Los

Angeles County and the towering Bank of America in San Francisco.

Balazs, who immigrated to the United States in 1957 after the Hungarian Revolution, is working on similar equipment which can be used to set off dynamite that will create barrier trenches around a forest fire.

One very special immigrant who has contributed much is Zsa Zsa Gabor. She is a member of the famous Gabor family and her sister, Eva, and mother, Jolie, are noteworthy immigrants also. Zsa Zsa has been an inspiration for women everywhere and her book, *How to Catch a Man, How to Keep a Man, How to Get Rid of a Man*, is a delight to read as well as being educational. Zsa Zsa as the beautiful actress is how most people know her. Some of her movies are: Lovely to Look At, We're Not Married, The Story of Three Loves, Lili, Moulin Rouge, Three Ring Circus, Death of a Scoundrel, and For the First Time. A talented stage star also, her performances in 40 Carats and Blithe Spirit entertained those fortunate enough to see her. Television is another medium she has excelled in. An insight into this charming person can be gained through the book: *My Story, written for me by Gerald Frank*.

The list of influential Hungarian immigrants could go on and on. Atomic physicist Zoltan Bay developed the first moon radar in 1946. Clara Szego, zoologist and educator, was named Woman of the Year for 1957-1958 by the *Los Angeles Times*. Fine artist, Zoltan Sepeshy, has been the recipient of many awards, and his paintings hang in museums throughout the world. Old-time movie greats like Bela Lugosi and Peter Lorre; movie producers and directors Joseph Pasternak and Adolph Zukor; guitarist, sitarist, and composer Gabor Szabo, a former Hungarian Freedom Fighter; wrestler Sandor Szabo (seven times World Champion!); and many others have made--and will continue to make--Hungarian names famous throughout the United States.

19

IRELAND

by

M. J. SAPERSTEIN

"It's a Great Day for the Irish, it's a Great Day for the Green...."The marching band blared, banners waved and crowds pushed and jostled, as hundreds of Irish patriots paraded down Fifth Avenue. It was 1852, and for the first time New Yorkers were observing Ireland's national holiday. Over the screams of the happy spectators, a young colleen was heard to exclaim, "Glory be, the whole town's turned Irish overnight!"

The celebration, of course, was in honor of that long ago day when St. Patrick was given the power to drive the snakes and toads from Ireland.

That's just *one* of the traditions we owe to the Emerald Isle. You may have known about St. Patricks Day, but did you know that we can also thank the Irish for some of our Halloween spooks?

"All Saints Day" was a holiday recognized by all of the Celts (British, Scotch, Welsh and Irish). In the Middle Ages it was a solemn religious holiday. But the night before it, "Hallow Evening," was a festive night of bonfires and masquerades. The Irish, a superstitious people, believed in what they referred to as the "little people." These were goblins, ghosts, elves, and leprechauns. So on Halloween night they would sit about the fire and embroider eerie tales of witches and goblins.

It was the Irish youngsters who clung to the Halloween legend and brought it with them to the New World. Soon they were entertaining their wide-eyed American cousins with old Halloween pranks, such as bobbing for apples and creating what they called a Jack-O-Lantern.

According to an old folk tale, Jack was a fearful and monstrous old man, so mean and hideous that when he died, neither the angels nor the devil would have him, and his spirit haunted the countryside searching for a home. The Irish children used to hollow out a giant potato and carve a scary face in it, to frighten their playmates on Halloween. In the New World, pumpkins took the place of potatoes, but the name Jack-O-Lantern remained.

Those two particular Irish holidays didn't become especially popular in the United States until the huge Irish immigration during the 1850's. However, there had been Irish immigrants in the U.S. since its inception. As a matter of fact, Irish-born Thomas Dongan was one of the first Governors of Colonial New York way back in the early 17th century.

REVOLUTIONARY WAR DAYS

"General Washington, you have been elected by the people of the United States to be our first President." Words to that effect gave George Washington the news of his new position, and they were spoken by the Secretary to the Congress which adopted the Declaration of Independence, Charles Thomson.

Thomson, who also signed the Declaration of Independence, was born in a cottage in Gorteade, near Maghera, County Londonderry. In Ireland, of course.

During the Revolutionary War, George Washington's army was said to be almost half composed of Irish immigrants! There were some 12,000 soldiers with Irish names listed on the muster rolls--695 of them were Kelly's!

Washington was so pleased with these courageous men that he made "St. Patrick's Day" a password in one important battle, and on that special day he served his men Irish Whiskey!

While Washington and his brave soldiers were fighting on land, an Irishman named John Barry was making a name for himself in naval warfare.

Barry had immigrated to the Colonies at the age of 15, settling in Pennsylvania. In time he became a merchant captain. When war broke out, he was assigned to command one of the Colonies' battleships, the Lexington, which became the first United States vessel to capture an enemy ship.

All during the stormy war years he battled heroically on the sea. Through hurricanes and rough waters he continued, winning battle after battle for the Revolutionary forces. Among the other ships he commanded were the Alliance and the Raleigh. He trained other young officers to fight at sea. During one daring naval engagement, he captured an armed schooner in Delaware Bay using only a few men in rowboats.

His fame spread far and wide so that eventually he was known as one of the two foremost heroes of the sea during the Revolutionary War.

It wasn't called The Navy then, but when Congress got around to giving a name to the organization of men who fought on the seas, John Barry was appointed its first commander.

His statue stands today in Independence Square, The Father of the United States Navy, John Barry.

Well, they've always been the "fightin' Irish." They were prominent in the War of 1812 and in the Mexican-American War and they were really outstanding in the Civil War.

When the call went out for volunteers during the War between the States, the scrappy Sons of Erin answered with flying green colors. They rushed to enlist, both on the sides of the North and the South; but due to the fact that the majority of them had settled in Boston and New York, most of the Irish-born fought on the side of the Union.

Erin John Shields was just one of the immigrants who fought in both the Mexican-American and the Civil Wars. In both wars he was a hero. But there were many Irish-born heroes in the Civil War. In that war, there were 38 Union troops with the word "Irish" in their titles. In each and every battle of that war were Gaelic (Irish) names.

POTATOES AND IMMIGRATION

Shortly before the Civil War took place, a dreaded plague had descended upon Ireland. Not a war, but an agricultural blight was to prove the most appalling disaster to ever hit that lovely land.

In the early 19th century in Ireland, a large part of the island was engaged in farming. It was a land of picturesque little farms, thatched roof cottages, and jolly people pursuing their chores. For most of them, this consisted of growing and cultivating the chief crop, potatoes. Potatoes was their food, their livelihood, and their medium of exchange. Potatoes could never fail them. Or so they thought.

Then the dreadful potato blight struck, so devastating that it left thousands without the means to support themselves, homeless, with no food to eat or money to buy any.

For five years it took its deadly toll. During that time other countries aided them, relief stations were provided and government agencies assisted. Through those long dim years, the Irish could see the golden land of America shining in the distance. If only they could somehow get to the land of opportunity.

But how? How could they possibly raise the necessary fare of $15 for passage to New York? At that time it was also required that they take enough food to sustain them on the five to six week voyage. It seemed an impossible task for the penniless farmers, and there was no way for an entire family to make the trip.

So, reluctantly the families split up, with the strongest and most able leaving his homeland first, promising his family that he'd send for them as soon as possible.

It was heart-breaking to say goodbye to his loved ones, but an immigrant, by his very nature, is determined to make a new life for himself. The immigrant was the one who would struggle in the face of terrible odds to earn a dollar or so a day in order to help his dear ones join him.

Sometimes at that tiring rate, it took a year or more to reunite the family, but they persevered. It's a tribute to their hard work that the mails to Ireland were heavy those few years with fat letters of hope and money.

They scrimped and they saved. And they triumphed! In about five years, the U.S. received more immigrants from Ireland than it had from the rest of the world since 1776!

The green tinted population found their way into every field of endeavor. There were Irish policemen by the score, soldiers, seamen, domestics, mine-workers, and track-layers. There were Irishmen who worked on riverboats and there were Irish adventurers.

Two such men were named O'Reilly and McLaughlin. These men had plunged headlong into the California Gold Rush. It isn't certain if they ever did discover gold, but O'Reilly and McLaughlin discovered the legendary Comstock Lode in Nevada, the largest known silver deposit.

The Irish liked the West, and they were capable Indian agents, trappers, guides, and cowboys.

As the Irish cowboys rode the plains and rounded up their cattle, they sang traditional Irish tunes. "Get along Little Dogie" began its life as an Irish lullabye. Country-Western and Nashville sounds are said to have roots in the ancient sounds of Ireland.

But perhaps more than other occupation at that time, the immigrants found their way into some form of labor.

MARY HARRIS

One champion of their cause was Irish born Mary (Mother) Harris. Mary was a small girl when her family moved to the United States. When she grew up, she became a teacher. After that, she moved to Chicago, became a seamstress and opened a dressmaking shop. She married and had three children. Her establishment was thriving when along came the Chicago Fire and wiped her out financially.

Then she turned to her real interest, the working people. She became a fiery crusader for the worker's rights. She also organized unions, pressed for better conditions, educated the laborers, and traveled about making speeches on rights and dignity.

Children were a very special concern of hers, as her own had died while very young, in a flu epidemic. She threw herself into the fight to ease the children's pitiful working conditions.

During this period, she organized what came to be known as The Children's Crusade. She gathered 75 boys and girls together; and, armed with knives, forks, and plates (for eating whatever food kindly people along the way would provide) and a drum and a fife for a band, marched to see the President. On and on, through Pennsylvania, New Jersey, and New York they walked. Food was forthcoming, as was money and clothing for the underprivileged children.

Her purpose was to let President Theodore Roosevelt see how badly the children needed labor laws to protect their health and well-being.

But when they finally reached the Oyster Bay, N.Y., home of President Roosevelt, he refused to see them!

By that time, however, public sympathy had been aroused and it wasn't long before Child Labor Laws were passed to eliminate the horrible conditions the working children suffered.

In 1930, Mother Harris died at the age of 100! She was often compared with Joan of Arc for the efforts she had expended on behalf of workers of all ages.

Those years, from the middle of the 19th century on, were the years in which the United States was making the change from a farming country, to an industrial one.

The Irish were responsible for many labor unions as well as being influential in other laws for workmens rights.

It follows, then, that because of their concentrated interest in laborers, and laborers rights, that they should originate another holiday we all observe today!

Patrick J. McGuire proposed that there should be set aside one day of rest for the laborers. You guessed it...Labor Day was declared a legal holiday soon after!

And so on up the ladder they climbed. In publishing, Peter Collier founded a magazine that was to enjoy many years of success and become a household word, *Colliers*.

Young William Grace landed in the United States penniless and alone. Hard work paid off: he became a noted financier, was twice elected mayor of New York City, and started the steamship company that bears his name: the Grace Lines

Robert Gregg gave us what we know today as the Gregg shorthand method. Perhaps he perfected it as a result of studying the ancient Irish alphabet caled Ogham, which is made up of squiggles and symbols that represent words.

There were Irishmen to be found in every area of occupation.

The Irish were rich in color and folklore, and exceptionally superior when it came to the gift of gab. They were articulate, witty, sociable, poetic and whimsical. Charmers, dreamers, musicians, and orators--no one could ever accuse the Irish of being either dull or stolid.

Their lilting way of speaking inspired one poet (Irish of course) to remark "It's well known that in heaven even the angels speak Irish."

Two world reknowned Irishmen still provide people with good reading. They're George Bernard Shaw, whose *Pygmalion* was made into the ever popular My Fair Lady; and Oscar Wilde. We still see their plays on the stage, and read their works. So highly was Shaw thought of in the U.S. that upon his death in 1950, all theaters were darkened for the night.

FROM MUSIC TO THE MOVIES

Music? That's another field where the Irish proved themselves more than able. Victor Herbert was a composer who became famous for his operettas: Naughty Marietta, Babes in Toyland, and The Red Mill. He founded and conducted the Pittsburgh Symphony Orchestra.

As for voices, the sweet Irish tenor is well known. One of the most famous, John McCormack, might well have inspired another Irish poet to say "There's no language like the Irish for soothing and quieting." McCormack became a U.S. citizen after spending much time and performing many concerts in the U.S.

Yes, music was part of the Irish tradition. Plaintive melodies, toe-tapping marches, tender ballads, and rowdy Irish jigs.

To get into Irish politicians would take more pages than there are in this book! Since they set foot on the shores of the United States, the Irish have all but dominated politics! Not too long before he was assassinated, John F. Kennedy made a trip to Ireland to seek out his Irish forebears. But the Kennedy name is just one of the Irish names among the congressmen and politicians of Irish descent that you'll read about in your history books today.

There are novelists, playwrights, poets, actors, and artists listed among the famous Irish. John Sygne, one of the most noted writers who ever lived, was born in Ireland. Tyrone Power, a well known actor from that little island, toured the U.S., performing in many plays. His grandson, Tyrone Power III, became a Hollywood movie star. Another actor of that time, John O'Neill, was a member of the Abbey Players, a company of actors in Ireland who revitalized acting. Up until their time, acting was a stiff and formal thing. They naturalized it, and toured the United States with their new form of theater. The Abbey theater still exists today. John O'Neill stayed in the U.S. and became the father of Eugene O'Neill, one of our marvelous playwrights. James Joyce, Sean O'Casey, Brendan Behan, and William B. Yeats are a few more of the silver-tongued word magicians who have enriched our literature. Some of the 20th century's Irish born actors and actresses who may have captivated you on television, the stage, or in the movies, are: Greer Garson, Maureen O'Hara, Stephen Boyd, Siobhan McKenna, Richard Harris, Peter O'Toole and Edward Mulhare.

Shure, you of Irish descent have lots to be proud of. *The Dictionary of American Biography* lists over 500 well known people who were Irish born!

In many cases they came to the United States, friendless, alone, penniless, and frightened. Through backbreaking work, wise saving and investing, they were able to make a place for themselves and their families in their newly adopted country.

It is true that they were given refuge and relief when they so sorely needed it, but we can plainly see that the green tinted gifts that the Irishman gave in return more than compensated for that.

The next time you hear the word "Irish," don't just think of corned beef and cabbage, leprechauns, and shamrocks. Remember all the notable men and women who immigrated, spreading their plentiful gifts out for the United States.

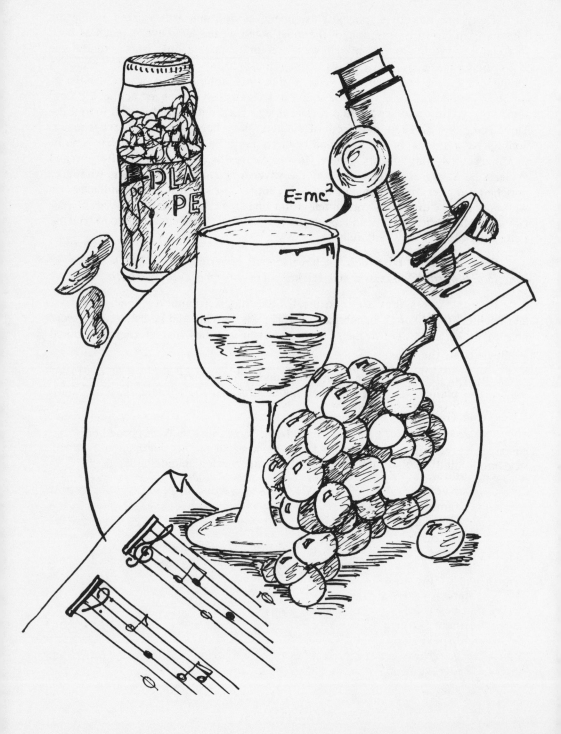

20

ITALY

by

LORETTA ROBERTS

When you think of things Italian, do visions of spaghetti with delicious sauce come to your mind? It's not very surprising because the United States imports annually from Italy, over five million pounds of pasta!

The Italians who immigrated to the United States have enriched their new land in many ways; including contributions in the fields of music, art, and science.

The Italian people immigrated in search of a brighter future. "The new country" promised something finer, something better--it was a force pulling them that they could not resist.

At first, the Italian immigrants took any ships that would grant them passage, landing at Boston, New York, Baltimore, or some other port. In New York, they landed at Castle Garden, a large round building which had once been used as a fortress and also as a concert hall. When the number of immigrants grew too large for Castle Garden to accomodate them (around 1892), the new reception center became Ellis Island, which lies in the middle of New York Harbor.

An Italian-born gentleman named Edward Corsi was appointed Commissioner of Immigration at Ellis Island by the President of the United States. Just twenty-four years earlier, he had passed through the same island as an immigrant, so he was familiar with, and sympathetic to, the problems facing new immigrants. He was, you might say, the perfect man for the job. During Corsi's term of office, the buildings on Ellis Island were improved and reforms were put into effect. When Ellis Island was closed in 1954, it marked the ending of mass migration.

Some of the first Italians--the first of over five million to immigrate to the United States--were farmers and artisans. In the New Jersey countryside, they developed berry farms, pepper fields, and vineyards. In western New York, they extended their farms into the Hudson River Valley, and in Arkansas they grew apples and peaches. In California, the Italian immigrants became successful viticulturists (grape growers and wine makers). Antonio Moramarco was at one time known as the Italian Vineyard King of California.

Other immigrants helped build cities, subways, and skyscrapers by laboring as bricklayers and stonecutters. They worked on the railroads and deep inside coal mines. Some found a place in urban life as owners of small stores, shoemakers, barbers, and tailors. They quickly overcame obstacles and found places of importance in almost every phase of life in the United States.

THE MICHELANGELO OF THE CAPITOL

Did you know that a West Indian and a Frenchman designed the U.S. Capitol in Washington, D.C., and that an Italian immigrant beautified it? His name was Constantino Brumidi. Take a minute to visualize this Italian gentleman in his sixties, lying on his back on a scaffold suspended 180 feet in the air. Does he remind your of another famous artist named Michelangelo? Constantino Brumidi was known as the "Michelangelo of the Capitol." The ceiling of the Capitol Dome is covered with his fresco paintings, and the entire masterpiece is called "Apotheosis of Washington." He signed it in 1865, after working on it for eleven months.

The colors of Brumidi's fresco paintings are as bright as if they had been painted yesterday. That is because he used a special technique that he had learned in his native Italy. This method is called fresco-painting. In fact it was the first time this method was ever used in the United States. "Fresco" is the Italian word for "fresh," and what Brumidi did was to actually paint on the fresh, wet plaster with water colors. Because it was done this way, the water colors permeated the wet plaster, resulting in the colors becoming more brilliant and permanent as the years go by.

Inside the nation's Capitol are many artistic works by Brumidi. In fact he devoted twenty-five years as he put it: "to make beautiful the Capitol of the one country on earth in which there is liberty!" He was proud of his new country, proud enough to want to belong totally, and so he became a United States citizen.

His last work was the band of fresco scenes encircling the Dome, depicting the thrill of the nation's history, from Columbus to the Wright brothers. His skill at the age of 72 made the flat figures look like sculptures. Unfortunately, while painting Penn's Treaty with the Indians, he slipped on the scaffold and hung helpless 58 feet above the floor for fifteen minutes before help came. The shock weakened him and he died a few months later. Another artist completed the band of frescoes.

Constantino Brumidi gave the United States a beautiful and lasting gift of the art form, fresco-painting. Today the word fresco is used to include mural decorations in general, but a true fresco is a mural painted on wet plaster.

Roman history reveals that fresco-paintings decorated the walls and ceilings of villas at Pompeii and Herculaneum. Both cities were destroyed in 79 A.D. by the volcanic eruption of Mount Vesuvius. One of the seaside villas, the Villa of the Papyri, has been reconstructed in full size and exact detail in Malibu, California, by the J. Paul Getty Museum as a setting for its art exhibits. The frescoes decorating the walls of this museum were beautifully recreated by Mr. Garth Benton, who used the seco or dry method. This method differs in that the water colors are applied on dry plaster.

Ancient marble quarries in Italy were reopened in order to duplicate the type of marble used in the original villa; and that marble was imported for use throughout the museum's construction.

Since the climate of Malibu is similar to the climate of that original seaside villa, it was possible to duplicate the trees, plants, and designs of the gardens that grew around the Villa of the Papyri nearly 2000 years ago.

FRANK CAPRA

Focusing in on more present times, we find one of the greatest, most creative, directors of the motion picture industry, an Italian gentleman by the name of Frank Capra. Always thinking, always coming up with new ideas for making scenes work, he helped the actors bring their best to a picture. A pioneer in his field, Capra developed directing techniques that are now standard procedure.

Frank Capra was born on May 18, 1897, and lived the first five years of his life in Bisaquino, Sicily. Then his family moved to the United States and settled in Los Angeles.

Going to school, whether it was high school or college, was important to him. And he gave it his best, always being in the top three of his class. After college, he enlisted in the Army.

In the early years of his career, Capra found a place with Mack Sennett as a gag writer for Hal Roach comedies. Remember the Our Gang comedies? Well, Frank Capra was responsible for some of the hi-jinks those kids got themselves into. Later when he went into directing, he was involved in the writing and re-writing of the scripts for the pictures he directed.

During his career, he brought home three Oscars for Best Director. The films he won them for were: It Happened One Night, Mr. Deeds Goes to Town, and You Can't Take it with You.

Before that, he had won something much more precious to him, a lovely lady by the name of Lucille Reyburn. They were married February 1, 1932.

Frank Capra retired after forty-five years in the film industry. He has written an autobiography, *Frank Capra, The Name Above the Title*, which has a message for the discouraged, doubting, or despairing. The same message he presumed to say in films, that is: "Friend, you are a divine mingle-mangle of guts and stardust. So hang in there! If doors opened for me, they can open for anyone."

MARCONI

Traveling into the world of science, we can see how the invention of a young man helped rescue seven hundred people. Have you ever heard of HMS Titanic? It was a luxury passenger ship that sank in North Atlantic waters in 1912, after colliding with an iceberg. Of the more than 2000 passengers aboard, only 700 survived. Those people owed their lives to the urgent messages sent out on the new wireless telegraph, the invention of Guglielmo Marconi. When the rescue ship Carpathian reached land, Marconi was there and rushed on board to shake the hand of Junior Wireless Operator, Harold Bride.

Marconi was not only an inventor but an electrical engineer as well. He had a theory that electric current could easily pass through any substance and, when started in a certain direction, would follow a direct course without the aid of any sort of conductor. In 1899, Marconi immigrated to the United States where he continued his experiments. The next year, his method was used in reporting the presidential election. Marconi was the first Italian in the field of physics to be honored with a Nobel Prize. From his inventions and experiments, radio and television have evolved as we know them today.

FERMI

Also in the field of science, there was a prominent immigrant who has been called The Architect of the Atomic Age. He is nuclear physicist, Enrico Fermi, who was honored in 1938 with a Nobel Prize. It was Fermi's experiments that paved the way for the atomic bomb, which he also helped design.

Enrico Fermi and his wife and children arrived in the United States in 1939. He went to work as Professor of Physics at Columbia University, engaged in uranium research. Then he directed the first controlled nuclear chain reaction, at the University of Chicago. In 1945, he became a United States citizen, and was appointed professor in the Institute of Nuclear Studies at the University of Chicago. Fermi was the first winner of the special $50,000 award, which now bears his name, for work on the atom.

Leaving science and moving to the field of religion, we find a woman whose entire life was dedicated to bringing people closer to God. Her name is Mother Frances Xavier Cabrini, and she was born on a farm in a northern province of Italy. Indefatigable, determined, and spirited, are but a few of the adjectives that describe her.

What was so special about this young nun's life that caused her name to lead the list of immigrants inscribed on the plaque at the Statue of Liberty? She wanted, for as long as she could remember, to become a missionary to China: "to convert those poor heathen who do not know our Lord!" And, she had a deep desire to help people, especially the orphans, the sick, and the poor.

There was not an established order of missionary sisters for her to join in 1899 because at that time only men were missionaries. This fact did not stop her, for with the Pope's approval, she gathered together a small band of sisters and the first order of women missionaires was founded. Instead of sending her to China as she had hoped, the Pope decided she and the other sisters were needed in New York. So it was to New York City they came to look after the orphans and tend to the needs of the sick and the poor. They often went into areas of the city where previously only policemen would enter. Surely the sisters knew God would protect them!

As the years went by, whenever a mission, convent, hospital, school, or orphanage that Mother Cabrini founded was in working operation, she moved on to start a new one somewhere else. This she did not only in the United States but in South and Central America as well.

Mother Cabrini had great courage and faith when it came to obtaining the finances necessary to build one of her hospitals or orphanges. She acted as though it was impossible to fail! Businessmen and bankers tried to look the other way when they saw her coming, but her cause gave her the necessary courage to face these people and ask for funds.

A story is told about the time Mother Cabrini and one of her sisters went into a Catholic Church to pray. They knelt before a statue of St. Anne reading to her child, the Virgin Mary. As they rose to leave, Mother Cabrini noticed the open pages of the book were blank so she took out her pen and wrote the figure $26,492 on the blank pages. As the other nun raised her eyebrows, Mother Cabrini said, "I just wanted to be sure she knew exactly how much it is I need." Two days later, one of the bankers cracked. He looked into her bright blue pleading eyes and could no longer say no. This happened in Seattle, Washington, the city where she asked for her papers to become an U.S. citizen.

Though Mother Frances Cabrini was frail in health from birth to her death in 1917, her spirit was strong and her faith sustained her. She was canonized in 1946, making her the United States' first saint.

THE KING OF PEANUTS

Another interesting story is about the success of an Italian named Amedeo Obici. It began with him selling peanuts at five cents a bag and years later, then known as America's Peanut King, heading one of the largest corporations in the United States.

Obici was born in 1877 and came to the United States with his family at the age of 12, settling in Pennsylvania. When he was 17, he decided to go into business for himself, selling fruit and peanuts. He rented a sidewalk space in front of a store and talked enthusiastically until he obtained enough lumber, on credit, to build. In the same way he managed to win over wholesale fruit dealers. "But for my peanut roaster I had to pay cash," he said. That $4.50 peanut roaster demanded constant attention or the peanuts would be scorched, so one day he got hold of an old electric fan motor and rigged up a set of pulleys. He then put that fan motor to work turning the peanut roaster. He just may have had the first electrically-operated peanut roaster in the world! Over his stand he put a sign reading "Obici, the Peanut Specialist." That was the beginning. Soon he was packing five-cent bags of shelled peanuts. The peanut specialist then experimented with salted peanuts and peanut candy bars. This led to his Planters Peanut Company. There is hardly anyone who is not familiar with the jaunty, monocled, and top-hatted figure of Mr. Peanut.

MUSIC

The Italian people are well known for their musical talents. Imagine yourself at the Metropolitan Opera in New York City in 1908. The lights are dimmed and a hush falls as the orchestra conductor enters, walks briskly to center stage, and raises his baton. Soon the auditorium is filled with beautiful music and the audience is enjoying the genius of Arturo Toscanini. For many years, he was the leader of the New York Philharmonic and the United States' most distinguished conductor of recent years.

The Italian composer, Lorenzo Da Ponte, loved the opera so much that he imported the first Italian opera troupe to New York in 1832, where it developed into a permanent institution. He had first come to the United States in 1805, and was considered one of the most worldly residents of New York City for the next thirty years. His collaboration with Mozart had produced such masterpieces as The Marriage of Figaro, and Don Giovanni. In the United States, he tried his hand at making a living in several ways but was most successful when promoting the Italian language and culture. He taught Italian privately for several years and was appointed the first professor of Italian at Columbia College.

Speaking of opera, a man called The Greatest Voice of This Century made his American debut at the Metropolitan Opera House in New York in the role of Duke in Rigoletto. This great Italian singer was Enrico Caruso. The phenomenal sale of his phonograph records did much to spread American interest in operatic music.

Other Italian born singers that have provided many hours of listening pleasure are Anna Maria Alberghetti and Caterina Valente. And the genius of conductor-composer Annuzio Montovani from Venice will live on forever, as will the dancing splendor of Jose Greco from Abruzzi, Italy.

These are but a small handful of the Italian people who came to the United States to make a new life for themselves and their families, and by so doing helped their adopted country grow in greatness.

21

JAPAN

by

JOAN S. FOLLENDORE

One little known Japanese person more than any other single individual, contributed towards the establishment of relations between Japan and the United States. That man was Manjiro Nakahama. He was born on the island of Shokoku and was the son of a fisherman. At the age of 14, he went to sea as a fisherman to help support his widowed mother. During a typhoon, his craft was wrecked against a cliff on Hurricane Island, east of Japan.

There was no habitation or vegetation and the only source of drinking water was from rain catches. For a considerable period of time, Manjiro and the four others of his party survived on a fare of albatross, seaweed, raw shell fish, and raw seafood.

One day, a whaling ship out of New Bedford, Massachusetts, the John Howland, stopped at this island in hope of finding some fresh water. But there was none. Manjiro and the others were afraid, at first, of the white men, since they had never known such men existed. In those days, any Japanese who went abroad was not permitted to return. Only three Whites were allowed in Japan and they were confined to a limited area in Nagasaki. Very few others even knew about the three Whites. Manjiro, from a small village on Shokoku, had never heard of them. The fishermen overcame their fear, and were grateful for being rescued.

A few months later, four of them remained in Hawaii when the ship touched there. Manjiro's destiny took a different direction. The youngest of the survivors, he elected to stay on the John Howland and went with Captain Whitfield and his crew back to New Bedford. Captain Whitfield, an ancestor of President Franklin Roosevelt, liked Manjiro and treated him as a son, especially after they arrived back in the United States.

Manjiro was intelligent and ambitious. Not only did he learn English well, but navigation and astronomy, too. He also learned the trade of a cooper (a person who makes and repairs barrels and casks). Subsequently he made a voyage on a whaler and worked himself up to the position of second mate and navigator.

However, he always yearned for an opportunity to return home. The discovery of gold in California gave him the chance. A whaler brought him to San Francisco in 1849. He staked a claim, and mined enough gold to exchange it for 600 pieces of silver, which he used to book passage for Hawaii. There he waited until he found a ship going close to Okinawa, a part of Japan. He bought passage and took along a small boat which he named the Adventurer.

He left the ship when it was about five miles off the southern tip of Okinawa, in 1851, with best wishes from his many American friends. He gradually worked his way from Okinawa to Shokoku, arriving home a year and a half later. The fact that he had been abroad caused him to be put into prison for awhile.

He was given many rigid examinations, was frequently cross-examined, and shared much of his knowledge of other parts of the world. The main thing he had to affirm was that he had not been converted to Christianity. Soon after he finally arrived home, he was called upon by the Governor to teach whaling and navigation to the young men of his province. He also enlightened many others regarding the foreign Barbarians, as Americans were called, who lived in the United States.

Manjiro's demonstration of the practicality of modern navigational methods more than any other thing, convinced the Japanese that they should open their doors to foreigners and learn what they could from them.

Shortly before Commodore Perry's visit to Japan, Manjiro entered the service of the "Yedo," or Tokyo government, and subsequently played a vital role in advising what the United States had to offer and what to expect from the Americans. What he said did much towards influencing governmental officials to change their policy with respect to the United States. Manjiro was designated official interpretor for the first Japanese Ambassador to the U.S., Shimmi-Buzen-no-Kami, and was commended by President James Buchanan for his invaluable service.

Manjiro definitely was a man of destiny who blazed a trail from one country to another.

Captain Katsu Kaishu's desire to meet Americans, and to have them get to know that Japanese people are really just like they are, led him to skipper the first Japanese ship to carry Japanese passengers to the United States. That was about 110 years ago. Their purpose was not commercial (to trade goods) but to get acquainted. On board was Yukiti Fukuzawa, who established Keio University, in Tokyo. He wanted to expand his knowledge by learning the ways of a completely foreign people.

A LONG LASTING GIFT

A beautiful gift immigrated to this country and has remained on the very same spot of earth for 64 years now. That spot is a around the Tidal Basin, at the Jefferson Memorial. The gift is the famous Japanese cherry trees which bloom at the same time in both Washington, D.C., and Tokyo. Three thousand of these special ornamental trees were presented to President and Mrs. William Howard Taft from the city of Tokyo. A Cherry Blossom Festival is held each Spring in both cities, attracting sight-seers from all over the world.

A great many Americans don't realize that they have Asian blood in their veins. Most of the whole blood used to make plasma comes from the rural areas of China and Japan. It's strong and more resistant to disease than American or European blood. Much of the weakness of western blood results from the preserved and non-natural foods westerners eat. But even more than that, the rural Japanese and Chinese, in overcoming many hardships, have developed certain immunities. This is very helpful to those receiving the blood. The product is good, the source certainly is plentiful, and the price is right. That makes it an excellent import. Dr. Jokichi Takamine developed a process that has also saved many people's lives. Adrenalin is injected into persons with heart and circulatory trouble, asthma, hay fever, and allergic reactions. In the past, adrenalin, which has to be kept refrigerated, was often unavailable in emergencies. Dr. Takamine produced *artificial* adrenalin, which accomplishes the same good and requires no refrigeration. What a great contribution!

Sometimes a contribution is an intangible thing, and perhaps only affects a few people, but the knowledge of the next gift could encourage many others to enjoy its positive results. What I'm referring to is a person-to-person exchange.

Kenzo Nanjo was eager and excited to visit a foreign country, the United States, but he was worried about the strangers with whom he would be staying. Would they speak too fast for him to understand them? And would they be able to understand his English? He had studied hard and his teacher said he spoke "well." Would they like him, however differently he looked and acted from them? He would try not to make noise when he ate, even though in his country, doing so means a person is enjoying the food. Could he manage a knife and fork properly? He would miss the "ofuro" (the square deep bathtub that one sits in), but he would try to have the hot water cover him by lying down in the American tub. He would have to remember to shake hands and not to bow when greeting someone. All these problems and more raced through his mind. His family had never even seen a foreigner, how could he possibly be going to a place filled with them? He was apprehensive, but it was part of his job to go. Kenzo was given the opportunity to visit because he was a policeman in Osaka at the time of Expo '70--the World's Fair there. The Japanese knew that many Americans would be visiting the "Fair," and wanted to accomodate them by having foods and facilities that they would enjoy.

During his one-week stay in the United States, Kenzo developed such a firm friendship with his American host family that flowing tears and long embraces accompanied his departure from all concerned: Grandma, Mom, Dad, and children.

He had taught the young daughter how to play a Japanese card game. He had taught the son the Japanese "Cherry Blossom" song, and had given lasting gifts of conversation and insight into the Japanese culture to the whole family.

He corresponded with them after his return home, and for six years that was the bridge across the ocean that kept him up on the growth of the children and the activities of his American family, while they learned of his marriage, job changes, and the birth of his daughter. Finally, the mother and father visited him in Osaka, and experienced such hospitality from their "brother" that it made them forget they were in a distant, strange land.

Inside the front door, they exchanged their shoes for slippers and removed those before going into an eating or sleeping room. They slept warm and snug on "futons," piled high with puffy quilts. In the morning, the "futons" were folded up and the low dining table set in its place. There were no chairs and the visitors changed sitting positions frequently on the large pillows, first legs tucked under them, then from one side to the other, and maybe cross-legged for awhile.

Sometimes they forgot when to put the slippers on and take them off, but all was taken with joy on the part of the Japanese hosts, and as a great adventure by the American guests. The food was as new to them as the food in the United States had been to Kenzo. He remembered going without rice the first couple days in America, and finally requesting some. The mother, remembering that incident, requested Japanese-style food for breakfast. She received that, plus ham and eggs and toasted giant bread. "Kompai!" was cheered as they raised their glasses, and then loving gifts were exchanged.

The relationship between these two families is strong because they took advantage of the opportunity to develop such a friendship. It is a wonderful feeling to have "brothers" and "sisters" in other countries. It proves that foreign cultures and modes of living cannot prevent brotherhood between persons who are open to experience the differences other countries offer.

The first Japanese to become a U.S. citizen, Hikozo Hamada, was brought to San Francisco in 1851 as part of a shipwrecked crew that had been picked up by the Auckland, when he was only thirteen years old. A year later he and his shipmates were shipped to Hong Kong via Hawaii. Because the Japanese ports were closed to foreigners, he was unable to get passage to Japan, and was returned to California. One day, while acting as an interpreter, Hikozo was noticed by a Collector of Customs, who befriended him, and offered him a home while he went to school.

He attended a Roman Catholic School in Baltimore, Maryland, where he became a convert. He changed his name to Joseph Heco. He was introduced to President Pierce and President Buchanan, and at the age of 21, became the first Japanese to gain American citizenship. He returned to Japan, and became an interpreter for the U.S. Consul, Townsend Harris, there. Harris was responsible for negotiating the Edo Treaty, allowing Japanese to immigrate to America.

In 1861, on a trip to the United States, Joseph Heco met with President Lincoln. Heco was an accredited representative of the American government, and again went to Japan, where he was refused positions in the Japanese feudal government on the grounds that he was a citizen of the United States.

He was responsible for writing several books describing America to the Japanese, and in 1865 he started the first Japanese newspaper in San Francisco.

ENTERTAINMENT

Two beautiful and talented American actresses, born in Tokyo, are Olivia de Haviland and Joan Fontaine. Sessue Hayakawa is the epitomy of the Japanese-American actor. One of the great artistic painters is Yasuo Kuniyoshi--a Japanese-born who the U.S. is now proud to claim.

You'd think that lovely actress Liv Ullman was born in Scandinavia, but she was actually born in Tokyo. And that dynamic superstar, Yul Brynner claims his birthplace as Sakhalin Island, Japan. Everyone's favorite Japanese actress is adorable Myoshi Umeki, the gifted star of television and films.

Among others who have made important contributions to their community we find Hachiro Onuki. Born in Japan, just before the signing of the treaty which opened up trade with Japan, he was one young man who had an opportunity to learn some English as a result of the teaching of Manjiro. Legend tells us that while shopping in Yokohama, he met a group of American Naval cadets who were having a difficult time because they couldn't speak Japanese. With his limited knowledge of English, he offered to interpret for them. They were so grateful that they asked him to visit the United States with them. They smuggled him aboard their ship, and he landed in Boston in 1876. He saw the nearby Philadelphia Centennial Exposition, and visited New York and Washington, D.C., before departing from his friends for San Francisco to get a ship home. Enroute to San Francisco, he learned about the silver strike in Tombstone, Arizona, and quickly forgot about Japan. We don't know if he ever found silver, but he settled in Phoenix, Arizona, and got his start there by selling drinking water. He Americanized his name to Hutchlon Ohnick (which shows his creativity--Hutchlon isn't your average American name!), and that seems to have led to the partnership which made him the builder and superintendent of the Phoenix Illuminating Gas and Electric Company. In 1886, he and his partners were granted a franchise by the city of Phoenix "to supply said City of Phoenix and its citizens and residents with illuminating gas or electric lights or both." He bought land downtown for $1200, and went to St. Louis to buy gas generating equipment, mains, and fixtures. A local editor writing of this momentous undertaking stated with pride, "It won't be long now before Phoenix will have illuminated streets and Phoenix will commence putting on the airs of a city in good earnest."

In the late 1890's, he visited Japan and returned to Seattle, Washington, in 1901. Together with two other Issei (Japanese-born Americans), he opened the Oriental American Bank.

These are but a few of the Japanese immigrants who have really proven that anything can be accomplished by anyone in the United States.

172

22

KOREA

by

JOAN S. FOLLENDORE

"From birth, each and every individual seeks freedom. I traveled all over the world and couldn't find as much freedom as the American government allows to individuals," said Dr. Ro Jeung Park.

"Of course, there are fallacies in the democratic system, but it is the best that one can have. In time, I found shortcomings in democracy, however this country's people try to correct their mistakes, and they recognize mistakes and don't hide them."

There is much room to grow in America, compared to overcrowded little Korea. He's proud of the Korean people because as a minority here, they try so hard. Koreans are some of the more recent immigrants, but they are not "the poor, the needy" (as the Statue of Liberty requests). They are educated, moneyed, and proud.

Dr. Park continues, "I hope all Americans accept Korean people as a part of their country. I will help them to become respected American brothers and sisters."

He would like to work not only for the Korean community, but Americans, also. Being Korean, he will dedicate the remainder of his life to the betterment of the Korean people.

Ro Jeung Park is a present-day humanitarian. At the age of seventeen, he left the place where he was born and reared, the Royal Palace of Korea, to go to Japan for higher education. He earned his doctorate degree in economics, and following World War II, he became leader of the Korean community in Japan, just as he now is in the United States.

There, as in America, he used as many Korean employees as possible and developed property and built office buildings, factories, hotels, resorts, and housing. He continues to encourage Korean immigrants to learn trades that will be of use in the United States, and to still retain some cultural aspects for ceremonies and special occasions.

175

In memory of his first wife, who died in Korea at the young age of 23, he dedicated a large Christian church to the Korean community of Los Angeles, where services are conducted in the native language.

Another instance of repeating an occupation of his adult life in Japan, is his American horse-breeding ranch, from which he derives, and gives, much pleasure.

His dream is to develop an Oriental Community Trade Center, with the help of his bright, ambitious, lovely wife, Kyung. At present, they have a small scale operation of this huge project, where Korean-Americans are learning to develop marketing techniques in order to import more goods from their mother country. They also counsel at the center, for family and employment problems and for problems in every area of life in the new, strange land.

Korea became a colony of Japan in 1910, then after 34 years, it was freed, but divided as a spoil of war. Soon the Civil War (involving United Nations troops), between the divided North and South, virtually destroyed the country. Five million lives were lost. The achievements made since the war ended in 1953, are remarkable. The people proved to be like elastic, and bounded right back to rebuild and improve their nation. Many of those resilient persons found their way to the United States.

A FAMILY CONTRIBUTION

Four brothers are all in the U.S. now, but they immigrated at different times, and each contributed in a different, but enriching way to his adopted country.

First to arrive was Lee Wook Chang, who came as a student in 1916. Working his way through college, he earned a masters degree in education. After ten years, he returned to Korea to his wife, and became principal of a prominent mission school. One of Lee Wook's visits to the United States was as a member of the six-man Korean Education Mission, to visit American institutions in various fields in order to arrange for student and personnel exchanges. He was selected to present a 600-year-old vase to President Truman from the Korean people. That vase is now in the Harry S. Truman Library, in Independence, Missouri.

When Dr. Chang came again in 1960, it was as the Ambassador from South Korea. In Washington, D.C., he began negotiations with Secretary of State Dean Rusk to formulate a Korean-American trade program based on a proposed detailed study of the Korean economy. Now a California resident, his latest book was published in 1976, stating his goal for the future: "To make public what he said, thought, and wrote during ten years of observation in Korea from 1961 to 1971."

The second brother found he could not earn enough money in Paris, France, to get through medical school, so in 1921, he joined Lee Wook, in Dubuque, Iowa, where they both completed college. Now in Houston, Texas, Dr. Sherwood Chang Lynn is still practicing medicine at 71 years old.

The youngest brother, Tae Wook Chang, has been with the Library of Congress in Washington, D.C., since 1966.

The last one to come to the U.S., in 1971, was Ki Wok Chang, now of Baltimore, Maryland. He had carried on the family business in Korea until his retirement. For four generations, the Chang family dealt in Chinese medicines (pharmaceuticals, as we know it).

There are hundreds of Korean immigrants who are medical doctors. Just one is James Chang, a heart specialist in Tuscaloosa, Alabama. His son, who is also an immigrant, is Dr. Seung Kook Chang and specializes in respiratory diseases, in Ohio.

The Korean-American history is less than 100 years old. It began with the signing of a Treaty of Commerce in 1882, which created an exchange of goods between the two countries. In 1887, the United States received the first Korean ambassador, Chung Yang Park. He and his couterie were the only Koreans in America until 1902, when the Hawaiian sugar plantation owners needed workers and sent representatives to Korea. A medical missionary, Dr. Allen, represented the United States on behalf of its territory's sugar cane growers and arranged a mutually beneficial plan. The workers earned 69 cents a day in Hawaii, and with that amount, enjoyed a beautiful life, and helped save the sugar industry.

All was going well until 1905, when Korea went under Japanese rule and they stopped immigration to the U.S. Seven thousand three hundred Koreans had immigrated to Hawaii during those three years. When their indenture was completed, two thousand went to the mainland United States. They were made up of scholars, farm hands, and unskilled laborers; all poor, illiterate in English, and sixty per cent were illiterate in Korean. These two thousand, along with a couple hundred others who had arrived earlier, saw the need to accomodate Korean immigrants, and organized the Korean National Association. Their leader was Chang Ho Ahn, who didn't have an extensive education, but was a born-intellectual and humanitarian. To raise the standard of living of the poor Korean immigrants, he went into many homes and swept them clean himself, teaching them to live cleanly and to eat regularly in a more American lifestyle. Ahn taught his fellow-immigrants how to work in the U.S. so that they could keep a job. They must be industrious and honest, and he set an example for them, working in the orange groves.

As is the way with many dedicated humanitarians, he had to neglect his wife and family, because he was sent to Korea and Shanghai to represent the Korean-Americans.

A Korean Provisional Government was established within the French Concession Area in Shanghai, China, which was a haven for political refugees for 30 years. Mr. Ahn served as one of its most influential cabinet members. Tribute is still paid to him, both in the U.S. and in Korea, as the "Founder of Korean Independence."

A HOME IN A NEW LAND

In 1912, the Korean National Association built a dormitory in Claremont, California, which during the ensuing ten years acted as a "half-way house" between the first day ashore in a strange land and finding a job or starting school. Five hundred college-age persons crossed the Yalu River and escaped through Shanghai, China, without passports. They were political exiles, but the United States didn't require a passport until World War I. About half of these young people continued their education in American universities. Many of them earned their living expenses by working on rice farms or in factories during their school vacations.

Chong Rim Kim founded a rice farm in northern California. He was so successful that he bacame known as the "Rice King." Korean experts are still hired to give advice on rice farming in America.

A popular singing group, the three Kim Sisters, have toured the world with their sensational act. The United States is happy to have these three lovely Koreans on her soil.

One of the world's top painters was Whan Ki Kim, whose art hangs in museums and galleries throughout the United States.

Pianist Dong II Hahn received rave reviews for his performance in London, in 1974. He also played for President and Mrs. Kennedy in the White House.

Korean immigrants may be found throughout the United States and they have learned the lessons well that were taught by Chang Ho Ahn, whose son, Phillip Ahn, has starred in countless American films. They are immaculate, hard-working, and honest--a genuine asset to American life.

23

MEXICO

by

JOAN S. FOLLENDORE

"G.T.T." scrawled on a cabin door meant, as everyone knew "Gone to Texas." Americans had been moving to the Texas Territory ever since Mexico became independent in 1821. Mexico included the frontier from Texas to California and was dotted with ranches and missions. More wild horses lived there than people. The first Americans were welcome, provided they became Mexican citizens and joined the Catholic Church. A man could have a bigger farm there than in the United States, besides thousands of acres for cattle. Some settlers tried to be good Mexicans. They told their families, "Speak in Spanish, learn the ways of the country, and obey its laws."

In 1836, after the Alamo had fallen and been retaken, Texas became an independent republic with Sam Houston as President. Ten years later, the U.S. defeated Mexico in a war to insure Texas' independence from Mexico. The Mexican-American Treaty was signed surrendering 525,000 square miles north ot the Rio Grande River to the U.S. in return for fifteen million dollars. In 1854, The Gadsden Purchase brought almost 30,000 more square miles into the U.S. That was Arizona and New Mexico. Thus Mexican-Americans came into existence because, rather than move back to Mexico, they became American citizens, and an important part of the population.

Today, every state in the union has residents representing the three major Hispanic American groups: Mexicans, Puerto Ricans, and Cubans. The largest Hispanic group, Mexican-Americans, or Chicanos, number some ten million. Their contribution to American heritage has been so great it is difficult to appraise. These people are warm, colorful, and possess a classical beauty rooted in antiquity.

Juan de Onate led a group from Mexico to the American Southwest, in 1597, for the express purpose of making it a colony. He took possession of New Mexico, which included much, much more than the state of New Mexico today. He was Governor and Captain-General for nineteen years. That gave him the right to conquer and settle the land, at his own expense, and he did just that. Being the son of one of the richest men in Mexico gave him that opportunity. Members of

181

his party spread out to parts of what are now Texas, Utah, Colorado, Kansas, and Nebraska.

The explorers taught the Indians about God, guns and horses. By 1630, there were 25 missions and 90 pueblos founded by Onate. He was a terrific planner and developer to be able to build 90 villages in about 32 years. Fifty years later, however, due to wars, almost all Spanish life in the Southwest was gone. Cattle and horses escaped from ruined pueblos and missions, and multiplied into vast wild herds. The mustangs and longhorn cattle of Texas are examples of those new wild breeds.

The Spanish-speaking came back after that disaster, and adopted a new system of settlement to be able to come to one another's aid quickly. Presidios (fortresses), pueblos, and missions were located about a day's march from each other--a system that worked, but was expensive. These settlements were made up mostly of Mexicans.

The Rio Grande is a shallow river that forms the border between Mexico and Texas. American trappers traveled as far south as the Rio Grande, camping for short periods in the wilds, then moving on to another spot for more wild game. They felt the life too rough for women, so gave up the idea of settling down and raising a family. But when they saw the beautiful Mexican women along the Rio Grande, they were captivated, and quit traveling. This also worked in reverse as when a handsome Mexican took off with the good-looking daughter of the Governor of New Mexico. These marriages tied the nationalities and nations together, creating more Mexican-Americans.

"Let it be remembered that the Mexican was the original cowboy," wrote Owen Wister. Cattle-raising became increasingly important in the vast rangelands of the southwestern part of the United States, and the hardy men who engaged in this occupation were known as cowboys. Trappings and techniques of the Mexican "vaquero" are basic in the folklore of the West. As a matter of fact, cowboys derived as much knowledge (in handling cattle) from the Mexican vaqueros as settlers on the Eastern seaboard did from the American Indians. Their contributions and vernacular to our cattle-raising industry are: lariat, rodeo, mesa, savvy, reata, high-heeled boots, chaps, and the knowledge of the multiple uses of the mesquite tree. Hawaiian cowboys are still called "panioles" because the originals learned cattle handling in the early nineteenth century from imported Mexicans who called themselves "Espanolos."

During the California gold rush, Mexican miners taught their techniques to the Anglo Americans, who had little knowledge of gold mining. The Spanish word "Bonanza!" means rich ore, and "placer" is the name for a mineral deposit which has particles large enough to be obtained by washing. "Staking a claim" is a Mexican concept, and led to laws being established similar to those in Mexico. The "arrastra," a machine to extract gold from quartz, was introduced by the Mexicans who came when the cry of "Gold!" was heard around the world.

TRANSPORTATION

Mexican-Americans combined the knowledge of Spain and the experience of the Indian. Before 1900, they brought the pack trains to Texas, and made the first transportation system throughout the Southwest. The trails they made from California to Arizona, (and) from New Mexico to Texas brought supplies to the mining camps and the settlements. Later these trails became the rail lines and turnpikes. Then it was Mexican labor which laid the ties and drove the spikes. They provided most of the labor force for the great agricultural development in the Southwest. Most of the nation has been well-fed due to their help, year after year.

Mexican-Americans also filled the need when the manufacturing industry was growing. Many of them grew too, into relatively skilled occupations in the mechanical revolution of our country.

In the 1920's, from north of the border, American industries: the railroads, and mines, the steel mills, the orchards, the farms, all needed workers. Labor agents went into Mexico, representing American companies and offered Mexican "peons" (people who are forced to work off debts or prescribed punishments and who had never earned more than 25¢ a day) as much as $1.25 to $1.50 a day. If that alone didn't bring them, there was also the excitement of a new experience, and the chance to escape from the hopelessness of peonage and the uncertainties of the post-revolutionary years in Mexico.

When twenty-five families of Mexican Mormons faced poverty and destitution, the Mormon church purchased 440 acres in Colorado, and gave it to them for farming. Those Mexican families have become independent. They know how to get the most out of each ray of sunshine and every drop of rain. They have rich harvests and put into the storehouses what they do not use themselves. Their produce helps to feed hundreds of people engaged in other work than farming, under the Security Program of the Mormons.

Intelligent young Americans know that being fluent in more than one language is normal in most other countries. It is a fact that Spanish is spoken by more people than any other language throughout the world. How fortunate to be raised in a home where one language is spoken, and go to a school where a different one is the rule. You would become familiar with the culture behind both tongues also, and your life twice as rich as that of a unilingual person. In this world made small by television and jet planes, career opportunities are fantastic for the bilingual young person.

A good example of making use of the advantage of being a Mexican-American is Raul H. Castro. As a child, his family moved to the U.S.

from Cananea, Mexico, seeking a better life. They found it, and Raul finished public school and entered college in Arizona, where he earned a law degree. He became a Judge, and later District Attorney in Arizona. His bilingual and bicultural environment led him into the United States Foreign Service, which took him to El Salvador and then to Bolivia, as Ambassador from the U.S. He has been a living bridge between cultures, and has served America well.

While still a young man, Frank Paz organized clubs for Mexican youths, at Hull House, in Chicago, and later continued his efforts in behalf of Mexican-Americans in San Antonio and Los Angeles. The U.S. owes a political debt to the early Mexican leaders, who along with other Mexican humanitarians, set the stage for civil rights for all minorities.

After Lee Trevino became the first man to ever win three major golf tournaments in one year, he said, "When they asked me what I was going to do with all that money after my first win, I said I'm going to buy the Alamo, and give it back to Mexico!"

Jim Plunkett, the football player, was offered $300,000 to play Pro-Ball after only his second year at Stanford. He turned it down because, as he put it, "we're always telling kids today--and I tell a lot of Mexican-Americans kids this--not to drop out, to finish school. Set a target and work toward it."

Notable contributions from Mexico to the U.S. in the art world are Rufino Tamayo and Jose Luis Cuevas. They have both taught and had "One Man Shows" in New York City.

A gift in abundance has been music in every form. All American school children must know the La Raspa, or Mexican Hat Dance. It's so much fun to sing and to dance to that quick beat. Mexican rhythm always brings out a smile in the listener. It's happy, celebration-style music.

California, Colorado, and New Mexico entered the Union as bilingual states. Their constitutions required that all laws be published in both Spanish and English. The flavor of Mexico was, and is, vividly apparent in the customs, manners, foods, and architecture of our Southwest.

The architecture of the American Southwest has been trememdously influenced by the Mexican tile roofs, balconies, plazas, and courtyards. You can see whole communities here made up of white adobe-type buildings topped with red curved tiles. Prominent today, Felix Candela's designs in architecture transcend national boundaries.

Kernels of the first corn, or maize, came from Mexico; as did the cacao nut, which makes chocolate. Today's food gifts from south of the border include chili, tacos, tamales, and tortillas.

Many talented Mexican-born members of the entertainment world have given America countless hours of pleasure. Some are actors Ricardo Montalban, Ramon Navarro, Anthony Quinn, Gilbert Roland, and comedian Cantinflas. Actresses are Linda Christian, Dolores Del Rio, Katy Jurado; and the marvelous choreographer Jose Limon. Not to be forgotten is Carlos Chavez, composer and conductor. Literary treasures came from novelist Mariano Azuela and Octavio Paz. In appreciation of their great contributions to lovers of art, we thank three outstanding Mexican mural painters: Jose Orozco, Diego Rivera, and David Siquieros.

It is certain that the Southwest as we know it would not exist without the Mexican-Spanish heritage. Their language and culture serves to provide the entire region with much of its distinctiveness. The American way of life has been, and is being, immeasurably enriched by their presence.

24

THE NETHERLANDS

by

IRENE L. JERISON

A May visitor to Holland, Michigan, might think that the little country of Holland (also known as the Netherlands) had been magically transported from the shores of the North Sea to the shores of Lake Michigan. Tulip fields blazing with color line the roads leading into town and border the city streets. Townspeople clump about in wooden shoes and Dutch costumes, looking as if they had stepped out of decorated Dutch tiles and cocoa boxes. At Tulip Festival time in the Michigan town, just as in Holland during holidays, people go all out for local color.

The dutch countryside, unlike its people, wears its age-old quaintness the year round. Dikes and windmills keep the sea from flooding the low-lying ("nether") land. Narrow streets and gabled houses line the many canals, the country's waterways. All these reflect Dutch history. Since the 9th century, the Dutch have been forced to battle both the sea and foreign armies. But in spite of hardship and disaster, industry, the arts, and religious tolerance have flourished in Holland. In order to prosper, the Dutch, crammed as densely together as people anywhere in the world, have had to reach out beyond their country's borders. For centuries, the Dutch have been the traveling merchants of the world.

This is how the first Hollanders came to settle in the New World. One of their settlements, New Amsterdam, became New York City over three hundred years ago. Their imprint on downstate New York and parts of New Jersey still remains. Peekskill, Catskill Mountains, and Rensselaer County are all Dutch names. Many well-known people from there--the Roosevelts, the Van Burens, the Vanderbilts--all have Dutch blood in their veins. Rip Van Winkle was a Dutch-American although his creator, the writer Washington Irving, was not. Harlem, named after the Dutch city of Haarlem, and the Bowery, which used to be the "Bouwerie" (farm) on which Peter Stuyvesant lived out his last years, are among the many New York landmarks with Dutch names.

The Dutch who colonized New Amsterdam were brought over by the Dutch West Indies Company to clear and farm the land; but more importantly because that trading company wanted to have a place from which their ships could pick up furs and grain on the new continent. Had things gone differently, Dutch might now be the language of the United States. The colony of New Amsterdam was a lively bit of Holland for decades. A traveler in about 1640 reported hearing 18 different languages spoken on the island of Manhattan. But Dutch was predominant, spoken even by French and German colonists. The Dutch, more easygoing than the Puritans of New England, led a pleasant life and introduced many customs. Ice skating and sledding are imports from old Holland, as are colored Easter eggs and Santa Claus.

The good life of New Amsterdam was a reflection of the life and culture of 17th century Holland, and because things were so good at home, few people wanted to leave. The colony could not develop. And so it happened that the Dutch lost out to the English. In 1664, Peter Stuyvesant gave up the colony to the British.

Stuyvesant, the peg-legged governor, is best remembered for his last official act. Even though he was less cruel and braver than the governors before him, he was a tyrannical boss rather than a true leader. In the end, he lost the support of not only the colonists but even the company he had served. Among the burghers (citizens) who might have clashed with him was Adrien van der Donck, the first lawyer in the colony of New Netherlands. He wrote the first book describing life in the colony and was a champion of the right of the people to govern themselves. He and other settlers felt that their standing as Dutch citizens entitled them to have much say about their taxes and self-government. Their "Remonstrance and Petition to the Director-General and Council of New Netherland" foreshadowed the Declaration of Independence...a century later.

For almost two hundred years, few Dutch people immigrated to the New World as Dutch-Americans blended into the American landscape, working and intermarrying. A group of Dutch Quakers did come over to found Germantown in Pennsylvania in 1684; and a Dutch revolutionary, Francis Adrian van der Kamp, found refuge in Virginia in the 18th century. He was described as "a star of the first magnitude" by John Adams for his great learning, and Harvard granted him a doctor's degree.

A WAVE OF IMMIGRATION

By the middle of the 19th century, however, the worsening economic and religious climate in the Netherlands led to a second wave of immigration, when groups of poverty-striken religious dissidents immigrated to the United States to better their lots and practice their religion as they wished. These newcomers founded their own settlements, such as Holland, Michigan; Pella, Iowa; and Hollandtown, Wisconsin. Most were smart enough to stop at places that were similar in climate and soil to what they had left behind, so that they were able to adapt their old-country skills in their new home. Since they knew how to grow flowers, it is no wonder that Dutch-Americans have become kings of that industry.

In the 1930's, Jan de Graaf grew six million daffodils in 700 acres in Oregon, and John Theodore Scheepers revolutionized the tulip bulb industry in the U.S. The Dutch also knew how to design and build furniture, and the furniture industry in Grand Rapids, Michigan, has long profited from their skills.

Not everything from the old country worked in the United States. The windmill, for example, could not be counted on to grind grain for flour, because winds in the U.S. are too changeable. Celery, on the other hand, which the Dutch discovered in their newly adopted country, became the All-American munch thanks to the ingenuity of the Dutch.

A Michigan settler by the name of Marinus de Bruin owned acres of mucky, mosquito-infested bog, in which his cows would sink to their bellies in wet summer weather. He decided to try some celery seed on it. He ditched and drained the swamp, and then hand-cleared every last root, working covered from head to foot in black ooze, to the taunts and laughter of passers-by. When at last he succeeded in raising the vegetable, his children sold tidy bundles of it door to door. Eventually the growing of celery became a profitable specialty of Dutch-Americans and a healthful contribution to people's diets as the one foodstuff that burns up more calories in the eating than are in it.

Both the founder of the Michigan settlement, Albertus Christian Van Raalte, and the founder of Pella in Iowa, Hendrik Peter Scholte achieved prominence in the United States. The latter became friendly with Abraham Lincoln, and it is said that his heart failed and he died of grief after Lincoln's assassination. The story of Scholte's wife, however, set down by her granddaughter, Leonora, is the story of all pioneer women. Most are not remembered by name. They worked too hard to keep their families going to make much of a mark in the wider world. Yet, of course, without them the country would not have been built. Better off than most, Mareah Scholte was still typical.

When Mareah Kranz married Hendrik Scholte in Amsterdam, she was young, beautiful, gay and spoiled, and just back from Paris where she had studied music, art, and dancing. Her husband was a stern dominie (minister), about twice her age and a widower with three daughters. He was also intelligent and wealthy, and his beautiful house in Amsterdam, filled with books, paintings, and lovely things, was a source of pride and joy to its new mistress. And so Mareah enjoyed life, always dressed in the latest Paris fashions, her hair just so, reading the latest books and playing the newest music on her piano.

Naturally, she dutifully went with her husband on the endless journey across the Atlantic and across half a strange, empty continent. But Mareah broke down and wept when she found herself in front of a crude one-room cabin that was to be her home. And she cried again when she unpacked the delicate Delft china they had brought with them and found it all broken. Many beautiful velvet drapes and priceless carpets had to be thrown out because they had mildewed.

It didn't take Mareah long, however, to recover and adapt. Soon both the house and her way of life were almost up to her old fashionable standards, so much so that some elders in the congregation complained to Scholte that it wasn't fitting for their dominie to have such a gorgeous clotheshorse for a wife.

Scholte heard them out, and then he said, "Brethren, I am deeply moved.... Now please help me further with your advice. What shall I do with her? Shall I poison her or drown her?"

Needless to say, Scholte did neither, and his wife contributed much-needed sparkle and elegance to a frontier on which such pleasant frills were in short supply.

EDWARD BOK

Edward Bok lived out his rags-to-riches American dream in the big cities rather than on the frontier. He was probably the best-known Dutch American of his day. His life story, *The Americanization of Edward Bok*, won the Pulitzer prize (1920) and sold over a quarter of a million copies. In it, he credits his success to the energy and solid self-discipline that are part of the Dutch tradition.

Bok found himself a paying job as window washer at a bakery at the age of ten. He then went on to being a messenger, newsboy, cub reporter and, at 21, editor. As a proper Victorian boy-hero should, young Edward left school after seven years in order to make life easier for his mother, whose sheltered European upbringing had not prepared her for the hardships of housecleaning and peeling potatoes. To continue educating himself, Bok studied the lives of the great men of his day in an encyclopedia. Whenever he had a question, he would simply shoot off a letter to the celebrity and ask for information. Since the reply carried the famous person's signature, this poor teenage immigrant soon became the owner of a very valuable autograph collection. Letters led to personal meetings, and Bok, still a boy, came to know personally many famous writers and even the President of the United States.

Bok's nerve, perserverance, and hard work, coupled with his ability to hit on popular ideas, led to an exteremely successful career as editor of the *Ladies' Home Journal*, a magazine which became a household fixture in the United States. His grandson, Derek, became president of Harvard University.

Bok was the first of many Dutch-Americans who have distinguished themselves as writers, a field in which it is unusual for people whose native language is not English to excel. Hendrik Willem van Loon wrote and illustrated biographies and popular history books, including the famous *Story of Mankind*. He was also a much sought-after lecturer. Pierre van Paassen was both a journalist and a Unitarian minister. Hilda Van Stockum, whose husband was a State

Department official, is the author and illustrator of many books for children and young adults, some of which describe her family's adventures around the world. Meindert de Jong is another Dutch-born writer of books for children. One of his books won the Newbery Award, the highest honor in the United States for children's literature. Jan de Hartog has written books and plays for children and adults. *The Fourposter* was first a play, then a film, and then the musical "I Do, I Do." *The Little Ark*, a novel about children, also was turned into a movie. Two Dutch-American writers, Arnold Mulder and David Cornel De Jong, have written novels based on their immigrant background.

Two famous artists from Holland lived in the United States: Willem de Kooning, whose blotchy, colorful paintings hang in many galleries and Piet Mondrian, whose bright canvasses, composed of patterns of colored rectangles framed in straight black lines, have been copied endlessly in modern interior decorating.

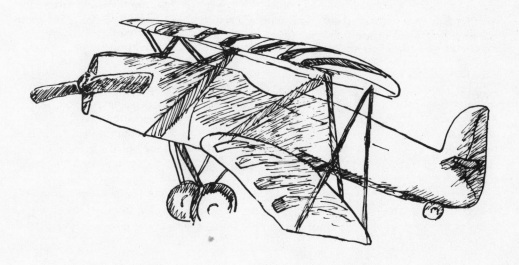

As all fans of Snoopy (and who isn't one, except Lucy?) know, the airplane the dreaded Red Baron flies is a Fokker. The designer and builder of this World War I German fighter plane was Dutch-born Anthony Fokker, who immigrated to the United States in 1922 to found the Fokker Aircraft Corporation. The Fokkers, the first planes with welded steel fuselages, were also the first to fly across the Pacific and to the North Pole. Like Edward Bok, Fokker recorded his life story in a book, called *The Flying Dutchman*.

But the most lasting Dutch contribution to the United States has probably been its export of scholars. Dutch universities have always produced more than Holland could use, to the advantage of the U.S. Dutch astronomers, such as Peter van de Kamp, Jan Schilt, and Dirk Brouwer, immigrated in the 1920's. So did physicists, such as Samuel Goudsmit. World War II brought the Nobel Prize chemist Peter Debye, oriental scholar Henri Frankfort, psychoanalyst Elizabeth Geleerd, and economist Tjalling Koopmans, among others.

A Californian since 1937, Aarie Haagen-Smit is a chemist who took up a new field of study in his new country. He investigated that plague of his adopted Los Angeles area home -- smog. Haagen-Smit proved that smog is made by the reaction of hydrocarbons and nitrous oxides in sunlight; that automobile exhaust is largely responsible for it; and that it can damage plant life. Without his work, we might not have clean air laws and regulations, and we might have kept on choking ourselves to death instead of trying to do something about it.

These are the gifts the land of windmills and tulips has given the United States. The tulips have thrived in the new country and the windmills are once again being considered as a source of energy. The immigrants from the Netherlands have thrived too and, from celery to smog control, have given their adopted homeland much that is useful and much that is gay.

25

NEW ZEALAND

by

JOAN S. FOLLENDORE

When you see pictures of beautiful New Zealand, you wonder why anyone would ever leave it. But because one New Zealander chose to look at the scenery of the United States instead of his native mountains and streams, the whole world is a different place. The stars are nearer earth. Outer space is not so far away. Men have walked on the moon and have seen the planets in color photographs.

That former New Zealander is William Hayward Pickering, born the day after Christmas in Wellington. A Christmas present to the universe, if anyone had had the foresight to know it on that day in 1910.

William Pickering became director of the Jet Propulsion Laboratory (JPL) in Pasadena, California, in 1954, after he had made a name for himself in several fields of research. He was graduated from the California Institute of Technology in 1932 with a Bachelor of Science Degree in Technical Engineering. In 1933, he earned his Master of Science Degree and in 1936, his Doctorate in Physics. He was invited to join the faculty of Caltech. It is hard to believe that the institute almost didn't accept him as a student seven years before that appointment!

Bill Pickering's mother died when he was a small child and his father sent him to live with his grandparents in the small seaside village of Havelock. The primary school that he attended had also given early schooling to Ernest Rutherford. Rutherford became a famous scientist, one of the founders of nuclear physics. The school was very proud that it had once enrolled him as a small boy and encouraged the other boys to try to be like Ernest.

Even though Havelock was small and it seemed like an unlikely place to develop another great scientist, it opened Bill's eyes to the great universe of science.

He was ten years old when he read about an astonishing new invention--a wireless system of communication called radio.

"Where can I find out more about it?" Bill asked his grandmother. Kate Pickering said she didn't know, but she tried to help Bill find out. Together they trudged through Havelock asking people. But no one had heard about radio.

Finally, Bill discovered that there were science magazines and he immediately bought some. In one he found a set of plans for the construction of a radio.

"Now we can have our own!" he said excitedly to his grandparents. But Havelock was too small for the merchants to carry the materials Bill needed to build a radio--his first space effort failed!

Although Havelock was a waterfront town, Bill never learned to swim until he fell out of a rowboat. Then it was either drown or swim--he swam. Swimming and rowing were fun but they were slow ways of getting around. Bill liked traveling with his grandfather on his business trips to other villages in the family's horse-drawn buggy. Horses were really fast!

When it came time for Bill to go to high school he returned to Wellington, happy that he would be reunited with his father. He was disappointed that his father was on government business in Samoa. Bill missed the warmth and love he had found in his grandparents' home. Life seemed dull. Even his school uniform was dull-grey, tight jacket and short pants, and a cap with a brim. Every student looked just like every other student--until he began to sort them out.

One of the teachers, A. C. Gifford, affectionately called "Uncle Charlie" by the boys when his back was turned, recognized that young Bill Pickering was not at all like every other student, and needed something more to occupy his mind than the routine lessons. He introduced Bill to astronomy and led him into a study of the solar system. Bill found other boys who were interested in radio, and in Wellington there were places to buy equipment.

A group of the brighter boys formed a radio club, equipped themselves with short wave radios and learned the Morse code. Bill appreciated the speed of radio waves. When he visited U. S. Navy ships that put in at Wellington, he discovered that they were even able to talk with Washington, D. C., on their ham radio outfits.

Bill expected to take his college studies at the Canterbury College Engineering School of the University of New Zealand at Christ Church. His uncle, Horace Douslin, who had worked in South Africa and maintained a home in Los Angeles as well as in Rotorua, New Zealand, urged Bill to complete his education at the California Institute of Technology.

Bill Pickering boarded a ship for the United States in March, 1929. He planned to return to New Zealand as an electrical engineer--*if* he were accepted by Caltech as a student. The institute wasn't at all sure that the university in New Zealand had given him an adequate education, and Bill was coming to a foreign country as an immigrant instead of on a student's visa.

His first examination convinced the board that they had one bright young student to enroll. Bill was accepted.

He did so well in his studies that in his junior year he was one of the two students given the Travel Award by an anonymous donor. He and Charles Jones, the other winner, and two boys who paid their own way, set out for Europe. There, they obtained a Ford car and spent a merry six months traveling in it for 16,000 miles. The Ford went much faster than the horse and buggy of Bill's childhood, but he could scarcely have foreseen the day when he would direct the construction of guided missiles and rockets that would whiz through the upper atmosphere at speeds greater than the speed of sound.

Bill served on the Caltech faculty under Dr. Robert A. Millikan, chairman of the Caltech Executive Council. He had been awarded the Nobel Prize for Physics in 1923, and he assigned Bill to work with him on cosmic ray analysis.

They went on numerous expeditions to other countries with enthusiastic young scientists, researching the upper atmosphere.

THE JET STREAM

They loaded Geiger counters in balloons and sent them up, sometimes as high as 100,000 feet to relay back information about the atmosphere. Bill first learned about the jet stream (a long, narrow meandering current of high speed winds, sometimes exceeding 250 miles per hour) when his group was in Agra, India, the site of the beautiful Taj Mahal. The balloons they sent up traveled to 30,000 feet straight up, then were suddenly seized by some strange current and pushed rapidly a great distance to the east. When the balloons had made it to 40,000 feet they again rose straight up.

This was a new lesson about the upper atmosphere. Bill didn't realize then how useful this knowledge was to be to him.

It was in the late 1930's that Bill was invited to join a group of a half dozen bright young scientists working under Dr. Theodore von Karman at the Guggenheim Aeronautical Laboratory of Caltech, in Pasadena, California. The group first called themselves "The Suicide Club," and did research in rocketry and propulsion technology.

News of the club leaked out and the citizens of Pasadena were angry. They held meetings for the purpose of having the club disbanded and the research stopped.

"I don't mind the noise!" said one protester, "But I can't bear to see those hearses coming out every night with the day's casualties in them!"

"Those vehicles are not hearses and they are not carrying bodies!" the spokesman for the Suicide Club declared. "They are carrying missiles to distant proving grounds under police escort!"

The protests stopped.

During World War II, Bill's work at the Caltech Laboratory was to find a way to combat the German rockets which were terrifying the population of England and her allies. The Corporal was the first rocket capable of carrying an attack warhead. It came from the laboratory. It was followed by the Sergeant, powered by a mighty solid propellant rocket engine.

Bill became a naturalized U. S. citizen in 1941.

All during the war, the research in rocketry progressed, to the point that after hostilities ended there was much knowledge gained for the start of space exploration for the benefit of mankind.

The team of William Pickering, Werner von Braun and James A. Van Allen put the first U. S. satellite into orbit on January 31, 1958. Bumbling on the part of the military had delayed the project so that the Russians had placed Sputniks I and II into orbit before Explorer I was launched from America. After that, the United States went on steadily to surpass the Russians in space exploration successes.

Some people were angry about the money spent in space exploration. "It should have been given to the poor!" was their outcry.

The money, of course, was not tied up in a leather bag and dropped into the ocean to disappear from sight. Space developments have kept thousands of people working and drawing paychecks; hundreds of new businesses have been spin-offs from space research.

Bill directed the JPL in the launching of more Explorers which discovered and measured the Van Allen Radiation Belt in the upper atmosphere. The JPL also developed several of the unmanned Pioneer interplanetary probes. The Surveyor missions returned more than 86,000 close-up pictures of the moon's surface and assured scientists that the moon's surface could support landing craft--and even men.

The Mariner spacecraft, developed at JPL, flew missions to the near planets and then went on to Venus and Mars, taking the first close-up pictures of planets other than Earth.

During all these years of active research, Bill was happy in another aspect of his life too--with his wife, Muriel, their son Balfour, and daughter Ann Elizabeth. He loved to garden, swim, fish, and hike with them.

He somehow found time to serve on the board of directors of the Boys' Club of Pasadena, the Pasadena Chamber of Commerce, and the Los Angeles World Affairs Council and to be active in the Los Angeles-Auckland (New Zealand) sister city program and civic groups. His professional appointments and his honors and awards fill pages and were given him by Italy, France, England, New Zealand, and the United States.

Bill Pickering planned to retire in 1976, but no one who is acquainted with him believed that he really can be content to fill his time only with gardening or rock collecting! Of course he has done an enormous amount of writing--and publishing--articles and papers on various aspects of science, and undoubtedly he will continue that activity. He will still be concerned about pollution, leisure, energy, and integration, all subjects that are being studied at JPL along with space projects.

Bill said, "The problem which mankind must solve if we are to continue to maintain any sort of civilization on this planet, is no longer the one of our struggle to provide food and shelter for the family, but the spiritual one of learning to live with the rest of the human species, in a world filled with the products of modern technology."

Machines now do so much of man's work, and computers are so busy telling the machines how and when to do it that men and women sometimes get the feeling that they have no useful place on this earth at all.

Bill believes that in the future, children will be educated in the sciences as they once were in literature so that the wonderful world beyond sight can be explored even further. The great reaches of space still stretch before us, the path already unrolled for long distances by that boy from New Zealand.

26

NORWAY

by

MABLE CORINNE PARRISH

Never in the history of the world has there been a more daring, venturesome breed than the Vikings of Scandinavia. Their long, swift ships flashed through the water, silently cruising the coasts of Europe, North Africa, and Asia. By using rivers and lakes and carrying their boats short distances where necessary, the Vikings traveled with the wind--to wherever adventure beckoned. Their sturdy, flat-bottomed boats (called Dragon Ships) could float on the shallowest of streams.

It was inevitable, then, that they would find their way to the eastern shores of North America--which they called Vinland. There is disputed evidence that, having arrived and landed somewhere on the southern shores of Canada, they entered either Hudson Bay or the St. Lawrence River and then sailed through the Great Lakes and on into the mid-western parts of the continent.

Disputed or not, a farmer near Kensington, Minnesota, while digging in his field, uncovered a stone slab on which was engraved a series of Viking runes--a story in picture characters. Noted archeologists were called in, and the writings were transcribed:

> We are 8 Goths (Swedes) and 22 Norwegians on
> exploration of Vinland. We had camp by two
> skerries (islands) on one day's journey from this
> stone. We were away and fished for one day.
> After we came home found 10 men dead. AVM
> (Ave Maria). Have 10 men by the sea to look after
> our ships, 14 days' journey from this island. Year
> 1362.

Some insist that this stone was probably carried to the Minnesota farm by Indians. There's no way of settling the dispute; but the stone slab *was* found. Exactly how far into the continent the Vikings traveled, we do not know; nor do we know for how long these adventurers lived along the rivers they explored. What we do know is that the 8th through 10th century Vikings did cross the

Atlantic in their Dragon Ships--that they did reach North America. We also know that from that day to the present, Norway has contributed more than her share toward the making of the United States.

Although they may not be considered immigrants in the true meaning of the word, the Vikings explored North America's rivers and lakes; and the bodies of many of these noble men lie buried on the eastern shores of that continent. Basically, they were adventurers--not warriors. Because their only weapons were their swords and knives, they were no match for the Indians, whose deadly accuracy with bow and arrow drove them back to Iceland, Greenland, and their homeland.

The Norwegian people--both from necessity and choice--have always been men of the sea. Andrew Fusureth was no exception. Born in a little Norwegian village--and named Andres Andreassen--he changed his last name to that of the cottage in which he was born. (In those small villages, the cottages had names instead of numbers. Many still do. For instance, instead of "1105 Main St.," they would say "the Cutter Cottage." In this case, it was the Fusureth cottage.) He probably made the name change because "Andreassen" simply means "Andre's son"; and Andre wanted his own identity.

At the age of 19, Andres took up the life of a seaman. From Oslo, he sailed the seven seas--north, south, east, and west. He signed on in every port and under every flag. In those days, the food aboard ship was abominable. Living and working conditions were unbearable. The crew received, besides their obnoxious food, a mere pittance; and the discipline was inflexible and cruel. Beatings and prison sentences--in some squalid port--were almost the order of the day. However, much as young Fusureth hated the conditions, he loved the sea even more.

In 1880, he landed for the first time on the west coast of the United States. From then on, he spent more and more time ashore. Because of his own bitter, deep-reaching experiences, he began promoting unionism among seamen. After being elected secretary of the Seamen's Union of the Pacific, he gave up the sea altogether and devoted all his time to union duties.

He went to Washington, D.C., where he helped push through the LaFollette Seamen's Act. One of the most important provisions of the act--and the one that gave Fusureth the most satisfaction--was the abolishment of prison sentences for desertion. The act also provided for better pay and better working conditions.

From that day, until his death, Fusureth was president of the International Seamen's Union. He worked unceasingly on behalf of the union members--living a solitary, lonely life; and although he could have demanded a phenomenal salary, he would accept only the union scale for able-bodied seamen.

His efforts and successes on behalf of U. S. seamen forced the other shipping nations to follow suit or lose out on crew recruiting. His influence was felt in every field of labor and brought about the passage of the Norris-La Guardia Anti-Injunction Act of 1932, which gives unions more liberal use of strikes, picketing, and boycotting. It outlaws yellow-dog contracts--contracts where a laborer agrees to not join a union if he is given a job.

After his death, Fusureth's body lay in state at the Department of Labor--the first time a labor leader had been given such an honor. His ashes were, by his wish, scattered in mid-Atlantic; a fitting burial for a man who had dedicated his life to the sea and to the betterment of seamen everywhere.

A FOOTBALL GREAT

To a sports fan, no list of Norwegian immigrants would be complete without the name of Knute Rockne, football coach.

Born in Voss, Norway, in 1888, he immigrated with his family to the United States in 1893. He attended school in Chicago, after which he worked at various jobs. In 1910, he entered the University of Notre Dame, where he starred on the football field. It was his brilliant use of the forward pass against Army that marked the turning point in football toward greater fan-enjoyment of the game.

After graduation, he became a chemistry instructor and assistant football coach at Notre Dame. It was inevitable that, four years later, he be made head coach.

In 13 years, his teams had 105 wins, 12 losses, and 5 ties! His particular brand of football used speed, agility, and deception--rather than following the previous notion that football was a game of brute force. Also, he was the first coach in the nation to substitute whole teams called "shock troops," during a game.

This great coach's pep talks were classics. Sometimes it was a scathing lecture. Sometimes merely, "You're a Notre Dame team! remember?" Whatever the pitch, it usually worked.

One game in particular was going pretty badly. At half-time he gathered his team around him and reminded them of George Gipp, who had recently died of a football injury. "Go out there and win this one for Gipp," he told them. Notre Dame won the game; and the saying, "Win one for the Gipper," was born and became a catch phrase that was to sweep the football fraternity.

Knute Rockne! His teams began the Notre Dame tradition that has given that university a national following that goes far beyond the confines of the Catholic Church and the University of Notre Dame.

Rolvaag was born on an island in Helgeland, Norway, where fishing was the only means of livelihood. By the time he was 15, he was sailing in the open boats that worked the fishing ground near his home. Young Ole dreamed of some day owning his own farm; and because farmland is so scarce in that part of Norway (and because most Norwegians must grow their own food) Rolvaag immigrated to the United States at the age of 20--joining other members of his family in South Dakota.

By the time he'd reached the age of 23, he decided that he wanted to do more with his life than work on his uncle's farm. So--after graduating from St. Olaf College--he took a professorship there in Norwegian language and literature. Rolvaag didn't believe in "Americanization." He believed and taught that people from foreign countries should retain their languages, customs, and religion; that by so doing they could make better contributions to their new country. It follows, then, that all his books were written in Norwegian and translated into English!

Some of the best of his books are *Giants of the Earth*, the story of immigrant life on the prarie; *The Third Life of Persmevik*, his own experiences as a farmer, a fisherman and professor; and *The Boat of Longing*, the story of the immigrant in the city. Even though his books were written primarily for Norwegians and for students of the Norwegian language, they have been translated into English and widely read.

Among the many women Norway has given to the United States, none has been more beloved than Sonja Henie. Born in Oslo, she became the Norwegian figure-skating champion when ten years of age!

Before immigrating to the United States, she won the women's figure-skating title ten times! She also won the Olympic figure-skating gold medals in 1928, 1932, and 1936--each time she won, the United States came in second! And it wasn't until Sonja Henie made the United States her home that it placed first in that category!

Upon her arrival in the U.S., Sonja turned professional. She was soon producing her own ice show spectacular. It was she who demonstrated that ballet and ice skating make a dazzling and exquisite combination. To her beautiful ballet numbers, she added clowns, skits, and even numbers that presented fairy-tale stories.

Sonja Henie will long be remembered by those who saw her skate as the little girl with the golden curls, whose artistry on ice was, to quote a scripture, "like an apple of gold in a picture of silver"!

Although Kirsten Flagstad had been singing professionally since the time she reached the age of 18, it wasn't until she sang her first Isolde, at 37, that she attained fame. Her singing at the Bayreuth led to an audition and a contract with the Metropolitan Opera in New York. From that time on, she was considered the greatest Wagnerian soprano of the first half of this century. She often sang opposite Lauritz Melchior--the Danish tenor--at the Metropolitan.

Following her New York debut, she had success after success in New York, London, and Vienna. In 1941, when the Nazis occupied Norway, Kirsten Flagstad returned to her homeland. She continued her singing performances, but only in the neutral country of Switzerland.

She fell into disfavor with her countrymen because she did not take an active part in Norway's resistance activities. We cannot judge either Flagstad or her countrymen. It must be remembered that Norway was at war--without an army--and the only way they could fight was by resistance. On the other hand, Flagstad was an artist--to her, war was just a plague that would pass.

Because of her alleged friendliness toward the invaders, her return to the United States was greeted with hostility. Reaction against her soon passed, however, and she sang two more seasons at the Metropolitan--her voice as beautiful at the age of 60 as it had been at 30!

This artist's career was exceptional. She did not become an international star until almost 40 years of age; and even in her 50's, her beautiful, clear soprano was unimpaired. Many contend that at the age of 60 her interpretative powers were even clearer and deeper than at age 40! And she did make reocrdings until she was well into her 60's!

KIRSTEN FLAGSTAD--a soprano whose star rose above wars and rumors of wars and nation against nation. She loved to sing, and sing she did!

27

THE PHILIPPINES

by

JOAN S. FOLLENDORE

Nature has been bountiful to the Philippines. It has endowed the country with physical beauty and great wealth. It has also given it a strategic position in Asian geography and politics. Nearly half of the land area is covered with thick green forests which provide valuable timber. Some thirty-five per cent is used for agriculture. The plains and valleys of the Philippines are dotted with many lakes and streams, which make them very fertile. These tropical islands are mostly mountainous, having been formed by volcanic eruptions. It is not a tiny group of islands, but is actually larger than New York and all the New England states combined. It has many areas that are completely unpopulated.

The relationship between the United States and the Philippines took on a personal meaning for many young Filipinos after the Spanish-American War. It was then that the U.S. began governing these islands. Missionaries and teachers brought an educational system similar to the one they had gone through in the United States. Physical education was emphasized, especially football, tennis, and boxing. The Filipino youth learned our Constitution. The idea that "All men are created equal" gave them hope and inspiration. They saw that the entrance into the modern world was through education.

The first twenty years of this century saw 5000 Filipinos immigrate to the U.S. Once here, their strong feelings for one another sustained them. Almost all these immigrants were men under 25 years of age. The men outnumbered the women (Filipinas) 143 to 1 in the states. It was considered inappropriate for young Filipinas to travel unaccompanied so far from their homes. Women are held in high regard and have considerable influence in family decisions, however, it was the young men who went off to make their fortunes and bring honor to their families by gaining a college education. They showed a marked preference for studying oratory and law. They made a fine impression on Americans, and they gained many friends.

From 1940 to 1950, our Filipino immigrants found work in three main areas: domestic and personal service, fishing and fish-canning in Alaska and on the west coast, and special agricultural work. After World War II, most became engaged in farmwork, many acquiring their own farms.

FROM HATS TO PSYCHIATRY

Stockton, California, has become the "Manila of the United States," and New York has many outstanding Filipinos. Among them are Remedios G. Cabachungan, who opened her own business· as a young woman, specializing in hats and Philippine novelties. Later she started a lumber and plywood agency, importing plywood from her homeland. Then she once again proved her courage and resourcefulness by organizing the Bayanihan Craft, Inc., supplying department stores with Philippine products.

Augusto Camacho is an accomplished architect, Emilia Villasenor is a registered physical therapist and registered nurse, Fred Rola has achieved prominence as an architectural and industrial photographer, Dr. Leopoldo Toralballa has specialized in that field of mathematics called topology, holding a position as a mathematical consultant to the U.S. Government. Marciana B. Cortes, as a member of the nursing staff at New York Hospital, was also president of the Filipino Nurses Association of New York. Educational psychologist Luz V. Datiles is always willing to make sacrifices and to work diligently.

Lorenzo J. Garcia overcame tremendous obstacles in pursuing his ambition to go to the U.S. to complete his education. Working as a waiter, he financed his schooling and achieved his degree in Civil Engineering.

Another Filipina, Josefina J. Hermoso, received her medical degree and then took advanced courses in psychiatry in New York. She· has the deep understanding, knowledge, training, and experience required to successuflly help the disordered and troubled minds of her patients. "Training in psychiatry has played an important role in my growing up, and a better understanding of human behavior is important to me," she said.

FROM INDUSTRIAL DESIGN TO PATHOLOGY

Manuel Rey Isip, with remarkable enterprise, has succeeded in two fields, industrial design and commercial art. Marcelino Monasterial honors his homeland as a sociologist, i.e. Professional Assistant, Bureau of Social Affairs, United Nations.

"Do not be ashamed to take any job in adversity or if compelled by circumstances, even if that job seems too low for your educational attainment, as long as it is honest, legitimate and remunerative. Have faith in yourself and in this United States of America. This is the best country in the world. Here you can become whatever you want to be, if you work long enough and hard enough to attain your goal," advises Professor Hernando Lopez, a Merchant Marine and an accomplished violinist, composer, and musicologist.

Jose Radovan's life is a fascinating story from poverty to success in the yo-yo business. Erlinda Cortes Zetlin was a dramatic actress, singer, and dancer on both stage and screen. During her appearances, she sang Philippine songs, acted in dramatic and comedy sketches, and danced Philippine dances to the great delight of her American public. Erlinda also worked as an undercover girl for the CID of the U.S. Army and at the same time served as a Censor girl. Another well-known actress from the Philippines is Brenda Marshall.

Another notable Filipina in the U.S. is Nobleza Asuncion Lande. She organizes conferences and prepares papers at the University of Kansas in the field of Speech and Intercultural Communication. Corky Dirnidad is a nationally syndicated editorial cartoonist: Ben Junaza is the Director of the State Immigration Service in Hawaii: Tino Calabia is with the U.S. Commission of Civil Rights as a Specialist on Minority Rights, in Washington, D.C. Also there, is Juanita Tamayo Lott as a Specialist on Women in HEW's Asian American Affairs.

Some Filipino writers worth reading are N.V.M. Gonzales; author and poet, Bien Benido Santos; and Carlos Bulosan who wrote *America is in the Heart.* Bulosan was also a California labor leader. In Los Angeles, as head of the Pathology department at Kaiser-Permanent Hospital, is Dr. Ramon Sison.

The Filipinos were determined to become a part of American society, and through patience and diligence they have achieved their desire.

28

POLAND

by

VIRGINIA STEVENSON

Of all the people who have immigrated to the United States, the third largest group are the people from Poland.

In September, 1608, Captain John Smith sent a plea to Europe for men who could handle the tough work of clearing the forests and tilling the soil. A few months later, a small ship named the Good Speed sailed up the James River. Among the passengers were six powerful young workers who were eager to reach the New World. Within three weeks of their landing at the crude fort that Smith had founded in the wilderness, their sharp axes had made inroads into the forest. They also started a glass furnace and the first factory in the New World; tapped the pine trees for tar and pitch to be distilled; and built a soap works and a saw mill. The English colonists, who were gentlemen adventurers, had brought America's first settlement to the edge of failure. Following the example of those hardworking new arrivals, they went to work. Those few men who saved Smith's colony, and in effect made sure that the colonies would develop as an English-speaking nation, were not Englishmen at all. Their names were Michal Lowicki, Zbigniew Stefanski, Jur Mata, Jan Bogdan, Karol Zrencia, and Stanislaw Sadowski--all Polish.

A few years later, Virginia's Governor George Yeardley authorized the election of the first legislative body in the colonies but ordered that only natives of England be allowed to vote. The Poles laid down their tools and refused to work until they were granted equality with the other colonists. Their righteous anger paid off. The strike was short as the workmen scored a quick victory. It is interesting that the first strike by workmen in the New World was not for money, but for equal voting rights.

The Court Book of the Virginia Company has the following entry: "Upon some dispute of the Polonians...it was now agreed that they shall be enfranchised and made as free as any inhabitant whatsoever."

Other colonies soon followed Virginia in welcoming the hardworking Polish people. Governor Stuyvesant of New Amsterdam was so delighted with the first Poles to come to his area that he repeatedly requested more of them be persuaded to come. By training, most Poles were skilled craftsmen such as carpenters, shipwrights, sail makers, and rope workers--all trades that were needed in the building of the New World.

In 1659 when the New Hollanders decided to set up the first academy of higher learning in the colonies, Dr. Alexander Kurcyusz was asked to be the head of the new school. He also taught Greek and Latin.

Oebracht Zaborowski landed in New Amsterdam in 1662. He shortened his name to Zabriskie, became an Indian trader, invested in huge land holdings on the west bank of the Hudson River and served as one of the first judges in New Jersey. He married a lovely young lady named Machtilt Van der Linden and they had five sons. Today the Zabriskie descendants in the United States number in the hundreds.

Another Indian trader, Jan Antoni Sadowski, soon became known as Jonathan Sandusky because that is how his name sounded to American ears. In the year 1735, he pushed through the Alleghany Mountains two hundred miles beyond the last English outpost. There he set up a fortified trading post near the western end of Lake Erie. Today, this is the location of Sandusky, Ohio. Two of Jonathan Sandusky's sons later went with Daniel Boone on his exploration of Kentucky and with Boone, they set up that state's first settlement, Harrodsburg. A little later the Indians attacked and James Sandusky escaped by going west instead of east which confused the attackers. Alone in a canoe, he paddled down the Cumberland, Ohio and Mississippi Rivers. He was the first man from the English colonies to arrive at New Orleans by way of the river route.

Haym Salomon was born in Lissa (now Leszno,) Poland on January 6, 1740. He immigrated to England in 1772 and then to America, where he opened a brokerage office in New York. Being naturally drawn to America's movement for Independence, he joined the Sons of Liberty and during the Revolutionary War he was arrested twice for his underground activities on behalf of Freedom.

Salomon was financial agent for the French government in America and a leading dealer in bills of exchange and other securities. As a result of his position, he was one of the largest depositors in Robert Morris' Bank of North America and thus contributed to maintaining the credit of the new government of the United States. He also advanced direct loans to the United States and gave generously of his own money to pay salaries of government officials and Army officers.

After the war, Salomon was almost penniless and the large debt owed by the government to him was never repaid, either to him or his heirs. Before he could rebuild his business, he died in Philadelphia on January 6, 1785.

In February, 1893, a bill was presented to the House providing for a gold medal to be struck in recognition of Haym Salomon's valuable contributions to

America's freedom--for which his heirs were to waive all claims--but the measure, although reported favorably, was too late for consideration.

At least one thousand names of clearly Polish origin can be identified in the muster roles of the Continental Army, choosing as they did to fight on the side of independence. The brave acts of many of these men have been overlooked by historians because they were overshadowed by the brilliance of two spectacular young volunteers from Europe, Tadeusz Kosciuszko and Casimir Pulaski. Both of these men were exiled from Poland for resisting Russia's, Prussia's, and Austria's wars against their country. Before the Declaration of Independence was signed, Kosciuszko sailed to America at his own expense. He offered his services to General George Washington and while we was waiting for the War Board to act on his appointment, he designed and built forts around Philadelphia. In 1777, he was appointed Colonel of Engineers and went north to build the breastworks (low barriers built to protect gunners) at Saratoga, New York. As Chief of Engineers, he fortified Ticonderoga and West Point. He fought as a cavalry leader through North and South Carolina and helped drive the British from Charleston, South Carolina.

Casimir Pulaski, driven from Poland where he helped to hold at bay the Czar's armies, fled to France. There he offered his services to Benjamin Franklin who was visiting in Europe at the time. He also offered his large fortune to America. Later, after Pulaski had arrived in America, when General Washington was forced to retreat from Brandywine, Pulaski was given credit for saving much of the Army with his rear guard action. Four days after the battle he was made a General by Congress.

During the Valley Forge ordeal, Pulaski led raids through the British lines time after time. He returned with captured food and supplies for the hungry infantry. He formed his own cavalry corps and spent sixteen thousand dollars of his own money to equip it. This group became known as Pulaski's Legion. At Savannah, Pulaski was hit by miniballs from cannon and fatally wounded. He has been memorialized by a bust in our nation's Capitol, and also with a statue of him on horseback, in one of the squares in Washington, D.C.

During the Civil War, the day after President Lincoln's first call for volunteers, Vladimir Kryzanowski enlisted as a Private. Within six months he held the rank of Colonel. By the end of the war, he was a Brigadier General. When the Civil War ended, Kryzanowski became the first governor of the Territory of Alaska.

Joseph Karge's career was much like Kryzanowski's and after the war he was appointed Professor of Literature and Languages at Princeton University.

SPORTS

Until 1915, only two Polish-Americans stood out as athletes; Frank Piekarski of the University of Pennsylvania who was named an All-American football player in 1905 and Stan Ketchel, middleweight boxing champion in 1907. Then the Coveleskie brothers came out of the coal fields of Pennsylvania. Harry Coveleskie was the American Baseball League pitching champion of 1916. Four years later his brother, Stan, pitched 315 innings for the Cleveland Indians, gave up only 65 walks and won 24 games. Was it any wonder his club won the pennant that year? In the World Series he pitched three full games and won them all.

After that, the baseball scouts haunted every Polish neighborhood and by the late 1920's, there were many Polish names on baseball rosters. Al Simmons, Joe Boley, Adam Comorowski, Ed Modjeski, John Grabowski, Billy Urbanski and others, who made opposing teams bow to their talent and desire to win. Who can ever forget "Stan the Man" Musial, Ted Kluszewski, Ed Lopat, Joe Collins, Jim Konstanty, Ray Jablonski, Tom Poholsky, Rip Repulski, Dave Koslo, Hank Majdeski, and so many other giants of baseball?

College football developed rosters of star players as did baseball. All-American honors have been awarded to Polish-American players almost every year since 1927, when Al Raskowski was a star at Ohio State. At one time the "fighting Irish of Notre Dame" had so many Polish players on the squad, their famous coach Knute Rockne, when asked how he chose his players, said, "It's a cinch. If I can't pronounce 'em, they're good."

Samuel Goldfish was hardly more than a boy when he ran away from his home in Warsaw, Poland.

Age eleven when he left home, he arrived alone at Ellis Island as a steerage passenger two years later, in 1896.

His first job paid three dollars a week and his formal education in the United States was one year of night school.

In 1902, he became a U.S. citizen and took the name Samuel Goldwyn.

He entered the motion picture field in 1913 as a partner in the Jesse Lasky Feature Photoplay Company and his first production was a silent film called "The Squaw Man."

Three years later he formed the Goldwyn Pictures Corporation which became a part of MGM.

No account of Samuel Goldwyn would be complete without quoting a famous "Goldwynism" or two. There was the time film producer Arthur Hornblow, Jr., and his wife had an infant son. Goldwyn called Hornblow to congratulate him and inquired what name the Hornblows had selected for the child. Upon being told that a family tradition would be continued by naming the child Arthur Hornblow, III, Goldwyn exlaimed: "Arthur? Why Arthur? Every Tom, Dick and Harry is called Arthur."

And there was the time Sam Goldwyn decided to clean up his office. He summoned a male assistant who'd been in his employ many years. "Listen," he said to the man, "we've got twenty-five years' worth of files out there just sitting around. Now, what I want you to do is go out there and throw everything out--but make a copy of it first."

Samuel Goldwyn was one of the first producers to hire famous authors to write scripts for Hollywood.

He was credited with having discovered, among others, Gary Cooper, Dana Andrews, Danny Kaye, and Eddie Cantor.

During the 19th century and the first part of the 20th American arts were enriched by such great musicians and conductors as Leopold Stokowski, Ignace Paderewski, Artur Rodzinski, and Jerzy Bojanowski. Opera stars Marcella Sembrich and Jan Kiepura thrilled their listerners. Helen Modjeska became famous as a Shakespearean actress and Pola Negri as a star of silent movies. In more recent years, Wanda Landowska has become well-known as a skilled artist on the harpsichord.

Adam Kurek was believed to have founded the first brass band in the United States.

Famed piano virtuoso Artur Rubinstein said in January, 1975: "I have never met a man as happy as I am," as he blew out the candles on his eighty-sixth birthday cake. Then he appeared as a guest with the New York Philharmonic.

Poles excel in other fields as well. Joseph Turkolski surveyed the states of Louisiana and Utah; and Captain Karol Radziminski had a hand in establishing the Mexican-United States boundary.

Emil Konopinski, a professor Physics at the University of Indiana, has been credited with much of the theoretical work that made possible the development of the H-bomb.

Casimir Funk, "Father of the vitamin", came to America under the sponsorship of the Rockefeller Foundation. His idea was that many illnesses are caused by not having certain chemicals in the diet. Dr. Funk studied all of the knowledge that existed at that time on diseases that were caused by poor nutrition. In trying to classify all the known food essentials, he coined the word "vitamine" (life amines) as the name for substances that up to that time were called "accessory food factors."

In 1976, at the 50th Annual Meeting of the Federation of American Societies for Experimental Biology, Dr. Stanislaw R. Burzynski presented a new theory of changing cancer cells back to normal cells by using a chemical found in human urine. This new theory was so exciting that news of it quickly spread around the world. Others working with Dr. Burzynski on the experiments leading to the dicovery of the chemical were Dr. Z. Stolzman, Dr. E. Lubanski and Dr. S. Gross, all Polish immigrants to the United States.

Stanislaw R. Burzynski was born in Lublin, Poland in 1943. He attended schools in Lublin and the Medical Academy, where he took a doctor's degree in medicine and a Ph. D. in Biochemistry. He began doing biochemical research in 1961 and by 1970 had published twenty-four papers. In 1970, Dr. Bruzynski immigrated to the United States. After a short stay in New York, he joined the staff at Baylor College of Medicine in Houston, Texas where he continued his research and by 1976 had published twelve more papers.

Much work still needs to be done on the Burzynski treatment to bring the cost down within reach of everyone, but it is one of the most promising treatments for cancer ever to be developed.

The first Polish settlement in the United States was in the state of Texas. Panna Maria was established in 1854. Its name means Virgin Mary in Polish. This town is rich in historic buildings, churches and schools, and is said to have founded the first Polish school in the United States. There are over fifty towns in the United States with such names as Pulaski, Warsaw, Carcow, Polonia, Poland and New Poland.

29

PORTUGAL

by

LELIA K. FLIGELMAN

I'll bet, like me, you didn't know that Portugal once discovered the whole world...

Or that more Portuguese have immigrated to the Americas than were alive during the days Columbus trained as a Portuguese seaman...

Or that the western part of the Iberian peninsula, first called Lusitania, was once one of the most powerful nations in the world, to which the United States owes its very existence.

How did it all begin? It began with Prince Henry the Navigator (in those days people were named because of what they did), son of King John I of Portugal.

Prince Henry built an observatory and established a school for seamen by gathering about him from all over the then-known world: explorers, navigators, geographers, cosmographers (scientists who had collected all that they could find out about the heavens and the earth), cartographers (map and chart makers), and even astrologers. Some information came from Marco Polo's Italian maps. From the island of Majorca, off the coast of Spain, came the Cresques family, father and son, who had written down almost all that was known about the earth.

Prince Henry gave up marriage and family life in order to devote himself completely to solving the riddles of navigation. He became known as Prince Henry the Navigator, the father of all modern discovery. Prince Henry paid for exploration, voyages, and colonization. If his mariners were lost at sea, Prince Henry took their wives and children into his palace to care for and protect.

Prince Henry's motto was a French one, "Talent de Bien Faire" (devotion to duty), and he lived up to the motto. A writer of his time illustrates this by describing Prince Henry like this: "Oh, how often would the sun find him sitting where it had left him the previous day, watching all of the night."

There were discoveries before and after Prince Henry, but his place in history is unchallenged. Many have written about his importance, but Adam Smith, the Scotch economist, perhaps said it best: "The discovery of America and that of a passage to the East Indies by the Cape of Good Hope are the two greatest and most important events recorded in the history of mankind."

Adam Smith felt that because of Prince Henry's inspiration for discovery, exploration, and colonization, all humans came to know that all men are brothers.

To Prince Henry's school of navigation came Christobol Colon, later known as Christopher Columbus. Although he was supposedly from Italy, Columbus had a Portuguese name and never spoke or wrote a word of Italian. He arrived in Portugal as a man of mystery. Apparently, Columbus had been washed up naked from a stormy sea without anything about him to show who he was or where he came from. Columbus lived in Portugal for at least eight years before his voyage of discovery, serving as an apprentice seaman upon Portuguese ships and inhaling the exciting air of Prince Henry's circle and school. This environment contained all of the electrifying plans and gossip of the kind that America's Cape Canaveral knew before the first flights to the moon.

It was to Portugal that Columbus first applied for funding. Only a matter of twenty-seven cents stood between him and the Portuguese financial backing. Twenty-seven cents, worth more to be sure in the 15th century than today, but still a trifling sum. But it kept bankrupt Portugal from the glory of financing Columbus' voyage.

In the 15th century, Portugal was bankrupt. The Turks had captured Constantinople (now Istanbul), a port guarding the eastern caravan route exit from the Mediterranean Sea to India. (This caused a crisis somewhat like our modern day one, when the Arabs shut off the Far Eastern oil supply.) The mariners everywhere, particularly in Portugal, Queen of the Sea, were out of work and starving. In order to get the ships sailing and the men back to work, new alternative trade routes to the Far East had to be discovered.

Remember, in those exciting days of adventure and exploration, airplanes, motor cars, trains, and submarines--not to mention dirigibles and space-ships--were yet to be imagined, much less invented. Only rivers and the Mediterranean Sea, an inland body of water, almost as calm as a lake, served as the main path of communication and trade between the then known continents. If you look at a map, you can see that Portugal guards the western entrance to the Mediterranean. At the same time Portugal had a long seacoast like a window facing into what the Greeks and Arabs called the sea of darkness, the stormy Atlantic Ocean with its undiscovered horizon. With all the resources of Prince Henry's world, still navigators had little to guide them across the wild Atlantic waters until Prince Henry's students perfected the compass; invented three-masted sailing ships called caravels; and discovered routes to the New World.

Around Africa, sailed courageous Portuguese navigators, touching the coasts of Arabia, India, and Ceylon (that island hanging like a pearl on the ear lobe of

India); and reaching eastward to the island of Malacca, to Siam, to Japan--even marching into China. Westward, rounding north around the Americas and Mexico, the Portuguese carved a new world for those safe at home, who believed that when the tiny open sailboats drifted out of sight over the horizon, sailors and ships dropped off the edge of the flat earth.

Compare the courage of those early navigators with that of the super-trained technician heroes of our present space-age. Until well into Prince Henry's time, sailors were so ignorant that garlic was hung on the starboard side of the ships and onions upon the port side. The ropes of the sails were posted with playing cards, and there would be shouts of, "Queen of Spades, King of Hearts, onion side, garlic side!" as the caravels set sail. The Portuguese had no instruments to communicate with home; no radio, radar, or telephone; no special vitamin diets or protective costumes. Into the tiny open holds of the caravels went cattle and sheep, water and men...and all that was needed for the long, unpredictable trip. Nor was their adventure reported to cheering multitudes in the news or relayed via television. No, the Portuguese set out into the loneliness of a voyage from which no Portuguese traveler had ever returned, guided only by the stars and the whims of the winds.

MANY EXPLORERS

Columbus had three caravels carrying his handful of men. Only the flagship was decked. The rest were open boats. Upon the deck of the flagship, it is probable that Columbus brought to the New World, cannon, which had been developed three centuries before, and also Portuguese gunpowder.

Columbus not only found the New World, but was its first colonizer. He called the natives "Indians" because he thought that he had discovered a new route to India.

Columbus, although the most daring, was not alone among discoverers of that great period of Portuguese exploration (1460-1524). Cabrillo, another of Prince Henry's graduates, discovered California. Ferdinand Magellan headed the first voyage around the globe, which revealed that America was a continent separate from Asia. The very name America comes from Amerigo Vespucci, an Italian navigator who sailed under the Portuguese flag around the shores of America, some eighteen years before Magellan left Prince Henry's school to round the world. Many other Portuguese played their part in making the times so rich in booty that it became necessary for Portugal and Spain to call in outside help to split the newly discovered lands between them with an incorrect geographic demarcation which was supposed to divide the discoveries in half.

Six cities in the United States are named after Portugal's city of Lisbon. Open any atlas and look at maps of the states and you will find hundreds more places named to honor Portuguese. An example is Duarte, California, a name which means Edward in Portuguese. Look in the phone book. How many names do you find that begin with the prefix "da"? These are all names of Portuguese origin. Is it possible that the early Portuguese could look ahead into California's smoggy future, when they Called Santa Monica Beach, "A prata dos fumos" (The Beach of the Smoke)?

An ancient Chinese said, "The Portuguese are like fish, remove them from water and they will die." And it is as whalers that the first modern day Portuguese immigrated to the east ard west coasts of the United States, probably bringing then what is still one of Portugal's major exports, cork (used as floats on the Portuguese fishing nets).

While there are Portuguese throughout the United States, most of the immigrants--as they did in Portugal--live off, and by, the sea as farmers and fishermen.

On the Atlantic Coast, Portuguese immigrants settled largely in cities. Already by colonial times, they were so well established and important, that a descendant of Portuguese immigrants was invited to George Washington's inauguration. While in California, where Portuguese ties go back 300 years, the immigrants settled mostly in the countryside, where at the turn of the 20th century, they and their descendants owned seventy-five percent of the states' cattle industry and were important members of the dairy industry. Many California communities not only have Portuguese names, but were founded entirely by Portuguese immigrants.

There is a saying in New England that "Potatoes will not grow unless you speak Portuguese to them." This is because of the large numbers of east coast Portuguese farmers. In the Cape Cod cranberry bogs, the dark skinned Portuguese from the Cape Verde Islands (discovered off the coast of Africa by Magellan and Cabral and remaining part of the undisturbed Portuguese empire ever since) do the lion's share of the crop picking. But most United States Portuguese have come from the Azores (discovered by Velho ten years before Columbus made his most famous voyage), which are islands lying in the Atlantic Ocean en route to the Americas and are also still part of Portugal.

Prince Henry the Navigator not only rediscovered the islands of Madeira (south of Portugal off the west coast of Africa) and the Azores, but he colonized and stocked them with cattle. Due to Prince Henry's insturctons, both island groups produced sugar and wine during his lifetime. It is from these islands that the majority of Portuguese immigrants to the U.S. have come. On both coasts of the United States, Portuguese labor in cotton mills, carrying on a home tradition.

Up and down the West Coast of the United States, the Portuguese founded whaling stations, dotting the countryside with names like Modesto, Mendocino, Lompoc, Portuguese Bend, and Castro Valley. The station in San Diego was in use until recently when tunny (tuna) fishing replaced the outlawed whaling. Bleached whale bones are still to be found there as well as old iron pots which renedered the whale blubber (fat) into oil and other products.

In spite of these largely rural California settlements, cities such as San Francisco, San Diego, and Oakland in particular, have large Portuguese populations. One of the very first newspapers printed in San Francisco was Voz Portuguesa, and it was followed within two years by two more Portuguese language journals, one of which continues in Oakland to this day.

In Southern California, Antonio Jose Rocha built a structure at Court and Spring Streets, which housed Los Angeles' first town hall. Rocha owned the La Brea Ranch and built the mill at the San Gabriel Mission. Possibly Mr. Rocha's descendants have now Americanized their name as have so many other Portuguese, such as Lazarus from Lazaro, Oliver from Oliveiro, Pine from Pinhuro, and Rose from Rosa, to name a very few.

Among the gifts that Portugal has given the U.S. is Madeira wine from Prince Henry's vines on the lovely Portuguese island for which it is named. Madeira Island is where Columbus sailed in search of a beautiful girl with whom he had fallen in love at first sight while she knelt praying in the chapel of her Lisbon convent school. Her name was Philippa and she was the daughter of Madeira's governor. After Columbus wooed and won her as her as his wife, he settled in Madeira where descendants of the pair lived for centuries. It was from Madeira that Columbus reportedly took the pigs from which have come all those of the West Indies.

From the Madeira of modern times, come the gorgeous Marghab embroideries found in the most exclusive boutiques in the United States: blouses, nightgowns, dressing-gowns, handkerchiefs, and table cloths--the finest in the world.

Port from the Portuguese city of Oporto has been an American favorite since the days of George Washington and Thomas Jefferson, who both ordered Port and Madeira for their wine cellars.

Fine gold and silver filigree jewelry is found on most jewelry counters. While Portuguese olives, olive oil, sardines, cod, and other dried fish make their way to our dinner tables and were in all probability first brought to the New World by the early navigators of Prince Henry.

A musical people, the Portuguese are skilled in using their crude version of the guitar with which they acompany the fado (folk) songs. These are old classical tunes from out of Portugal's oriental past, which are constantly up-dated to current lyrics. Probably modern day Caribbean Calypso singers evolved from the fado. Fado songs, once heard, can never be forgotten and seem to echo into our present day rock music up from the Caribbean, by way of Basin Street. Origin of America's first spirituals is traced to the lonely songs of the black slaves first introduced into Portugal.

Folk dances, mostly Moorish in origin, have been carefully preserved and performed by the Portuguese-American immigrants. If you enjoy folk dancing and folk dance music, perhaps the oldest of all, the Chamarrita, a dance of celebration, is among your favorites.

NATIONAL CHARACTERISTICS

The Portuguese are a clannish people, faithful to traditional ways, songs and dances. Although fifty per cent more men than women immigrate, the great majority return to Portugal to bring back the sweetheart they left behind to find a home in the U.S. But alongside these qualities, the Portuguese seem to have forgotten the color line. Possibly this tolerance is their most unusual quality: the way in which the Portuguese have handled integration with the large numbers of blacks brought into their territories, as well as the way in which they intermarried with the people of Hawaii.

Brazil alone imported millions more black slaves than did the United States. This slave trade was begun by Prince Henry the Navigator, but also stopped by him in his lifetime. Apparently the Portuguese are completely lacking in racism. One of the reasons for this is that their folklore tells many wonderful tales about a beautiful (North African) Moorish Princess, who is held up as a model for Portuguese dream fantasies. Possibly another reason is that the Moors, who lived among the Portuguese were superior to them in education. At any rate, the result seems to have been a strong, passionate, moral and beautiful people. Among the American-Portuguese immigrants, alcoholism and tangles with the law are almost unknown. Portuguese workers are among the most highly prized are preferred. Industrious and skilled, Portuguese workmen have formed a strong unit of the very backbone of the builders of the United States, and their descendants have excelled in many fields.

And now the next time you hear Joaquin Miller's poem about Columbus, or recite it yourself in school,

> Behind him lay the great Azores...
> Behind the Gates of Hercules...
> Before him only shoreless seas...

you'll remember the Azores are Portuguese islands, lovely islands, rising high on palisades out of the sea, wild cyprus-wooded islands, that mark the start of the beginning of the discovery of what became the United States.

30

ROMANIA

by

VIRGINIA STEVENSON

Two men from Romania who took part in the Civil War and won a place in history for their outstanding records are Captain Nicolae Dunca and General Gheorghe Pomutz. During World War II, a Liberty ship was named for Pomutz.

Romanians did not begin to come to the United States in large numbers, however, until after 1880. They immigrated because of wars and persecution in their own country. Most of them moved to cities where they went to work in mills and factories; or they found jobs in mines. The largest number settled in six states: New York, Ohio, Pennsylvania, Illinois, Michigan, and New Jersey. A few, who became farmers, settled in California, Indiana, Minnesota, North Dakota, and Missouri.

Not all Romanians who immigrated to the U.S. were workingmen. There were also leaders in the arts and sciences. George Julian Zolnay, a talented sculptor, designed and built monuments and memorials in several sections of the United States. In charge of sculpture for the art department at the Louisiana Purchase Exposition at St. Louis in 1904, his work won world-wide fame. His monument to Pierre Laclede Liguest, founder of St. Louis, is one of that city's proud possessions. He also created the stone lions that guard the entrance gates of University City, Missouri. For the city of New Bedford, Massachusetts, he created a stone group commemorating the whaling industry. In Nashville, Tennessee, is his memorial to the Private Confederate Soldier; and in St. Louis is the Confederate memorial, The Call to Arms. For Richmond, Virginia, he did the Jefferson Davis and Winnie Davis memorials. He also did a memorial to Woodrow Wilson that was sent to Rumania.

Bernard Reder, another sculptor, immigrated to the United States in 1943. Another immigrant, Andre Racz, was a talented painter and engraver. Saul Steinberg's satirical art began appearing in the New Yorker in 1941.

Jerzy Neyman, renowned statistician and mathematician, was born in Romania. Before he immigrated to the United States in 1938, he spent four years in London. Upon his arrival in the U.S., he joined the University of California at Los Angeles faculty, and stayed there until he retired.

In addition, Romania gave the U.S. such great people as Alma Gluck, who sang with the Metropolitan Opera thrilling audiences with the brilliance of her performances. Konrad Bercovici, while very young, left his family and settled in New York, where he had a hard struggle to survive. Then his talent as a writer of short stories and books brought him world-wide fame and financial success.

Dr. Trajan Leucutsia studied in Vienna and Paris, and when he immigrated to the U.S., became director of the X-ray department of Harper Hospital in New York.

The first petroleum engineer to take a doctor's degree at the University of California was Dr. Ionel Gardescu. He was the son of a general in the Romanian Army. After receiving his degree, he was employed by the Texas Oil Company in Houston, Texas.

Eugene Ravage, a gifted writer, was the author of *An American in the Making*, the story of an immigrant family. This book, which was very popular, helped the people who already lived in the U.S. to understand the feelings of new arrivals to the United States.

A young boy left Iassy in order to study in the U.S. He was graduated from Williamette University and took his doctor's degree in law at the University of California. His name was Leon Rene Yankwich and he became a respected district federal judge in Los Angeles.

Also from Romania, the U.S. received C.D. Barbuiescu, a genius in aeronautics and ammunitions and Peter Neagoe who wrote several novels about Romanian peasant life. Dr. Dagobert Runes, who took his doctor's degree in Vienna, became very successful in the publishing business and founded the Philosophical Library.

Jean Negulesco went into movie making with Warner Brothers and became a very successful producer of short features, directing over fifty of them.

31

RUSSIA

by

VIRGINIA STEVENSON

The one invention that has had the greatest effect upon the way people live, since the invention of the automobile, is television.

One of the fathers of television is Dr. Vladimir Zworykin. He is credited with being the first to recognize that an electronic system, rather than a mechanical one, should be used. It was under Dr. Zworykin's direction that such a system was perfected at the laboratories of Radio Corporation of America (RCA). Zworykin was a seventeen-year-old student in Leningrad when he began to work with a professor named Boris Van Rosing on an electronic eye, a primitive television tube. The invention was patented in 1907 by Dr. Van Rosing. In 1912, Zworykin went to Paris to study with Nobel prize-winner physicist Paul Langevin. After World War I, he left Russia and immigrated to the United States. He went to work for Westinghouse Laboratories in Pittsburgh.

Television was not the aim of the early pioneers in his field; they wanted to reproduce the human eye. But in 1929, Zworykin put together a complete television system with cameras. Also, that same year, he filed the first patent for color television. The government divided the field of electronics between Westinghouse and Radio Corporation of America at that time. Dr. Zworykin was transferred to RCA and appointed director of electronic research. David Sarnoff was then president of the company. Recognizing that television could be used for entertainment, he urged Dr. Zworykin to perfect the system; but it was not widely used until after World War II.

EARLY COLONIZATION

Going further back in history, in 1697, William Penn was at home in England. He was a devout Quaker and traveled around the country as a minister of that church. When he heard that Czar Peter (later to be called Peter the Great) of Russia was in Europe to learn shipbuilding and other skills he could take back to his own country, Penn arranged to meet him. He arranged the meeting hoping to persuade the czar to adopt the Quaker faith. This idea failed, but Peter became very interested in the New World through his talks with Penn. The czar was especially interested in learning about the colonies established in the New World by England, Spain, and France. It is probable that he thought Russia, too, should start colonies in the new land.

Although Russia itself had not been fully explored and no one knew its true size, many people in St. Petersburg believed that a new land, which could be a part of the New World, existed somewhere off Siberia. They thought that it might even connect with Siberia.

Czar Peter did nothing immediately about his idea of colonizing in the New World, but when Captain Vitus Bering, a Dane serving in the Russian Navy, came to his notice he made plans for an expedition. Unfortunately, Czar Peter died before the expedition got underway. Catherine I succeeded him and she also was in favor of the expedition. In 1728, Captain Bering sailed from Kamchatka on his first voyage, and when he returned to Russia he had gained much valuable knowledge about the North Pacific. Captain Bering discovered the strait separating Russia from Alaska, and the sea below it. Both are named for him. He also found the islands which lie at the tip of the Alaska Penninsula in the southern part of the Bering Sea. He called the islands the Catherine Archipelago in honor of the Empress, but during World War II, they became known as the Aleutians.

In the 1740's, Bering organized a second expedition which was cursed by ill luck and ended in failure. But he had cleared the way for the many Russian adventurers, hunters, fur traders, soldiers, and priests who headed for Alaska and the islands. Adventuring south along the coastline of the present states of Washington and Oregon, some of them wandered into northern California where they established military and fur trading posts, towns, and agricultural colonies.

There, a faltering Russian America existed twenty-five years before the Revolutionary War. At that time the Pacific Coast of North America was still unknown in New England. Russia claimed the territory by right of discovery, exploration, and settlement.

The Russian colony in California lasted until 1841, when the land was sold to a Mexican citizen of German birth named Johann Augustus Sutter. Just a few years later, this area became the site of California's famous gold strike. Many of the Russians stayed there, were Mexicanized, and became vaqueros (the Spanish word for cowboy).

There is a part of the city of San Francisco that is still called Russian Hill. Just north of the Bay region are the Russian River and the town of Sebastapol, named for a city in Russia which was the birthplace of some of the hardy souls who ventured to California.

After the sale of the California settlement, Russian America was restrictd to Alaska and its coastal islands. In 1867, under the terms of the Monroe Doctrine, the United States purchased the territory. For $7,200,000 this area came under the ownership of the United States.

Among Russians making major contributions to the United States was a pharmacist named Charles Thiel from St. Petersburg, who immigrated to Philadelphia in 1769. He succeeded in the printing and publishing business under the name of Charles Cist, but his chief claim to fame was that he was one of the first men to see that stone coal (anthracite) could be used as fuel. During the years the U.S. was growing into an industrial power, this coal was used as fuel for the mighty steam engines on the railroads. The possibility of an energy shortage in recent years has caused a new interest in mining coal. Since a large supply of anthracite coal exists in the United States, it is quite possible that Charles Cist's discovery could benefit people once again in the present day.

In 1792 in the city of Baltimore, a young man appeared who could speak half a dozen languages. Claiming to be Augustine Smith, he was actually a Russian nobleman named Prince Dimitri Augustin Gallitzin. Converted to Catholicism, he became a missionary in Maryland and Pennsylvania. The town of Gallitzin, Pennsylvania is named for him. Chalres M. Schwab, a steel magnate, erected a statue in his honor in Loretto, Pennsylvania.

A young Russian engineer, John B. Turchin, a former member of the Imperial staff and a veteran of the Crimean War, immigrated to the United States in 1855. He found a job with the Illinois Central Railroad. At the outbreak of the Civil War, he was appointed colonel of the 19th Illinois Volunteers which became one of the most famous, battled-scarred Union regiments. By personal order of President Lincoln, Turchin was made a brigadier general. After the war he wrote a book called *The Battle of Chickamauga.*

The Mennonites were a group of German farmers, noblemen, teachers, clergymen, and mechanics who were lured to the Lower Volga and Don Rivers in Russia by Catherine the Great. There they fought off many nomadic robber bands and made the rich valleys productive. Around 1870, they began to hear of a utopia in the United States where one could progress as far as common sense and hard work would take him. Also, they heard that freedom of religion was a firm actuality. About 1874, they began to pull up stakes and sail for the U.S. In the new land they became farmers in Kansas, Oklahoma, Nebraska, Minnesota, and Wisconsin. Many of them went into the sugar beet industry in Colorado, wheat farming in Washington, and fruit growing in California. They brought with them seeds of "kubanka" and "arnautka," types of wheat that resist rust. The bread you eat today probably was made from flour milled from this type of wheat.

The Mennonites are the most picturesque group of the Old Order of Amish. Removed from the mainstream of life, they shun the use of automobiles and other motorized equipment. They still depend upon horses for work power and transportation. They follow the teaching of Jakob Amman, who was very strict in his beliefs. He thought that men should wear beards and broad-brimmed hats, and women should wear long dresses, plain black bonnets and shawls, and even now this is the way they dress. Since the Amish children wear the same type of clothing, they are small beardless copies of their parents. Groups of these people still live in Pennsylvania, Ohio, and Indiana.

THEY BROUGHT THEIR CULTURE

Sol Hurok, theatrical impressario, did more to make classical music popular in the U.S. than possibly any other individual.

When Sol was a teenager, his father, a hardware merchant, gave him a thousand rubles and sent him to learn a trade in the city of Kharkov. Rather than face life as a tradesman, he ran away to the United States.

In May 1906, with less than three rubles in his pocket, Hurok was one of thousands of immigrants admitted through Ellis Island. He went to Philadelphia because he wanted to live in the city where the Declaration of Independence was signed. He sold needles, drove streetcars, washed soda bottles, and bundled midnight editions of newspapers.

Moving to New York, he found a job in a hardware store and went to night school to improve his English.

His spare time was spent attending every concert he could afford. He would wait in line for hours at the box office of the old Hammerstein Theatre, and stand at the back of the balcony through five-hour performances.

On a small scale, Hurok began to organize musical events himself, such as concerts for workingmen's clubs. By the time he was twenty-one, Sol was renting the old New York Hippodrome and Madison Square Garden.

Tickets were sold at local groceries, cigar stores, and newsstands--with a percentage going to the owner for each ticket he sold.

Sol Hurok proved there was a mass market for culture and for over half a century he presented to U.S. audiences such stars as: Chaliapin, Pavlova, Isadora Duncan, Marion Anderson, the Bolshoi Ballet, and the Royal Ballet with Margot Fonteyn and Rudolph Nureyev, to name a few.

Sol Hurok did so much for international culture that he received many awards, including: the French Legion of Honor, the Order of the British Empire, and the Austrian Cross of Honor.

Peter Demyanov, from St. Petersburg, became a successful businessman and railroad builder in the United States under the name of Peter Demens. He established St. Petersburg, Florida.

There are towns named St. Petersburg or Petersburg in fourteen other states; towns named Moscow in ten; Odessa in nine; and two states have towns named Kremlin.

Architect Vladimir Stoleshnikov, who was a refugee from the Russian revolution, helped design Carnegie Hall in New York City. Dr. George W. Raiziss, who died in 1945, was one of the pioneers in sulpha experiments. He took part in finding sulfapyrazine, one of the first drugs developed to fight pneumonia.

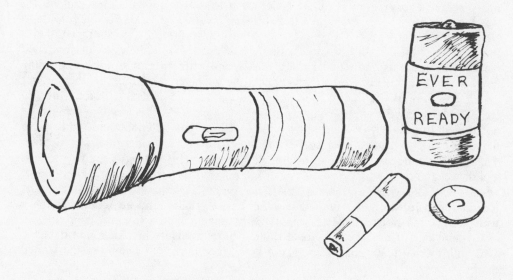

In 1890, thirty-five year old Akiba Horowitz arrived in New York City from Minsk. He changed his name to Conrad Hubert and went into various undertakings such as operating a cigar stand, owning a restaurant, delivering milk, and managing a jewelry store. Then he invented and patented an electrical gadget for lighting gas, which at that time was used for illumination. Later he patented an electric time alarm, a small electric lamp, and an electric battery. The two resulted in a "portable electric light" which contained the basic patents of today's flashlight. He organized the Yale Electric Company and the American Ever Ready Company.

Igor Stravinsky's influence on U.S. composers for over fifty years changed the course of music in the United States. He was born in Oranienbaum, Russia in 1882, son of the leading basso of the St. Petersburg Opera. Stravinsky studied law at the University of St. Petersburg; but because of his outstanding musical talent, he was encouraged by Rimsky-Korsakov, the famous composer, to study music with private tutors. His first symphony was performed a few years later. In 1919, Stravinsky left Russia for France where he lived in Paris for the next twenty years. In 1939, he moved to Hollywood, California, and became a U.S. citizen in 1945. Most of his major works were based on religious or biblical subjects. Stravinsky combined a career as a composer with that of a conductor, mainly of his own compositions. In 1970, he left California because he felt that Los Angeles had never given him the tribute he deserved. He died on April 6, 1971, only one week after arriving in New York.

One remarkable person who has brought hours of beauty into the lives of many people everywhere is famed ballet artist Rudolph Hametovich Nureyev. He was born on March 17, 1939, on a train passing Irkutsk, on Lake Baikal, enroute to Vladivostok. His father, a soldier in the Russian army, was stationed there. Nureyev first took ballet lessons at the age of eight. His father was disappointed since he wanted his son to be more manly and ordered him to stop taking the lessons. In order to keep on studying ballet, he deceived his family, taking his first part in an opera at the age of fourteen. The next year he danced with the Corps de Ballet and attended dancer's classes at the Ufa Opera. At the age of seventeen he auditioned for and was accepted by the Bolshoi Ballet School. He didn't have money to attend the school so he auditioned for the Leningrad Ballet School, which trains dancers for the Kirov Ballet. Nureyev refused to join the Communist Youth League and was constantly in trouble with the Kirov authorities. In 1961, when the ballet was on tour in Paris, he sought asylum. He escaped from the Russian security men by jumping over an airport railing and he found sanctuary with the French police. In February 1962, he appeared in a full-length production in England performed by the Royal Ballet. Nureyev made his American debut in 1962 with the Ruth Page Chicago Opera Ballet, and is now a resident of the United States.

AVIATION

The contribution of Igor Ivan Sikorsy was in the field of aviation. Sikorsky was graduated from the Naval College of St. Petersburg and completed his education at the Kiev Institute of Technology in 1908. At the age of twenty he tried to build a helicopter that would fly. He failed, but he soon had success in building other planes. From 1912 to 1918, as chief engineer in a Russian aviation factory, he built and flew the first multi-motored airplane. The year was 1913. During World War I he built bombers for Russia. Sikorsky arrived in the United

States in 1919 almost penniless. With help from friends, he formed the Sikorsky Aero Engineering Corporation which produced one of the first twin-engine planes made in the U.S. This company built the S-38, a flying boat, and then the first United States four-engine flying clipper, the S-42. This plane was a pioneer of transpacific and transatlantic commercial flights. The first successful helicopter of the western hemisphere, the VS-300, was produced in 1939. This was the first of a long line of helicopters. Besides his work in aviation, he wrote devotional and autobiographical works. Sikorsky was a citizen of the United States for 44 years.

Svetlana Alliluyeva-Stalina, the daughter of Joseph Stalin, a top political leader of Russia, was born in 1925. She was raised in the Kremlin in Moscow. Her mother died when Svetlana was quite young and her father was very devoted to her. Even though his political duties were very demanding he tried to find time each day to spend with her. As a young woman she was interested in history, music, and the arts and learned to cook and to sew at an early age. She attended the Moscow University. At the age of seventeen she was married to Grigory Morozov, later a professor at the Moscow Law Institute. The marriage was not approved by her father and ended in divorce two years later, after the birth of a son, Joseph Alliluyev. In 1948, at the age of twenty-three, she married Yuri A. Zhdanov, later President of the University of Rostov. The marriage was approved by her father because Zhdanov was considered to be "offically acceptable." Unfortunately, this marriage, too, ended in divorce, after the birth of a daughter, Ekterina Zhdanova. In 1963, Svetland met Brijesh Singh, a man from India, and for the first time married a man with whom she was in love. This marriage was doomed, also, since Singh died shortly after they were married. In 1967, Svetlana immigrated to the United States because she wanted to become a writer and she felt there was more freedom of expression in the U.S. She moved to Arizona and married an architect, William B. Peters. In 1971, their daughter Olga was born. They now live in California, and she has found that the United States is truly a country of freedom. Her contribution to her newly-adopted land is that of an author.

Many other Russian immigrants have made valuable contributions to the United States. There are far too many to list all of them, but some of the best known are Ayn Rand, Max Lerner and George Sokolsky in literature; and Dmitri Tiomkin, Andre Kostelantz, and Jascha Heifitz in music. Irving Berlin's beautiful songs have become modern classics. David Sarnoff, Efrem Zimbalist, Louis B. Mayer, and Nicholas Schenck contributed much to the field of movies and entertainment. Alexander de Seversky achieved fame in aviation. Norman Rosten, the poet and Jan Peerce, the tenor of Metropolitan Opera fame were also valuable contributors to the arts.

32

SCOTLAND

by

EVELYN ISAACS

Can you imagine a billionaire described as a lovable old Scotsman? Well, that was Andrew Carnegie's image all over the world. He wanted his magic formula of how to make money, lots and lots of money, to be placed within reach of all of the people who did not have the time to study how men make money. He believed the formula should be taught in all public schools and colleges, and he felt if it were properly taught that the time children spent in school could be reduced to less than half!

THE FORMULA TO GET RICH

Every person who acquires the secret and uses it, finds himself swept on to success. Alexander Graham Bell and John Muir, two other famous Scots who immigrated to the United States, had the very same philosophy.

What is the Carnegie secret? Simply this: All achievement, all earned riches, have their beginning in an IDEA!

Decide what the chief aim in your life is. Write it down. Say it over and over again. Never stop trying until you have reached your goal. You have to be sure of yourself. If you think you'll lose, you're lost. If you think you're outclassed, you are. If you think you're beaten, you are. Even if you like to win, but you *think* you can't, it is almost certain you won't. Success begins with will power.

Andrew Carnegie had three specialties; making steel, making money, and then giving it away. He was the son of a poor weaver, and when he immigrated to the United States, his father went back to weaving and his mother went back to stitching shoe leather. But twelve year old Andy was as bright as a silver belt buckle and as frisky as an otter. He went right to work. From a bobbin boy, to telegraph messenger, to railroad clerk, to superintendent, to director. Then iron entered his career, and finally, steel. He saw the infinite possibilities of steel for steamships, forks and knives, elevators, and bridge building.

239

He decided to make steel and make it cheap! Before he was thirty, he was building and buying up iron and steel mills and their coal and iron fields. He had his own steamships and railroads, besides.

He created one of the largest and greatest industrial enterprises in the United States, Carnegie Steel Company. He sold out to United States Steel Corporation in 1901. He retired at age sixty-five, a full fledged billionaire. Now, at last, Andy was free to do as he liked. He had written an article in which he explained that Darwin's theory of evolution proved that life was a struggle among species for existence. Only the fittest survived. Business life, too, was a war for survival. Those who came out on top of the competitive heap were naturally the fittest. It was the law of nature that some men became wealthy. They were gifted with a natural talent for outstripping others in money-making, under the law of competition. But they had a duty to perform. They must use their surplus wealth to promote the good of the community. They must not squander their money in piece-meal charity, but instead support those activities that helped the "fittest" of the next generation to emerge. "The man who dies rich, dies disgraced."

As a boy he had loved to read, so he gave $60,000,000 to build some 2,800 library buildings; $30,000,000 to universities: $22,000,000 each to Carnegie Institutes in Washington, and another in Pittsburgh; and $125,000,000 to the Carnegie Corporation of New York. All three promoted research, not only in the natural and social sciences, but in the legal and educational fields as well.

In a letter to a friend in Pittsburgh, who criticized him for "not giving with his heart as well as his head," Carnegie answered, "My friend, the heart is the steam in the boiler; the head is the engine that regulates dangerous steam and prevents disastrous explosions. So, far from my heart being allowed to more control, I see that wisdom requires it to be more and more repressed."

He shared his secret and his wealth with his adopted country. He probably gave away more money that any man who ever lived

A GREAT CONSERVATIONIST

John Muir's family moved from Dunbar, Scotland, to Wisconsin, when he was eleven years old. He grew up on a farm and developed a great love of nature. When Muir was twenty-one, he left home with only fifteen dollars in his pocket. He spent four years at the University of Wisconsin, and earned enough money during the summer vacations to pay thirty-two dollars a year for instruction and books. He had to cut down all other expenses to fifty cents a week.

During this period he invented an apparatus that attached to a bed. It would not only wake you up, but light a lamp at the same time. He also invented a desk that pushed a book up from a rack below the desk top, opened it, allowed it to remain there for a certain number of minutes, and then closed the book and dropped it back inside the desk.

From the university, John set out on his travels. He was very upset by the indiscriminate slaughter of the California Redwood trees, the largest of living things. Thousands were cut into shingles or blasted into smithereens to supply grape stakes for the winegrowers. Of this wholesale destruction, Muir wrote: "As well sell the rain clouds, and the snow, and the rivers, to be cut up and carried away, if that were possible."

Muir loved trees--trees of any sort--particularly during a storm. Once, when a windstorm erupted while he was exploring the Yuba River Valley, he climbed to the madly-swaying top of a Douglas Fir and "clung with muscles firm braced, like a Bobolink on a reed," remaining there for hours and hours, to hear the needles chorusing in the wild wind.

During his lifetime, he kept numerous journals of his travels, and wrote hundreds of articles. His most eloquent plea for conservation, entitled "The American Forests," appeared in the *Atlantic Monthly Magazine*.

> The outcries we hear against forest reservations
> come mostly from thieves who are wealthy, and
> steal timber wholesale....The people will not
> always be deceived by selfish opposition; whether
> from lumber and mining corporations or from
> sheepmen and prospectors; however cunningly
> brought forward underneath fables of gold.
>
> Any fool can destroy trees. They cannot run
> away; and if they could, they would still be
> destroyed--chased and hunted down as long as
> fun, or a dollar, could be got out of their bark
> hides, branching horns, or magnificent backbones.
> Few that fell trees plant them; nor would planting
> avail much towards getting back anything like the
> noble primeval forests.

The names of parks created because of Muirs' efforts are: Yosemite, Sequoia, King's Canyon, Rainier, Petrified Forest, and Grand Canyon.

He was also the guiding light behind the Antiquities Act, which gives Presidents the power to proclaim national monuments. Two years after Muir died, another of his dreams came true. A National Park Service was created to protect the parks for the recreation and enjoyment of everybody.

He founded the Sierra Club in 1892, and for eight decades that conservationist organization, fired by Muirs' ideals, has stood watchdog against those who would destroy all the land, water, trees, and animals. A beautiful redwood forest in northern California's Coast Range near San Francisco, was named Muir Woods, in honor of his contributions to forest conservation, and a glacier he discovered in Alaska also bears his name.

At the age of 74, two years before his death, he was still traveling to Europe, Asia, South America, and Africa. "The world's big," he said, "and I want to have a good look at it before it gets dark.

John Paul Jones is often called the Father of the American Navy. John was a very real and very brave hero. His heroism in fighting against a larger and much better equipped enemy fleet has made him famous in naval history. Maybe you are familiar with his reply to a British demand to surrender, "I have not yet begun to fight."

In 1776, Jones was promoted to the rank of captain. He took as his flagship the frigate Ranger. He was the first to fly the new United States flag while he was aboard this ship. The Ranger was also the first U.S. man-of-war to receive a foreign salute.

Duncan Phyfe made some of the most beautiful furniture in the world. His gracefully proportioned, yet soundly made, pieces were so original that people call the design by his name. His work was as good as any of the furniture then being imported from London, and he became the leading U.S. furniture maker of his time.

Philip Murray immigrated to the United States and began working in the mines at the age of ten. He got into an argument with his employer soon after he started, and quickly lost his job.

The other miners went on strike in sympathy with Murray, but they lost the strike. From that time on, Philip worked as a labor union organizer and leader. He alone was responsible for the C.I.O. unions "no-strike" policy pledge during World War II. He fought for the workers in the mines to have better safety devices, pensions and, union security.

Thanks to Alexander Graham Bell, all nations have telephones. Today, scientists and engineers at Bell Laboratories, birthplace of the first electrical digital computer and the transistor, are working on transmitting telephone calls on a beam of light. They expect to put it into operation by the year 2000.

The first detective agency in the United States was formed by Allan Pinkerton. He helped organize a federal secret service and he became its chief.

After the Civil War, Pinkerton helped management break up labor strikes. He smashed Western gangs, and went after train robbers. Later on, he wrote books about detective and spy work.

Golf was probably developed in Scotland about 1100, from a Roman game called Paganica. Golfers played with a leather-covered ball stuffed with feathers, called the "feathery," until 1848. In that year a ball of solid gutta-percha was used. Gutta-percha is a milky juice from certain trees that grow in the Malay Peninsula. It is like rubber but it doesn't last as long. The present type of golf ball was invented fifty years later by a golfer from Cleveland, Ohio.

Be it telephone or steel; national parks, or golf; or detective agencies or libraries, the Scottish immigrants to the United States changed its face and future.

33

SPAIN

by

JOAN S. FOLLENDORE

Imagine being shipwrecked in the Gulf of Mexico, off the coast of Texas. You swim to shore to find a tribe of Indians looking at you as if you were from another planet. They are frightened, and so are you. You are exhausted and wet and hungry besides. They have you warm yourself next to a fire, and they serve you strange, but delicious, meat and vegetables. You are a well-treated prisoner, but their prisoner just the same. They mean to study you. You are a strange creature, with pale skin, speaking a foreign language. You sit differently, and can't dance or sing like they do.

You finally escape, with others in your crew, and hide in the forests. Everything is new to you--the vegetation; the change as you travel from woods to desert, then hills; the wildlife; not knowing if a plant is edible or poisonous, but you must eat or starve.

You and your companions struggle on. You're all strong, and determined to explore this wild land. The year is 1527. You cut trails through the thick forests, drag yourselves through soggy swamplands, experience heat and loneliness crossing deserts, climb up and down mountains, fight rapids in rivers, and walk and walk and walk. The challenge of discovering the unknown drives you on. You keep a journal which tells the direction you travel and the distance. This is the first mapping of North America. It is in Spanish, your native tongue, of course. Your group is the first of the white men to explore the Southwest. With "Cabeza" (Alvar Nunez Cabeza de Vaca) as your leader, you and a couple others, wander through Texas for eight long years. When you finally reach Mexico City, you tell of seeing abundant herds of strange, enormous animals, which were excellent for food and for their fur skins. You were the first Europeans to see buffalo and Pueblo Indian communities built around plazas (central squares), with some houses rising to five stories in a staggered sort of way.

These stories became exaggerated with each telling, and led other Spaniards to go to the new land looking for the fabled "Seven Cities of Cibola." Because of their curiosity, we now have tile roofs, balconies, Spanish music and dancing, and countless influences that give our lives that Latin flavor. Well, the seven cities turned out to be seven mud villages of the buffalo-hunting Zuni Indians, and you guessed it, Cibola translates to "buffalo." Today, if they would come searching, they would find that the fable has come true.

EXPLORERS

Now put yourself on board Juan Cabrillo's ship. After the rough Atlantic, he couldn't believe the calmness of the passive Pacific. He kept going north along its coast. When it seemed endless, in what is now Oregon, he came about and set sail to return home and report his glorious discoveries. That was 1542, the same time Francis Coronado explored the deserts and mountains of Texas with the same eagerness as astronauts explore outer space. He mapped and charted the unknown all the way to Colorado and Lower California.

The Spanish moved northward from Mexico in two ways: to the Southwest and to Florida. St. Augustine, Florida, was founded then in 1565, by Pedro Menendez de Aviles, explorer and governor. It is the oldest European settlement that still survives on this continent. The city grew slowly because it changed hands so often. Florida belonged to England for awhile, then it was traded back to Spain, and finally ceded to the United States in 1821, after which it began to develop. The greatest Spanish gift to the U.S. was the opening of a large part of North America to travel and settlement by pioneers.

As a boy, Juan Ponce de Leon sailed with Columbus on the second voyage to Hispaniola (New Spain), in 1493. They landed on what is today the Dominican Republic, and Ponce was appointed governer of the province a few years later. An Indian came to see him, traveling by canoe, from Puerto Rico. The Indian brought him gold, and said there was much more where that came from. Ponce immediately set sail for Puerto Rico. When he returned, he was appointed to the well-paying positon of governor of the island. But a son of Columbus wanted the position, and won out after a long dispute. Ponce next became fascinated by Indian tales of an island called Bimini, where not only gold, but everything else a man might desire could be found, including the Fountain of Youth, which could make an old man young again. Ponce boarded his ship again, and reached land on Easter Sunday. So he named it Pascua, Florida, in honor of the holy day. He sailed through the Florida Keys at Key West, but couldn't find the fabled Bimini. Spain made him governor of the "island of Florida." He is remembered as the discoverer of Florida, which he hoped someday to explore and determine whether or not it was an island. He died before he could.

Although he never really set foot in North America, we must give Christopher Columbus credit for proving that future exploration in that part of the world would be worthwhile. But, he never would have made the trip if the Spanish hadn't come through with the money to make it possible. After being turned down by the King of Portugal in 1485, he went through six years of frustrating negotiations with Queen Isabella and King Ferdinand of Spain before they finally agreed to finance his expedition with Spanish ships and crew.

Columbus proved to be a successful admiral. He found lands on the other side of the water, but had trouble maintaining control of them because he was always sailing off and leaving them in weaker hands. When the Spanish seamen finally reached North America, without Columbus, they put up their country's flag on Hispaniola, making it a colony, after which they established many others as well.

Friar Junipero Serra, the walking priest, was bitten on the leg by a rattlesnake, and the wound gave him much difficulty during the thousands of miles he walked to perform religious duties. Although he was always in weak health, he still set up twenty-one missions, and journeyed from Mexico City to California, and back to Mexico City, on foot. He and Friar Francisco Palou established the presidios (fortresses) and pueblos (villages) of San Diego, Santa Barbara, and Monterey. In 1781, the pueblo of Los Angeles was founded. Most of these settlements were manned by people born in Mexico.

Spanish exploring along the Pacific ended with Alejandro Malsapina, who sailed in 1790 mapping the coast as far as Alaska.

The Spaniards brought us horses, burros, sheep, goats, and tools made of iron. They can be thanked, therefore, for wool, pack-animals, and horse power, as well as mapping out a great deal of the land.

The discovery that soon tilted the country west was made in the hills northeast of Los Angeles by a Spanish ranch-hand who dug up a clump of onions and saw gold in the dirt. During the next three years some $8000 was washed out of the local soil. That was in 1842, however it wasn't until six years later that the gold rush began, when an American claimed the strike on Sutter's land. The man's name who found the first gold in California was Francisco Lopez.

MUSIC AND THE ARTS

This century too, Spain sent Jose Iturbi, the world-reknown pianist. He studied in Barcelona, and at the Paris Conservatory, then appeared with numerous symphony orchestras, thrilling audiences wherever he went. When he became a conductor, he often played the piano and conducted at the same time. His sister, Amparo, was also a brilliant pianist, and they gave many recitals of music for two pianos. The Iturbi duet had listeners breathing in rhythm, so as not to break the spell cast by the performers.

Other accomplished musicians from Spain are cellist and conductor Pablo Casals; lyric soprano Victoria de los Angeles; and composer and pianist Isaac Albeniz. One of the world's finest guitarists is Andres Segovia; and you all must know beautiful, wiggly Charro, and her bandleader-husband, Xavier Cugat.

The movie story, Man of La Mancha, is a Spanish classic. One can't get much more famous than Cervantes (Saavedra), who wrote the original *Don Quixote de la Mancha*, in two volumes. Cervantes didn't rush through things, as most of us are tempted to do today. It took him over ten years to complete this work, and that was in the early 17th century. It was worth it, for everyone still knows the story of Don Quixote, the tall, skinny man who fought windmills, with his short, fat assistant, Sancho, at his side.

More recent, brilliant, contributors of our literary world are novelists Pedro Antonio de Alarcon and Vincente Blasco-Ibanez and dramatist Pedro Calderon de la Barca.

Whether you like them or not, art critics acclaim the works of artist Pablo Picasso. An unusual man who probably produced more paintings than anyone--one big reason is because he lived so long. Shortly before he died, he is supposed to have said that his "modern abstract" art, which he gave birth to, really was not good art! Two contemporary surrealist painters, whose work you may like to try to figure out, are Salvador Dali and Joan Miro.

Another Spanish first for the United States was the elevated railway in New York, constructed in 1878. It was the brainchild of Jose Francisco de Navarro. Nineteen years earlier, he had built the first sea-going iron steamship. Quite a construction engineer!

Jinx Falkenburg is one of the loveliest and most talented of actresses. We enjoy her in all mediums of entertainment.

Another great Spaniard, Severo Ochoa, studied the chemical causes of heredity. In his experiments on the reproduction of body cells, he made the key breakthroughs that were to change the course of future work in biochemistry. He created an artificial virus--the important step toward creating life in the laboratory out of lifeless material. This is now solving life-support problems of future long distance space travel, which takes hundreds of years to go to distant planets. He created a new life for himself when he became a naturalized citizen in 1956. Three years later, he shared the Nobel Prize as a physician and biochemist.

Most natives of Spain desire to remain in their country, and that is not surprising. It's called "sunny Spain" with good reason. It is the southernmost European country, with the warmest climate. Yet there is skiing on the snowy slopes of the Sierra Nevadas, while the broad beaches on the Atlantic coast are sandy and suntanned. From the "Costa del Sol" on the clear Mediterranean Sea,

Africa can be viewed almost every day. In all but the large cities, the pace of life is slow and relaxed. The people are content and smiling, showing love to each other. One can hear singing everywhere, from construction workers to housemaids and gardeners. Life is good in Spain, and the immigrants to the United States from there are good, too.

34

SWEDEN

by

JOYCE B. SCHWARTZ

Do log cabins remind you of Abraham Lincoln? Or the American frontier? And what about the iron-sided ship Monitor that turned Confederate ships into bonfires during the Civil War and so helped the Union win the war. And what about a mysterious film star whose "I want to be alone" became a household slogan? Or an early attempt to use solar energy? How about sculptors who create art in the form of ten-foot ice-cream cones? How often have you heard the phrase "pie in the sky"? Think of your home television set and remember films dealing with the conflicts of our emotions.

That's quite a bit to think about. Quite a bit for one group of people to have contributed to the vast country called the United States of America. All the things just mentioned were contributed by Swedes who immigrated to the U.S. when life in Sweden began offering less and less. They came here seeking the opportunity to provide a better, more secure life for themselves and their families. They found that better life, and the U.S. is immeasurably richer for their seeking.

GEOGRAPHY

Who were the Swedish immigrants and what of the land they left? Located on the Scandinavian Peninsula, Sweden is in the far northern part of Europe. It is a land of great contrasts, a democratic welfare state that still maintains its monarchy. From the sea-wild shores of a hauntingly beautiful coastline to the widely wooded interior, it is long on lakes and short on farmland. Highly industrialized, its territory ranges from lowlands to mountains. In area, it roughly equals that of Missouri, Arkansas, and Louisiana combined.

Lying east of Norway, Sweden is Europe's third largest country, but has a smaller population than New York City. Sweden has a shape similar to California, but is larger in size. One-seventh of it lies above the Arctic Circle, frozen half the year, but warmed by the Gulf Stream. In the north, winter lasts for seven long, cold months. The short Swedish summer is known for its intense light. Traveling through the moody, lonely countryside, you absorb the feeling of herds of

251

reindeer, fairy-tale castle-turrets, unfolding vistas of bodies of water, and cliffs and woodlands everywhere.

People from this peninsula traveled south to the cradles of Western Civilization and helped to shape European history. The Vikings were Scandinavian bands of sea rovers who tried to establish settlements in North America. They did not succeed. (However, in 1892, a farmer near Kensington, Minnesota, discovered a stone slab that indicated the Vikings had explored the Minnesota region as early as 1362.) These Nordic people who were the ancestors of the Norwegians, Swedes, and Danes of today, were skillful, daring seamen and fierce fighters. They were feared wherever they were known. They were also the most efficient shipbuilders in Europe. Their fast, high-prowed ships carried raiding parties to most of the known world at that time, and across the Atlantic to the unknown.

Sweden was not influenced by Central European culture and was less touched by the social and political unrest of Europe than other countries. Because of improved health standards in Sweden during the 19th century, there was a population explosion similar to what the world is facing today. Since less people were dying, more were becoming landless and unemployed. From the 1860's up to World War I, about one-fifth of Sweden's people left their homeland. Most of them immigrated to the United States, where they cleared land for cultivation, and formed communities, many of which still retain a Swedish flavor.

In the 17th century, British and French colonies became securely established in North America. Along the eastern seaboard, new settlements arose as Europeans settled in new colonies such as Pennsylvania and Carolina. There were Swedes in the New World even before this mass migration. The brief colonial try by Sweden started at the invitation of the founder of the Dutch West India Company, a trading and colonizing company.

After establishment of Fort Christina on the Delaware River, Sweden bought out the Dutch interests, but peg legged Peter Stuyvesant, who had lost a leg while storming a French fort in the West Indies, was governor of New Netherlands (New York). He and the Dutch colonists considered the Swedes as rivals, and in 1655, the Dutch captured Fort Christina, ending Sweden's colonization in the New World. Fort Christina is now Wilmington, Delaware.

But those Swedish people, then consisting of only two to three hundred, had brought with them the knowledge of building log cabins. These structures proved to be so well-suited to the pioneer way of life that log cabins spread all over the North American frontier.

Good music did not become popular in the United States until P.T. Barnum, that great promoter, brought Jenny Lind, the "Swedish Nightingale," from Sweden in 1850. Then as now, people could be lured by showmanship. Her tour was a fantastic success. People talked of little else. She made front-page news in the papers. Thousands followed her from her arrival by steamship until she reached her hotel. Crowds followed her wherever she went. Her fine soprano voice had great range. After she retired from the stage, she continued to work by teaching singing.

IRONCLAD SHIPS

Shortly after Jenny Lind's American triumph, the Civil War broke out. Confederate forces captured the partly burned United States steam frigate Merrimack. They decided to cover the ship's upper parts with heavy iron plates. Nine months later, renamed the Virginia, she was ready for action, the first ironclad ship in naval history. She found the Union's blockading squadron, all wooden ships, off Newport News. In a few hours, she sank the Cumberland and put the Congress and the Minnesota out of action.

All Washington panicked. The Merrimack, officials predicted, could end the blockade of the South, sink every Union ship, bombard every coastal city, come up the Potomac to Washington, and even destroy the government buildings. But Secretary of the Navy, Gideon Welles, wasn't so sure. He had confidence in a new little ship he had ordered, the Monitor. Invented by an engineer who had emigrated from Sweden, John Ericsson, this ship had a revolving turret on a low deck, above an iron hull. She was no match in size for the Merrimack, but she mounted two heavy guns and would be hard to sink.

The two ships met on March 9, 1862, and fought the famous battle of Hampton Roads, the first battle in history between ironclad ships. The Monitor steamed around and around the Merrimack doing about six knots. She was faster than the Merrimack. The sailors on the Monitor longed to begin shooting, but their captain asked them to hold their fire, promising to put them alongside the Merrimack quickly.

Thousands of soldiers, sailors, and civilians were watching the battle, many through binoculars. The two ships fought up and back over a four-mile range. After the first firing by the Monitor, the Merrimack came close but could not knock out the guns in the Monitor's revolving turret. The captain of the Monitor said, "Keep cool. Don't lose a shot." The ships came closer and closer to each other. Twice they touched, and shots and shells flew around each of their decks.

Then the Monitor's captain was wounded. Instead of following the Merrimack, the Monitor returned to save the ship Minnesota. Cheers rang out from other ships, and from the shore, as the men of the Monitor passed. The excitement was electric. The Monitor's crew and the people on shore cheered and cheered.

While historians think this famous battle was a draw, it prevented the South from getting through the blockade that the North had set up. And so the Union Army was able to deliver its knock-out blows to the Confederacy and the war ended.

John Ericsson's Monitor opened the age of modern warships. From that time on, ships were powered solely by steam and propeller (also an Ericsson invention). They were constructed of iron, heavily armored, and armed with heavy guns mounted in revolving turrets. This began a revolution in naval warfare. The use of wooden ships for combat was over. Ericsson became famous and continued to design and build ironclads throughout the Civil War. Later he launched the Destroyer, a ship capable of firing underwater-torpedoes from its bow.

Since childhood, Ericsson had been fascinated by machinery. He was particularly interested in developing mechanical sources of power. He made many improvements in steam-engine design and construction. But he felt certain more was possible. There must be, he felt, a more direct and efficient means of using the energy of heat. Throughout his life, he constructed many kinds of what he termed "caloric" engines. But none worked as well as the steam engine.

When he turned to ship design and propulsion, he hit on the idea of placing the engines below the water line. It was then he began using a screw propeller instead of the paddle wheel. His ship, Novelty, was the first propeller-driven commercial vessel. His propulsion system was quickly adopted for a number of commercial steamers and then for warships. But Ericsson was not satisfied. He was still intrigued by the possibility of finding other sources of power. The idea of using solar energy fascinated him, although he was never able to make it work. Perhaps someday soon there will be a ship named the Ericsson that will use solar energy to run its engines. However, the great number, variety, and importance of his many inventions have marked him as one of the most creative, far-sighted engineers of his time.

JOE HILL

There were people who discovered new lands or new things, or whose talents enriched the culture of the United States. There were people who contributed in other ways, people who wanted to improve life as it was lived, where it was lived, because for many, even in the U.S., the choices were still limited. Joe Hill was one of those people. A song writer and labor leader, he came to these shores from Sweden at the beginning of the 20th century. He was a member of the Industrial Workers of the World (IWW, nicknamed Wobblies). The "Wobblies" never gained popular support. But Joe Hill's songs became the motto of the American labor movement in the years before World War I. They remain popular today.

Hill organized striking activities among the dock workers. He roamed the country almost as a hobo but serving also as one of "Wobblies" staunchest supporters.

It was the typically American songs that won him great attention. One of the most famous, The Preacher and the Slave, contained the phrase "pie in the sky" that became a part of American speech.

Hill's songs were sung by a movement that loved to sing. Songs were sung at many labor rallies. Many of the popular labor songs were reminiscent of the gospel songs of a generation earlier so that the tunes, at least, were familiar. Hold the Fort, another popular Joe Hill song, was originally an English version of a gospel song, adopted and sung by American workers. Other of his most popular songs were Casey Jones--The Union Scab, Coffee An', and The Rebel Girl.

In many ways Hill's songs held the labor movement together, not always a popular position. In January, 1914, he was arrested in Salt Lake City, Utah, on a murder charge. He was tried in June, quickly convicted on evidence that left, for many, considerable doubt of his guilt.

Hill and the IWW claimed that the charges against him had been manufactured. He remained in prison for twenty-two months while appeal after appeal was entered and denied. The Swedish government, Samuel Gompers of the American Federation of Labor, and President Woodrow Wilson tried without success to secure a new trial.

Joe Hill was executed by a firing squad. The night before his death he wired the head of the IWW, William "Big Bill" Haywood. The wire said, "Don't waste any time in mourning. Organize."

That message and huge funeral observances in Salt Lake City and Chicago confirmed his martyrdom and his reputation which grew to be a legend.

Today, with seeming appropriateness, he is also remembered by a song. It's words are:

> I dreamed I saw Joe Hill last night
> Alive as you and me.
> Says I, "But, Joe, you're ten years dead."
> "I never died," said he.
> "I never died," said he.

"The copper bosses killed you Joe,
They shot you, Joe," says I.
"Takes more than guns to kill a man,"
Says Joe, "I didn't die."
Says Joe, "I didn't die."
And standing there as big as life
And smiling with his eyes,
Says Joe, "What they can never kill
Went on to organize,
Went on to organize."

From San Diego up to Maine,
In every mine and mill
Where working men defend their rights,
It's there you'll find Joe Hill.
It's there you'll find Joe Hill.

I dreamed I saw Joe Hill last night
Alive as you and me
Says I, "But, Joe, you're ten years dead."
"I never died," said he.
"I never died," said he.

ACTRESSES

In the world of the theater and motion picture, personalities come and go quickly. Some however remain famous. The names keep a definite meaning to audiences. You may have enjoyed films starring Ingrid Bergman or heard about or seen films with Greta Garbo. And the name of the great film-maker Ingmar Bergman is one you can see daily when you look at film listings. These three celebrities have at least one thing in common besides films. They were all born in Sweden.

The uniquely lovely Ingrid Bergman turned up in Hollywood in 1938, a beauty of twenty-three, and made a film for David O. Selznick called Intermezzo. All Ingrid Bergman wanted to do was act. But at first, the film industry in the U.S. was not certain what to do with her. She seemed a different type to them and therefore difficult to cast. She complained. Nothing happened. She did good stage productions. Still nothing happened. Three years passed after her success in Intermezzo. Then she made two films, but they were not box office hits. A third, a remake of Dr. Jekyll and Mr. Hyde, did better.

And then it was 1942. She was cast opposite Humphrey Bogart in Casablanca. She played a warmly feminine role of a woman torn between duty and emotion. That film, shown and reshown on television and in theaters even today, made her a star. A line from that movie, "Play it again, Sam," became the title of a recent Woody Allen film. Look for Ingrid Bergman today as the star of a play or movie. Her performance will not disappoint you.

From somewhere in the Hollywood Hills, the great Greta Garbo said, "No!" No, she would not appear. No, to film offers. No, to interviews. "Fire and ice," the newspapers called her. She wanted privacy so much she was described as being a hermit. But Garbo felt her private life was her own. And in the United States, she knew few people and spoke English only with difficulty. Terribly shy, she was torn between her wish to perform and her dislike of the spotlight.

On her first visit to the United States, Garbo was a tall, slim, unhappy-looking Swedish girl. She took no interest in her clothes, did her hair in an unbecoming way, and seemed to do nothing to try and make herself appear attractive. That plain girl became the glamorous, mysterious Garbo. She was to fascinate people all over the world.

Born in Stockholm as Greta Louisa Gustafsson, she left school at fourteen because she had to go to work. That proved to be a fortunate step for her. While working as a department-store clerk, she met a motion-picture director who gave her a small part in his movie, Peter the Tramp. For the next two years she studied at the Royal Dramatic Theatre School in Stockholm, and then was given a major role. That film's director gave her the name of Garbo and helped her secure a contract with Metro-Goldwyn-Mayer in Hollywood, which stated that she would become the world's greatest actress. She remained with MGM for sixteen years and made twenty-four films, establishing herself as a star with a subtle and baffling charm. She was one of the few stars who was successfully able to switch from silent films to the new ones with sound. Her first talkie, Anna Christie, revealed a low, husky voice to match her beauty.

Her following films, among them Mata Hari, Grand Hotel, Anna Karenina, and Camille, won her almost faddish devotion. In Ninotchka, she also displayed an unexpected gift for comedy.

She always worked hard, concentrating on the character she played, the scene, and the feelings and relationships between all the characters in the film. She was said to inspire everyone who worked with her to do their best. She was the screen star men saw once and never forgot.

Two-Faced Woman did not have the success of her other films. At thirty-six, Garbo committed herself to never work again. She became a near recluse, living mostly in New York City, traveling under different names and refusing interviews or publicity of any kind. Her films, frequently revived, became classics, and many continued to think of her as the height of glamour. Her insistence on complete privacy recalled a famous line from one of her films, "I want to be alone." That line helped make her a legend in her own time.

What you enjoy doing when you are young can determine your future work. There is another famous Bergman whose work in films comes to us from Sweden.

INGMAR BERGMAN

Ingmar Bergman was born in 1918, the son of a Lutheran clergyman who later became Court Chaplain to the King of Sweden. Ingmar grew up in a fourteen-room apartment with his grandmother. His other companion was an old servant, full of fairy tales and country stories. Later in life when he wished to describe a sense of security in a film he was making, he did so by referring to that part of his childhood.

Bergman's attraction to the stage and screen started when he was ten years old. It was then he received his most remembered toy, a magic lantern and puppet theater, for which he made scenery, dolls, and wrote plays. Later he used these toys in film scenes in which the characters relived their childhoods. Throughout his adolesecence, he used much of his allowance to buy film and to go to the movies.

Bergman studied literature and art at the University of Stockholm, but he was more deeply involved in amateur theater groups than in his formal studies. Those years at the university gave him a chance to try out his creative and directorial talents, however, and led to his first contacts with film producers.

As a director, he became known as having both a magic touch and a quick temper. According to one young actor describing Bergman, "His face always seemed to have an angry expresssion...He directed the play, holding a hammer in his hand, and he threw it from time to time at the young actors."

Success followed success for Bergman. One theater was almost at the point of economic collapse, but in two years he saved it. He staged more than seventy-five productions in addition to many radio and television plays.

Success in film-making followed that of the stage. For years he has made on the average of one or two films a year. A film-maker who creates his own scripts, Bergman says, "Making films has become a natural necessity, a need similar to hunger and thirst."

Bergman's films are strongly personal. He is a master of the film techniques of expression. He has the ability to create characters, and intensely emotional situations which have meaning for all of us. He shows character by the way he focuses on faces and facial expressions. His eye is focused on the soul of modern men and women today. He is concerned with the rootlessness of people in a world of changing values. His films brood over questions of guilt, punishment, and forgiveness. It is the inner life of people that interests him, not social issues; the problem of the individual rather than that of large groups. He believes that the only subjects which can, and should be, handled in dramatic form are "What is good and what is bad"--that is--moral values. Our lives, he feels, are built around the idea that there are things we may do and things we may not do, and it is this conflict that always troubles us.

Bergman's films have made him prominent. Some of them are: The Magic Flute, Through A Glass Darkly, and The Silence.

In order for us to be able to enjoy seeing and hearing stars on radio and television, someone had to have mastered the electronics that made those marvels possible. Ernst Frederick Werner Alexanderson was one of those people. A Swedish-born electrical engineer and inventor, Alexanderson immigrated to the United States with the hope of working with Charles P. Steinmetz at the General Electric Company in Schenectady, New York. They must have been delighted to have him. He designed and constructed a powerful high-frequency alternator for use in radio experiments then being made. (An alternator creates power to send radio waves long distances.) The Alexanderson alternator made possible reliable radio communication across the oceans. Through the next forty years he made important contributions in electrical and electronic research, including electronic amplification (can you imagine rock music without it?). He was one of the first to get results that could be used in the field of television. He sent the first transatlantic picture message in 1924; three years later he constructed a working home television receiver. By 1930, he was able to show a complete television system, decades before the television set became standard equipment in so many homes. More than twenty years later it was again Alexanderson who developed a color television receiver. In all, he was granted over 300 patents. Think of him the next time you casually flick on your television set and sit back to enjoy your favorite program.

AN ATTITUDE OF PEACE

There are other arts in which Swedish immigrants excel. Cloes Thure Oldenburg is the son of a Swedish diplomat. The elder Oldenburg was Consul General for Sweden in Chicago, Illinois. Cloes studied at the Art Institute in Chicago, supporting himself by working at odd jobs and as a police reporter. He moved to New York City just as new forms of art were becoming popular.

Ideas can come from unlikely sources. The works for his first exhibit were mostly bundle-like sculptures made of paper, wood and string. Oldenburg said the inspiration for these works were the heaps of rubbish he saw as he walked the streets of his poor New York neighborhood. He began to produce what has become characteristic of him, soft sculptures. These are made of cloth, plastic, foam rubber, or other pliable materials, and represent objects in every-day life, but in gigantic size--a ten-foot-high ice-cream cone, a five-by-seven foot hamburger, a nine-foot-high slice of cake, a folded shirt the size of a double bed. He wanted to create what he called monuments, of ordinary useful things.

A huge lipstick was erected on the Yale campus as a gift to his former college. Considered one of the most successful and exciting of American artists, his works appear in permanent collections of museums in both the United States and abroad.

Swedish creativity seems unlimited. Juvenile literature from Sweden has also found its way to the outside world. Selma Lagerlof scored a world wide success with *The Wonderful Adventures of Nils*, and *Further Adventures of Nils*. These are imaginative stories of a young boy's adventures as he travels through Sweden on the back of a wild goose. And the towering figure among a whole group of talented writers of books for children has been Astrid Lindgren. With *Pippi Longstocking* and other eccentric characters, Lindgren has become a guest in homes all over the world.

Some say that World War I can be traced back to the time when Swedish chemist Alfred Bernhard Nobel cut his finger and dabbing it with collodion (cellulose nitrate) got an idea. He used this combination as the starting point for the blasting gelatin which made dynamite and other explosives possible. Adaptation for mining and military use quickly followed.

Nobel left a fortune to finance the yearly Nobel Prizes held in Stockholm for outstanding achievements in literature, physical sciences, or work toward world peace. (Sweden, itself, has been a neutral nation since 1814, rejecting war as a political policy.)

Perhaps that is why so many Swedes have been prominent in the United Nations. One of them, Dag Hammarskjold, was twice elected Secretary General of this world-wide organization.

Thinking about Swedish contributions to the United States, there is the sound of airplanes in the sky, people traveling everywhere. Charles A. Lindbergh was brought to the U.S. as an infant, reared on a farm, and elected to the House of Representatives. His son, also Charles A. Lindbergh, became one of the most famous of all air heroes. He thrilled the world with the first New York to Paris non-stop flight in a plane called The Spirit Of St. Louis. Nicknamed the "Lone Eagle," he made flying seem respectable and safe for the first time.

Sweden has had other influences upon us. Its good taste and flair for design have inspired many countries. Swedish modern furniture, also made in the United States, is made of light or bleached woods. With typically clean smooth lines, it has little decoration and is upholstered in pleasant bright colors.

Think also about what the United States represented to the world. The new beginning which it offered, attracted many to these shores. The ability of the Swedish, as well as other immigrants, to use that opportunity to create the American way of life has helped us all. As the United States passes its two-hundredth year as a nation, may it learn from the experiences of the past to keep alive hope, freedom, and opportunity for all individuals.

35

SWITZERLAND

by

IRENE L. JERISON

The tiny country of Switzerland lies like a jewel near the heart of Europe. It is a land of snow-crowned peaks and glittering lakes, where slant-roofed chalets hug mountain slopes; where cows graze in alpine meadows dazzling with flowers, and the mellow sound of their bells is punctuated by the shrillness of yodeling; and where the best chocolate, watches, and cheese with the biggest holes come from.

Switzerland is also the oldest existing democratic republic in the world. Its confederation of 25 independent states, called "cantons," had its beginnings almost seven centuries ago, when three cantons united and declared their independence. The Swiss passion for freedom found an echo in ideas of American freedom-seekers. The American confederation of the early days of the Republic was not unlike the Swiss system.

Switzerland sounds so ideal that it is surprising anyone would want to leave it for an uncertain future in foreign parts. But until it adopted a position of neutrality in the 19th century, the little country was often torn by other nations' quarrels. Frequently, also, its mountainous land and moody weather failed to provide enough to feed a growing population. Although some Swiss immigrated to the United States to seek religious tolerance in their own communities, most, like immigrants from everywhere, wandered away because the grass was said to grow greener elsewhere.

The first record of intended Swiss immigration to the colonies is a petition by a group of Swiss citizens in 1525 for permission to leave their country. The trail stops there, however, and it is not until 1562 that we find the record of the death in Florida of Diebold von Erlach, a Swiss mercenary soldier in the service of Spain. Hiring out to other governments' armies was common practice among the Swiss, and to this day the guards at the Vatican in Rome bear the name "Swiss Guards." Of the Swiss mercenaries who served in North America under the flags of foreign empires, the best known was Henry Louis Bouquet, who fought with the English against the French and the Indians in the 18th century. There were Swiss fighting under the Marquis de Lafayette during the Revolutionary War. Many more, by far, crossed the Atlantic to ply their old-world trades or to seek their fortunes as pioneers.

It is hard to determine how many Swiss have immigrated to the United States. Surprisingly for a country with such a long history of nationhood, in Switzerland, where variety has been the spice of existence, the different ingredients have never lost their distinct flavor. Each ethnic group speaks its own language: French, German, Italian or Romansch (a relic from the times when Rome had a province there). As a result, Swiss immigrants tended to be counted among the nationalities whose language they spoke and thus records do not show them as coming from Switzerland. Even so, it is known that at least 300,000 Swiss immigrated to the United States.

Three Swiss immigrants stand out as giants in U.S. history: Albert Gallatin, a statesman; John Sutter, a pioneer; and Louis Agassiz, a scientist. A fourth, Albert Einstein, is usually counted among Germans, but he was a Swiss citizen. Einstein, whose theory of relativity revolutionized physics, joked in an essay that his origins might someday become "an application of the principle of relativity." If he were worthy, the Germans would call him "a German savant," if not, they would disown him as "a Swiss Jew." He himself preferred to be viewed as a citizen of the world.

ALBERT GALLATIN

The issues of citizenship and foreign origin plagued the early career of Albert Gallatin. Gallatin was a high-born and well-educated nineteen-year-old, when, in 1780, he left home in a fit of anger against his family. He took off for the Colonies, attracted by the romantic pull of high adventure and the democratic idealism of the New World.

Arriving during the hard times of the War of Independence, Gallatin briefly eked out a living as a soldier, then as a wood chopper, and finally as a tutor in French to Harvard students. Soon, however, he made a successful life for himself as a businessman in Pennsylvania and Virginia. Always an outspoken opponent of concentrated executive power, Gallatin became an outstanding anti-Federalist during the Pennsylvania Convention that debated the ratification of the Constitution. Eventually he became the leader of Jefferson's party, the Whigs, in Congress.

Gallatin believed that the central government should be simple, economical, and free of debt; that Congress had a part to play in foreign policy; and that the people should have more to say about their own taxes. This political philosophy, which prevailed in the United States when Thomas Jefferson was president and Gallatin his secretary of the treasury, is popular once more now, one hundred and seventy years later.

Before either Gallatin or Jefferson reached the peak of their careers, Gallatin's fiery defense of his convictions got him into hot political water. It is easy to see that Gallatin, an imposing figure with his burning dark eyes, hawk nose, and black eyebrows and with his patrician bearing and sharp intelligence must have been an irritating thorn in his opponents' sides. In 1793, they forced him to resign his Senate seat on the technicality that he had not been a citizen for the nine years prescribed by a purposely anti-foreign law. The Constitution itself was not yet nine years old then.

Two years later he was elected to the House of Representatives. This time a citizen by any yardstick, Gallitan became the leader of the opposition to the John Adams administration. This was a period of hate of foreigners that was being inflamed by the government in power. The excesses of the French Revolution and the shabby treatment of American diplomats in France in the so-called XYZ Affair almost led to a war between the United States and France. Gallatin, who considered any war an obstacle to progress and prosperity, became the object of attacks as a French agent, because of his French-speaking origin. The Sedition Act of 1798, which the Federalist majority pushed through Congress to stifle freedom of action and expression by the opposition, was considered by some, including Jefferson, an attempt to get rid of Gallatin. The move backfired, because its oppressiveness shocked the country, and Gallatin was free to lead the successful effort to elect Jefferson president in 1800.

After he left the Cabinet in the administration of James Madison, Gallatin served in several diplomatic posts, founded New York University, and participated in scientific research.

JOHN SUTTER

To catch a glimpse of the life of another famous Swiss American, we must jump across the continent to Sacramento, where the state of California runs a historical park. You enter the gate through a gap in a stockade and find yourself inside a frontier fort, exactly as it used to be, with living quarters, stables, stores of rifles, powder and staples, a distillery, a tannery, and looms for blanket weaving. This was the domain of an extraordinary adventurer, for a time master of all he surveyed in his own colony, John Augustus Sutter. Sutter was a Swiss soldier of fortune, and Fortune helped both make and break him.

After having tried his luck in wine-making, beaver trapping, and shipping, Sutter happened to ask the Mexican governor of California for a land grant for a ranch just when the governor feared that recent Russian colonists would pose a threat to Mexican California. He gladly granted Sutter thousands of acres of land on the condition that Sutter build a fort. Soon thereafter fate once again played into Sutter's hand as he learned that the Russians were about to abandon their colony. He simply took over what the Russians had left behind: huge herds of cattle and horses, a dozen fierce-looking cannon, and muskets that had been used against Napoleon in Moscow, among other treasures.

For ten years Sutter prospered. His colony was the center of trade and industry, a shelter against hostile Indians, and a meeting place for travelers where they could always find a generous and hospitable welcome. But in 1848 fate turned against Sutter.

Two years before, foreseeing that Mexican rule, and with it his land grant, would soon come to an end, Sutter had a saw mill built in the Sierra Nevada foothills. There, in January 1848, the gold that started the California Gold Rush was discovered. Sutter rushed to obtain a title to his land only to be told that nothing could be done because the area was still occupied territory. This bad timing led Sutter to ruin as his New Helvetia (so named after the Roman name for Switzerland) was overrun and trampled by hordes of forty-niners, who squatted on his land and slaughtered his cattle. In spite of a long court battle, all Sutter ended up with was a meager government pension.

ARTISTS . . . ZOOLOSIST

Unlike Sutter or Gallatin, Louis Agassiz did not seek the United States. Rather, the U.S. sought him out. Agassiz may have been the first example of the so-called brain drain, the immigration of intellectuals from abroad, which reached a peak during World War II. Soon after Agassiz accepted the chair of zoology at Harvard, which had been created especially for him, Arnold Guyot, a geologist, and Leo Lesqueureux, a paleobotanist (a student of fossil plants), also took academic posts in the U.S.

Born in 1807, Louis Agassiz was already a famous man when he accepted the Harvard professorship in 1848. He was handsome and kind, with a charming smile and a knack for attracting disciples. Every professor of zoology in U.S. colleges and universities for about forty years was a pupil of his. Young Swiss and other Europeans flocked to study under him. His fame grew out of his theory that thousands of years ago much of the earth's surface was covered with glaciers in what he termed an Ice Age. Agassiz's more particularly American contributions were his inspiration for the founding of an American Academy of Sciences and the first American natural history museums, and his insistence that one must "read nature, not books," which took natural scientists out of libraries and into the field and laboratories.

Many other Swiss-Americans became known in their adopted country. A pioneer in Sutter's mold but on a smaller scale was Jules Ami Sandoz, who, like Gallatin, gave up a good education and a promising future to go to the United States in the wake of a family quarrel. Sandoz traveled west until his money ran out, which happened in northeastern Nebraska. "There," writes his daughter, author Mari Sandoz, in her award-winning biography, *Old Jules*, "he filed on a homestead and became a landed man, with twenty dollars, a stamp collection begun as a boy, a Swiss army rifle, and a spade." Energetic and eccentric, this trapper, surveyor, nurseryman, and vocal citizen was the western pioneer personified.

Another whose story of lifelong pioneering in the West has made its way into print is Elise Dubach Isely, who left Switzerland at the age of 12. At the end of a long trek by ship and then covered wagon, she suffered, in turn: taunts from schoolmates who were amused by her broken English; danger from the Border Ruffians (Confederate sympathizers in pre-Civil-War Missouri); and years of anxiety while her Swiss-born young husband fought in the Union Army. After the Civil War, she lived a long and prosperous life, farming on the rolling prairies of West Kansas.

Among distinguished Swiss immigrants were several churchmen. Philip Schaff is considered by some to be the foremost American theologian of the 19th century. Father Martin Kuendig tore out the pews of his church and converted it into a hospital when a cholera epidemic struck Detroit in 1834. He worked day and night organizing nursing care for the sick and later built a poorhouse for the invalids, widows, and orphans left by the epidemic. It took him years to pay off the huge debt he had incurred for the poorhouse.

Swiss-American contributions to science and art in the United States have continued. Unlike his father, Louis Agassiz, who before he immigrated had barely been able to support a family on his professor's pay, Alexander Agassiz lived a life of both learning (as an oceanographer) and wealth (as a coal mine owner). The Louis Agassiz Museum of Comparative Zoology at Harvard benefitted greatly from his contributions. A Swiss-American surveyor, Ferdinand Hassler, succeeded in promoting a survey of the Atlantic coast, which ultimately led to the establishment of the U.S. Coast and Geodetic Survey. The Survey has charted and studied the North American coast for almost 150 years. Swiss-born physicist Felix Bloch shared the Nobel Prize in physics in 1953 for having succeeded in measuring with extreme accuracy the magnetic characteristics of atomic nuclei. Several Swiss immigrant physicians, Senn, Banga, Detwiller, and Stam pioneered in surgical methods, the use of antiseptics, and medical education. The most prominent among artists of Swiss birth is the surrealist painter Kurt Seligmann. Film actress Ursula Andress has often adorned the screen.

A man who used his thorough European training well, but in a peculiarly American way, was the mechanic and inventor John Kruesi. Kruesi was the assistant whose job it often was to turn Thomas Edison's ideas into working models. One day, Edison left a crude sketch with a note saying, "Kruesi, make this," on the latter's workbench.

"What'll it do?" asked Kruesi, who not surprisingly wanted to know.

"It'll talk back," was Edison's reply.

A few days later, the gadget was ready. Edison sang a tune into it. "Mary had a little lamb," it sang back in a scratchy voice. Kruesi had built the first phonograph and record.

Many early Swiss immigrants, including Gallatin and Hassler, had dreamt of starting Swiss colonies. These two soon turned to other pursuits, but gradually bits of Switzerland sprouted across the United States, until now there are sixteen Genevas, a handful of Switzerlands, and many other places with Swiss names. The people who settled in them soon turned to occupations in which their countrymen had long excelled. They developed the cheese and silk industries; tried their hand at grape-growing and wine-making in Switzerland County, Indiana; introduced unsweetened evaporated milk and Swiss-type Wittnauer watches; and ran banks, hotels, and restaurants. Even Swiss chocolate became a household word in the U.S. when a descendant of a Swiss immigrant, Hersche, decided to try his luck at candymaking under his Americanized name of Hershey. Swiss chalets dot the United States landscape, especially in ski country. And the language even has taken on an expression from a Swiss name. "Ritzy" -- after the world-renowned hoteliers -- signifies the quality and know-how that have long been a landmark of the Swiss contributions to the United States.

36

TURKEY

by

MARILYN D. HALL

The Middle Atlantic

July 1895

My dear Cousin Ahmed:

I am sitting on the deck of our floating prison. The captain allows us to surface for two hours a day from the choking hold where we eat, sleep and live. Sometimes we children are allowed above longer. We suck in deep breaths of salty air, trying to clear our heads of the stale, rancid smell below. Even then, we consider ourselves fortunate; word has it that some masters keep their steerage passengers below decks for the whole journey of forty days.

Events have happened so fast since we left our village: the civil war, the crop failure. My father had long spoken of joining his brother, Uncle Mustafas, in New York, and now we're sailing to that dream. And yet I still dream about my village--the minarets on the mosque, the Roman ruins, the creaking of the carts, the Angora goats bleating near the parched wheat fields. When we left our village, the journey to Constantinople was hard and long. My father hoped we could take advantage of the Mediterranean trade ships to America that left from Naples and Genoa, the main ports of Italy. We wended our way to Constantinople by railway--a coal-burning locomotive that generates enormous clouds of thick black smoke, but very little power. The colorful bazaars of Constantinople were full of wares from Persia: buttons, laces, rugs, coins, pottery, jewelry. It was so exciting. I hope there will be the same thing in America. We had to spend a week in a lodging house in Constantinople before we made arrangements to catch a coal freighter to Naples. We were told our chances of a sailing vessel to America would be the greatest there--a vessel that knew its destination and not an itinerant ship picking up cargo where it could. My father was wary of the ship quickest found and was very careful, having heard of many tragic consequences. Many brokers oversell tickets of passage and then flee with the money.

In Naples we found our ship. My father was wise enough to have quantities of Turkish tobacco with him, and there was a great deal of bargaining for our departure on a cargo ship carrying leather to New York. We gathered our packets of straw to sleep on, the men heaving the chests with our belongings, and large awkward barrels that would hold our water, and Mother with her sacks of potatoes to supplement the meager ship's rations, and climbed to our temporary home.

How can I describe a sea voyage to you, my dear Ahmed? There is a constant motion beneath my feet. Above me rise three stately masts puffed by the wind. When the wind dies, the sails hang in great folds. There is a web of rigging, ropes, and pulleys are everywhere. And there is always the sound of wood creaking and groaning as the bowsprit dips into the waves. The seemingly endless ocean. Is there really land over there?

But it is below, in the hold, where our life is lived. The area is about 75 feet long, and in the dim light you can see a middle aisle five feet wide. There are water closets at each end, reserved for the women; the men must go above deck. Several cooking stoves and tables stand in the aisle. Two rows of bunks form either side of the aisle. If you were to examine a bunk, you would find 18 1/2 inches of sleeping area for each person. We have our daily ration of water, and larger and larger doses of vinegar are added to conceal the odor. We are stifled at night, the only air coming through the hatches. The babies cry, and some babies have been born during the journey. It is most uncomfortable. Sometimes the sea seeps in during a storm; and many a night we hunt the rats that scurry across our path. There is an epidemic of dysentery--and food is the furthest thing from our thoughts.

I have made friends with one of the crew, an Italian from Genoa. I taught him to play our Turkish game, Captain's Hole. He really caught on fast and got the marbles into all five holes. He gives our family extra rations, and Father gave him a fez and a meerschaum pipe that he made from sea foam while we were in Constantinople. It looks like ivory, and Father has arranged for a broker to send us meerschaum in New York so we can sell his pipes in the streets.

I cannot believe I am going to America, and I can only hope and pray that you and your family will join us soon in Uncle Mustafas' house in New York. I hope you'll be lucky enough to cross in those new steamships everybody is talking about.

And so my village will always be in my memory. I know we will never find it in New York.

I hope to see you soon, my dear cousin, so we can enter a mosque and pray (if they have mosques in New York) and then share lokoum together.

Your cousin,

Mehmets

Mehmets and his family left their floating home and began a long process of red tape. Officials peered at their papers, asked questions through an interpreter; and where there was no interpreter, the officials put down what answers they expected from the new immigrants. They had to prove that they would not become a burden so that the state would have to pay for their support. Fortunately Mehmets' family had a letter from Uncle Mustafas. They were then examined from head to toe--chests were thumped, throats looked down, ears peered into and eyes examined for trachoma, an infection of the eyelids. And a strange thing happened to Mehmets. Up until 1935 a Turk was known only by his first name. Now there happened to be next to the immigration entry where Mehmets and his family were processed, a man who owned a factory that made barrels. A man whose occupation is making barrels is called a coopersmith. In large letters on his building, the man advertised his craft: "Coopersmith" in clear view of many of the officials. Frustrated that Mehmets' family did not have a last name, the customs official looked up at the building and disgustedly wrote "Coopersmith" on their papers. When Mehmets Coopersmith was a man of fifty and the owner of a large Turkish rug importing business, he changed his name back to a Turkish name. He called himslef "Menderes" after the river Menderes that ran through the countryside of the village where he was born.

The Turkish people have enriched the culture of the United States in many ways. For centuries, Turkish rugs have been cherished as decorative and functional. They are an expression of art brought to the U.S. In the Islam religion, rugs are used in great quantity. The Moslems take off their shoes, and put their foreheads on the prayer rugs. The Turkish prayer rugs are rich reds and light and dark blue. In the center is a pointed arch called a "mihrab," and in the center of the mihrab is a reproduction of a hanging lamp that hangs from the main arch in the mosque. The rugs are always laid down with the mihrab pointing outwards Mecca, their holy city. Many of the rugs have the "Tree of Life" design and rosettes of flowers. However, reproduction of any living thing--a bird, insect, animal or human--is forbidden in Persian designs. The rugs are woven in painstaking detail, and the craftsmanship is something we admire. Some of these carpets are made with as many as 200 to 300 knots to the square inch, individually tied by hand. Many times a rug was a family effort, with different members of the family weaving different parts of the rug. Many of the weavers were very superstitious and often changed the design within a border to avoid being found stricken by the Evil Eye.

The lokoum that Mehmets mentioned at the end of his letter is the delicious candy called Turkish Delight. If you want to make lokoum, the following is a recipe. Some of the unfamiliar ingredients may be obtained at a grocery store carrying middle-eastern delicacies.

275

LOKOUM

1 3/4 lbs. granulated sugar
1 tsp. almond oil
1 pint water
1 tsp. cream of tartar
2 Tblsp. pistachio nuts, finely chopped

4 Tblsp. cornstarch
2 tsp. rosewater, triple strength
Few drops cochineal
8 oz. icing sugar
6 Tblsp. juice of white grapes

Boil sugar and water over moderate heat for 20 minutes, stirring until sugar is dissolved. Mix cornstarch with grape juice and add this, a little at a time, to the syrup. Add cream of tartar and stir continuously. Boil until mixture is thick and no smell of cornstarch comes from it, then remove from heat. Add rosewater and a few drops cochineal and pour into a long, shallow tray well brushed with almond oil. Leave till chilled. With a sharp knife, cut into one-inch squares, roll in icing sugar and pile on a serving dish. If liked, some of the sweetmeats may be rolled in a mixture of half icing sugar and half ground coconut. To serve six.

There is a Moslem mosque in Washington, D.C., built in Arabian style. The majority of Turkish people in the United States live in and around New York, Washington, and Baltimore, and many attend this mosque, where they worship and receive spiritual advice. It is also a community center for all Moslems. Many of the Turks in the United States represent the best brains their country has to offer; usually the professional men, doctors and engineers come to the U.S. for their doctorate degrees. They had to pass a very competitive examination in their own country to qualify for the American universities. Kemal Dirioz is a career diplomat in the Ministry of Foreign Affairs at the Turkish Embassy in Washington. He attended Robert College, an American-operated school in Istanbul.

Many of our everyday customs had their beginnings in Turkey. The coffee grinder was originally made of brass and was used to make the strong aromatic coffee that is associated with Turkey. The ottoman--named from the Ottoman Empire that originated from Turkey--is a low cushioned seat without back or arms. We sometimes call it a foot stool. The custom of the Turkish bath and its accompanying Turkish towel came from a medieval belief that taking hot baths preserved one's health. The bather first enters a sweat room which has dry heat in temperatures of about 160 degrees Fahrenheit, then passes to a room which has steam. This causes the bather to perspire freely. After being completely scrubbed with warm water and soap, he is dried off with the rough Turkish towel. This is followed by a cold shower, and the bather emerges purified.

Turkish tobacco is well-known in the United States. It has a strong rich flavor, and the Regieottoman tobacco is very popular with the Americans who roll their own cigarettes. Turkish tobacco is blended with American in the manufacture of commercial cigarettes.

Since the Ottoman Empire consisted of many lands, the Turks brought back with them many foods that have become Turkish. The delicious baklava, rich soups, shish-ke-bab, and many other dishes are associated with Turkish cuisine and are favorites in the U.S.

One Turkish-born actor--Turhan Bey--was kept busy playing middle-eastern and Indian characters in the movie industry during the forties and fifties. He occasionally wore a fez and was featured in many romantic costume adventures.

At one point in U.S. history, an Ottoman citizen who immigrated to the U.S. decided to introduce the camel to the West, and this beast of burden was seen in the fields and mountains of Utah, getting strange stares from the palomino ponies. Perhaps the most famous role the camel played was in the Camel Corps of the American Cavalry which was established in the 1850's to transport cargo from Texas to California: but the Civil War and the growth of the railroad rendered the camel obsolete.

Now there are 378,000 Turkish-Americans. If you should chance to meet one, say "Teshekkur Ederim" for enriching our culture and adding color to our life.

37

WALES

by

NEDRA WOOLF

There is a legend about Prince Madoc ab Owain Gwynedd, son of the ruler of North Wales and rumored descendent of King Arthur.

Prince Madoc, the legend says, was a lover of the sea, a courageous sailor and explorer. He sailed into unknown and unchartered waters. He studied the movements of the ocean waters, becoming familiar with the great currents of the Atlantic Ocean. He experimented in building boats, boats that were strong and able to endure the stresses of the unpredictable sea.

Growing tired and discouraged of the constant wars and quarreling in Wales, Prince Madoc decided to find a land where one could live out a peaceful life. He had heard stories of a great land beyond the sea. A land discovered by the Vikings. A land, it had been reported, that was green and where all things grew in abundance.

Prince Madoc, after much preparation, and accompanied by a band of followers, sailed out into the Atlantic Ocean. The year was 1170 A.D.

The legend goes on to say that Prince Madoc did find such a place and returned to Wales and told of his discovery. It was a land, he said, that was so large it could hold a thousand times all the people of Wales. A land so beautiful with clear streams and with rivers filled with fish and game so plentifully that no one need ever go hungry.

He invited those who would, to return with him. This group of Welsh men and women set sail, and it was believed by those remaining behind, that the group reached their new home. No word of the settlers ever came back to the homeland.

Historians dismiss this legend to some degree but scholars have argued about it over the centuries. The belief still exists that the land Prince Madoc and his people found was North America.

Stories kept appearing during the 16th and 17th centuries of Indians speaking Welsh. One story that seemed most credible was the story concerning the Reverend Morgan Jones.

The Reverend Jones, a Welsh minister and chaplain to the Governor of Virginia was sent by ship to the Carolinas as a missionary. Rev. Jones and his companions were traveling back to Virginia by land, when they were captured by hostile Tuscora Indians. They were informed that they were to be put to death the next morning. The Reverend Jones, in his anguish, spoke out in Welsh, "Have I escaped so many dangers and must I now be knocked on the head like a dog?"

An Indian approached him and began questioning him in Welsh! He told Reverend Jones that he was from the Doeg tribe and was intrigued to find a white man speaking his language. The Doeg Indian arranged ransom for Rev. Morgan Jones' release and took him back to the Doeg tribe.

Rev. Jones stayed with the Doeg tribe for months, preaching to them in Welsh, sometimes three and four times a week, at their request. They told him they were descendents of white men who had come from the other side of the big waters many, many moons ago.

This story had wide circulation as it carried weight, coming from such a respected man as the Reverend Morgan Jones. When this story reached London, Englishmen claimed that based on this evidence of Prince Madoc's discovery of North America in 1170, it was clear that Great Britain had an earlier title to the land than either Spain or France.

Welsh-speaking Indian stories continued to appear from time to time. There was the story about Francis Lewis who was Welsh born, and one of the signers of the Declaration of Independence. He had been taken prisoner by the French and given into the hands of Indians. To Mr. Lewis' surprise he found them speaking Welsh. When they discovered that he, too, spoke Welsh, they teated him with kindness and much consideration.

Another story that circulated was one about Maurice Griffiths. Griffiths left Wales at the age of 16, and shortly after his arrival in North America went to the Virginia frontier. There he was captured by the Shawnees. He lived with them for five years. One day he and five Shawnee braves were sent to explore the Missouri Territory. While on this mission, they were captured by hostile Indians, and to Griffiths' surprise, heard them speaking pure Welsh. When he answered them in Welsh, the Indians were so pleased that they were given their freedom instead of being put to death.

A group of Welshmen living in London, and well acquainted with the legend of Prince Madoc, became so excited when they heard these stories that they decided to finance an expedition to North America. This expedition would search for these Welsh-speaking Indians who were the descendents of Prince Madoc and his band.

JOHN EVANS

John Evans, a young Welshman, had just arrived in London and was eager to join the expedition. When the time of departure drew near, other members of the expedition couldn't or wouldn't go. John Evans volunteered to go by himself, and he set sail.

He arrived in Baltimore, and instead of the help he had expected from the Welsh community, he received only discouragement. He was strongly advised to give up the search because the Indians were especially hostile and dangerous. Furthermore, they felt, the stories of the Welsh-speaking Indians were not too reliable.

John Evans had lived with his dream too long to turn back now. Ignoring their advice he slowly made his way to St. Louis. The most recent information that Evans had gathered seemed to show that either the Padoucas or Mandan tribes might be the Welsh-speaking Indians. Studying his maps carefully, he was sure that the tribe he was looking for would be somewhere along the Missouri River.

Evans crossed the Alleghany Mountains and then sailed down the Ohio River to where it joined the Mississippi. Then up that great River until it meets the Missouri River at St. Louis.

In that year of 1793, four nations were fighting for the right to rule the North American continent: the young American nation, the British, the French, and the Spanish. Spain at this time was strong in the south, and completely in control of St. Louis.

The Governor of St. Louis and the French Governor of New Orleans were working together to find a route across the Rocky Mountains. They needed a quick way to link their Mississippi Valley with California. Their plan was to build a series of forts along the route. This was a top secret project. Strong methods were taken to prevent even a hint of this mission getting to the English. John Evans arrived in the middle of this, and he was suspected of being an English agent. He was put in jail while the Spaniards checked his story. He told them that his only interest was finding the Welsh-speaking Indians. When the Spaniards found he was telling the truth they decided they could use him to serve their purpose.

The route that the Spaniards were seeking to California depended upon following the Missouri River to its source. To do this it was necessary to win over the Mandan Indians, in order to pass through their lands. John Evans seemed just the man they needed. Here was a man who possibly was related to the Mandan Indians and spoke their language. The Spaniards worked on Evans and convinced him to become an agent for Spain.

He was made second in command to James Mackay, the Spanish agent, who was to lead the expedition. They were also instructed to drive the British out of the Mandan territory.

Starting out in the heat and humidity of August, the expedition headed up the strong-moving river. They had to winter in an Omaha Indian village. There, news reached them that a British post had been set up on the Missouri River in Mandan territory.

Evans and a small group of Spanish were sent to remove the English from their position. Evans was also instructed to make a detailed survey of the territory and a map of their route. They were reminded that all land was to be claimed in the name of the King of Spain. They worked their way far up the Missouri until they were forced to turn back in order to escape the Sioux Indians who were on their trail.

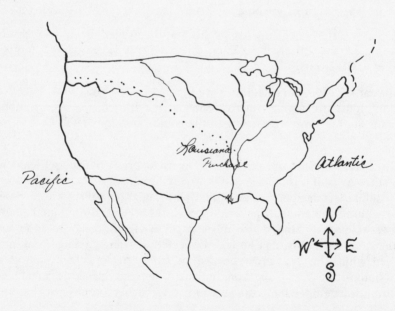

The map that John Evans had drawn came into the hands of President Thomas Jefferson, who was of Welsh ancestry. Jefferson found the map so good that he sent it to Meriwether Lewis, another Welsh-American. The President thought that Evans' map would help the Lewis & Clark expedition. He was right, as the map proved to be so accurate, only a few small changes had to be made. The map certainly helped the Lewis & Clark expedition in making their way up the Missouri River to its source.

The following year, John Evans began again. He started out, and did get to the Mandan territory. He lived with the Indians for six months but when he came back, said that he had not found the Welsh-speaking Indians.

Questions have been raised about John Evans' statement. Why did he stay with the Mandans so long? They were not a friendly tribe, why did they allow him to stay with them? Is it possible they were the Welsh-speaking Indians he had been searching for, and he gave this information to the Spaniards? Spain would not be anxious to give out any information that could establish Prince Madoc's landing in North America as happening before Christopher Columbus. Interesting questions, are they not, and your answers are as good as mine. John Evans died a few years later. However the legend did not die.

If you should find yourself on a road not far from Mobile, Alabama, at a place called Fort Morgan, Mobile Bay, you will find a marker which reads: "In memory of Prince Madoc, a Welsh Explorer, who landed on the shores of Mobile Bay in 1170 and left behind, with the Indians, the Welsh Language."

Wales forms part of the western coast of Great Britain. A small area crowded with mountains, waterfalls, and valleys. The Welsh fought off invaders for hundreds of years. It took all the force of a combined England to conquer them. It was during this period that King Arthur and his Knights of the Round Table were reported to have lived. The King Arthur tales may or may not be legendary, but what excitement, color, and imagery these Welsh tales have given us.

Although Wales, legally and politically, is part of Great Britain, it has its own language and culture. Fiercely, its people kept their personal independence, feeling themselves to be a separate people. Proud of their heritage, they had a legal code as far back as the year 925 A.D. This code was considered one of the first and best during the Middle Ages. They had a wonderful collection of music and literature that went back to the earliest of times. We still sing some of the old Welsh songs like "All through the Night" and "Deck the Halls."

The Welsh who immigrated to the United States brought this heritage with them. This background was a strong influence in the political thought and action that led to the Declaration of Independence. Five of the signers of the Declaration were of Welsh stock. Francis Lewis, who was born in Wales, was a successful businessman in New York. He willingly gave all his time and all his money helping the revolution. He was a delegate from New York when he signed the Declaration. Lewis Morris, also of New York, was a grandson of Welsh immigrants. Thomas Jefferson and William Floyd were of Welsh descendents. The fifth signer was Button Guwinnett, Governor of Georgia and a general in the Revolutionary army. He was born in England of Welsh parents. Recently Button Guwinnett's autograph was sold at auction for $28,500.

Throughout the colonial period of U.S. history one finds Welshmen in all areas of leadership: Roger Williams, founder of Rhode Island; Nicholas and John Easton, both governors of Rhode Island; John Evans (not the explorer) governor of Pennsylvania; Joseph Jenks, inventor and ironmaster; and Morgan Edwards, founder of Brown University.

Morgan John Rhees, a distinguished Welsh immigramnt, was forced to leave Wales because he spoke out against the established Church. He was a champion of the enslaved Blacks and the American Indians. He hated political and religious oppression. He loved democracy and had faith in the common people.

RIVERBOAT CAPTAIN

The Welsh were found across the country. Many of them migrated with William Penn. Welsh settlements were found throughout the Pennsylvania Territory. At one time it was common to hear Welsh spoken on the streets of Philadelphia. Welsh were found as far west as Utah. The Mormon-Welsh story must start with Captain Dan Jones.

The Captain owned a river boat which went up and down the Ohio and the Mississippi Rivers. His main cargo was made up of settlers going west. On one trip his cargo was a group of English converts to the new religion, Mormonism. When he brought them to Nauvoo, he met Joseph Smith, founder of the Mormon faith. Smith converted the little Captain to Mormonism. Captain Jones took to the new religion with such enthusiasm that he soon held an important place in the church. He was sent to Wales to make converts. He did this so well that he converted about 5000 Welshmen. Most of them immigrated to America. Captain Jones arrived back in Utah with 249 in his party. This group was the first foreign-speaking group to settle in Utah. Captain Dan Jones is known as the "Father of the Welsh Mormons."

There were Welshmen who followed the seductive call of the "Gold Rush" in California. However, only a small number went the gold rush trail. Perhaps the cost of the trip, $600, stopped most of them. After all $600 was a very large amount of money in those days. The Majority of the Welsh immigrated to the U.S. in the 19th century and went into the steel industry and coal mines in the eastern part of the country. Welshmen were among those who helped develop these two industries. David Thomas, who has been called the "Ironmaster of America," was brought to the U.S. to introduce his hot blast method. Coke had been used before then, but Thomas proved the advantage of using anthracite coal as a fuel. His method reduced the amount of fuel needed to manufacture steel. It allowed larger furnaces to be built and it increased productivity. David Thomas built the first hot blast furnace in the country. Throughout the steel and coal industries, Welshmen were in positions of supervision and administration.

The Welsh belief in personal dignity drew many of them into areas of social justice. Samuel Milton Jones was one of those. He came to the U.S. with his family when he was three years old. His family could only afford to allow him to have thirty hours of schooling. At the age of eighteen he was working in the Pennsylvania oil fields where he invented a sucker rod which improved the method of getting oil from the ground.

He opened his own factory to manufacture this invention and did what was considered "socialistic" at that time. He did away with child labor, had an eight-hour work day, gave his employees paid vacations, and established a minimum wage. He gave them a Christmas bonus of 5% of each worker's annual wage.

This was in the late 18th century, a time when the working man had no rights and children went to work at the age of eight. The workers in the U.S. had been fighting for almost fifty years for the right to collective bargaining, for better wages, and for decent working conditions, without success. A few states had passed laws to forbid children to work under the age of 12 and not to work longer than a 12 hour day. Most of the child labor was in the mines where the children went to work at the age of 8 and worked 12 to 14 hours a day for a gross wage of about $2 a week.

Samuel Jones, in the face of popular practice, did what he felt was the humane method and the only way to run a factory. After four years of this type of operation, he said, "The Golden Rule works, it is perfectly practicable and is worthy of a trial." After that saying he was known as "Golden Rule Jones." Sadly, other employers did not take his suggestion or follow his example.

He was elected Mayor of Toledo, Ohio, and at once put in reforms. He pushed through the eight-hour-work-day, and minimum wages for all city employees. He promoted civil service and established parks and started kindergartens. All of these things we take for granted now, but in Samuel Milton Jones' day they were non-existent.

The Welsh were also journalists. At one time there were 65 journals in the United States just to serve the Welsh-American community. One of the most colorful Welsh journalists was Henry Morton Stanley, who also was a famous explorer.

Stanley was born in Wales, an illegitimate child, deserted by his mother; and at the age of six was placed in a workhouse which was where the poor were housed. The children worked from six in the morning until eight at night. They were fed the poorest of foods, and little of that. They received two hours of schooling a day, taught by untrained and ignorant teachers. Beatings were constant and at the age of 15 he ran away. He stayed with an unwilling aunt and at the age of 17 he hired on a boat going to New Orleans.

In New Orleans, he began a more pleasant life. He was befriended by a kind merchant and his wife, who legally adopted him and gave him his name, Henry Morton Stanley. When Stanley grew older, he began to write for newspapers in the West about life there, but mostly about the Indian Wars. His real career started when he went to work for the *New York Herald* and was sent to Africa to search for David Livingstone, a famous missionary and explorer. Dr. Livingstone had gone to Africa to search for the source of the Nile River and had not been heard from for several years.

Stanley set out to search for the missionary. It took two years to find him. Most of Africa at that time was unexplored. Stanley was impressed with the superb scenery: the great mountains, the deep green of the jungles, and the many animals. His way was a difficult one. The jungles were infested with insects, snakes, mosquitos and the deadly tsetse fly. The expedition suffered from malaria and dysentery. They were attacked by bandits and the native carriers deserted the group. But Stanley, five feet five inches tall, unusually strong, and with a will-power that would not let him rest, pushed on. He found Livingstone on the eastern shore of Lake Tanganyika and greeted him, "Dr. Livingstone, I presume?" These words flashed out over the world and became part of the everyday conversation.

The two men, Dr. Livingstone, 58 years old, sick, and exhausted and the 30 year old Stanley became very close friends and together they explored the surrounding area. This began a love affair with Africa which stayed with Stanley all his life. He established the fact that Lake Victoria was a single body of water and the largest lake in Africa. He traced the course of the then unknown Congo River. He was responsible in encouraging King Leopold of Belgium to establish the Congo Free State. He wrote many books about his explorations and adventures. His best known book is *Through the Dark Continent.*

THE ARTS

There is yet another gift the Welsh have contributed. They created the "Eisteddfed." This is a competition for honors in singing and peotry. It is still held in Wales. There is a special part reserved for "Welshmen in Exile." This is for those emigrants who have returned to attend the festival. The United States is always well-represented.

In the United States, the "Eisteddfed" has been converted into the "Gymanfa Ganu." This is a Welsh singing festival. It is the largest and strongest association formed by the Welsh in the U.S. This is the only successful attempt at forming national associations of Welsh-Americans, probably due to the fact that the Welsh feel themselves completely American.

The Welsh introduced music wherever they settled. The Welsh choral singing is, and was, outstanding. It has been said that "When a Welsh choral group sing, the angels stop to listen."

How many of us and the rest of the world have laughed and been entertained by Bob Hope. He was born in England, son of Agnes Townes, a Welsh concert singer. Reginald Trescott Jones is a familiar face and voice. You probably know him better as Ray Milland. What about Billy DeWolfe, another actor, who has excelled in both TV and movies.

In the footsteps of Henry Stanley is Robert John Hughes, Pulitzer Prize winner for international reporting and then we have John Vipond Davies builder of the Hudson River tunnels...all Welshmen.

The *Dictionary of American Biography* lists 328 outstanding leaders of Welsh extraction. This is a list only of those no longer living. It includes U.S. Presidents, Governors, Senators, jurists, physicians, composers, inventors, and scientists.

Names like Thomas Jefferson, Abraham Lincoln, John L. Lewis, William Green, Jack London, Frank Lloyd Wright, and Daniel Boone light up our history pages. In the face of such accomplishments, the legend of Prince Madoc ab Owain Gwynedd is completely possible.

EPILOG

This book by no means covers all the major contributions of the immigrants to the United States. It doesn't even include all the countries.

According to the *U.S. Statistical Abstract*, each nation represented herein sent the United States at least 100,000 immigrants, from 1820 to 1972. Countries with fewer than that number of immigrants are not included in this book.

A good part of the credit for the accomplishments of the foreign-born, to American culture, goes to America's generosity in having offered opportunities to anyone, provided that he made intelligent use of them.

The immigrants came knowing that they could not achieve as much in their home country. The mixing of ideas and backgrounds in such an inviting, fresh, young environment made the miracle that is America.

BIBLIOGRAPHY

GENERAL

Adamic, Louis, *A Nation of Nations*, New York, Harper & Brothers, 1945.

Beard, Annie E., *Our Foreign Born Citizens, What They Have Done for America*, New York, Thomas Y. Crowel Co., 1968.

Cooke, Alistair, *Alistair Cooke's America*, New York, Alfred A. Knopf, 1974.

Eaton, Allen H. *Immigrant Gifts to American Life: Some Experiments in Appreciation of the Contributions of Our Foreign Born*, New York, Arno Press, 1971.

Fermi, Laura, *Illustrious Immigrants: The Intellectual Migration from Europe, 1930-1941*, Second Edition, Chicago, University of Chicago Press, 1971.

Kennedy, John F., *A Nation of Immigrants*, New York, Harper & Row, 1964.

Wittke, Carl, *We Who Built America, The Saga of the Immigrant*, Cleveland, The Press of Western Reserve University, 1964.

AFRICA

Bennett, Lerone Jr., *Before the Mayflower, A History of Black America*, Chicago, Johnson Publishing Company, Inc., 1969.

Faulkner, Harold Underwood, and Tyler Kepner, *America, Its History and People*, New York, McGraw-Hill Book Company, Inc. 1934.

Franklin, John Hope, *From Slavery to Freedom*, New York, Alfred A. Knopf, 1963.

Lynd, Staughton, *Class Conflict, Slavery, and the U.S. Constitution*, Indianapolis, Bobbs-Merrill, 1967.

Myrdal, Gunnar, *An American Dilemna*, New York, Harper & Brothers, 1943.

Strausz-Hupe, Robert, and Harry W. Hazard, *The Idea of Colonialism*, New York, Frederick A. Praegar, Inc., 1958.

AMERICAN INDIANS

Dozier, Edward, *The Pueblo Indians of North America*, New York, Holt, Rinehart and Winston, Inc., 1970.

Hillinger, Charles, *Los Angeles Times*, June 16, 1974.

Kroeger, Brooke W., *Los Angeles Times*, June 23, 1974.

Stubbs, Stanley, *Birdseye View of the Pueblos*, University of Oklahoma Press, 1950.

AUSTRALIA

Kenny, Elizabeth, and Martha Ostenso, *And They Shall Walk*, New York, Dodd, Mead, and Company, Inc., 1943.

Ladies Home Journal, "The Girl Who Wants to Swim," August 1910.

Ladies Home Journal, "How I Swam My Way to Fame and Fortune," July 1915.

Mattox, *Readers Digest*, "Sister Kenny vs. Infantile Paralysis," December, 1941.

Pollard, Jack, *Swimming Australian Style*, Lansdowne Press, 1963.

AUSTRIA

Guzzardi, Walter, *Fortune*, "An Architect of Environments," January 1962, p. 77.

Hornbeck, J.S., *Stores and Shopping Centers*, New York, McGraw Hill, 1962.

Spaulding, E. Wilder, *The Quiet Invaders*, New York, Frederick Ungar Publishing Co., 1968.

BELGIUM

American Men of Science, A Biographical Directory, edited by James McKeen Cattell and Jaques Cattell, New York, The Science Press, Sixth Edition, 1938.

Billings, Victoria, *Daily Breeze* (Torrance, California), "Decade of Adventure Souvenir of Congo," March 14, 1971, p. C1.

Borth, Christy, *Pioneers of Plenty. Modern Chemists and Their Work*, New York, The New Home Library, 1942.

Dosti, Rose, *Los Angeles Times*, "Belgian Waffles Are Goodwill Ambassadors," April 10, 1975, Part VI, p. 26.

Memo from Belgium: Belgians in the United States, Belgian Ministry of Foreign Affairs, Brussels, 1976.

Newsweek, "Lessons from History", April 28, 1947.

Smerk, George M., *Urban Transportation: The Federal Role*, Bloomington, Indiana University Press, 1965.

CANADA

Newhan, Ross, *Los Angeles Times*, February 19, 1976.

Stefansson, Vilhjalmur, *My Life with the Eskimo*, New York, MacMillan, 1951.

Stefansson, Vilhjalmur, *Unsolved Mysteries of the Arctic*, New York, MacMillan, 1939.

THE CARIBBEAN

Peoples of the Earth, The Danbury Press, 1973.

CZECHOSLOVAKIA

Wholrabe & Krusch, *Land and People of Czechoslovakia*, Philadelphia, J.B. Lippincott Co., 1966.

DENMARK

Buehr, Walter, *The Viking Explorers*, New York, G.P. Putnam's Sons, 1967.

Hoehling, A.A., *Great War at Sea*, New York, Thos. Y. Crowell Co., 1965.

Lobsenz, Norman M., *Denmark*, New York, Frankling Watts, Inc., 1970.

FRANCE

Avery, Elizabeth H., *The Influence of French Immigration*, University of Minnesota, R & E Research Association, 1972.

Bakeless, Katherine and John, *They Saw America First*, Philadelphia, Lippincott, 1957.

Durant, Will and Ariel, *The Age of Louis XIV*, New York, Simon, 1963.

Forbes, Ester, *Paul Revere and the World He Lived In*, Boston, Houghton, Mifflin Co., 1942.

Gottschalk, Louis R., *Lafayette Between the American & French Revolution*, Chicago, University of Chicago Press, 1965.

Havighurst, Walter, *Three Flags at the Straits*, Englewood Cliffs, Prentice-Hall, 1966.

Kraus, Michael, *The American Mosaic*, Princeton, Van Nostrand, 1966.

Maisel, Albert Q., *They All Chose America*, New York, T. Nelson, 1957.

Neidle, Cecyle S., *The New Americans*, New York, Twayne Publishers 1967.

Richmond, Jack, *Immigrants All--Americans All*, New York, Comet Press Books, 1955.

Tardieu, Andre, *France and the Alliances*, New York, The MacMillan Co., 1908.

Woodward, W.E., *Lafayette*, New York, Farrar & Rinehart, 1938.

GERMANY

Gotz Fehr and Heinz Moos Verlag, *1776-1976 Two Hundred Years of German American Relations*, Munich, 1976.

GREECE

Adamic, Louis, *From Many Lands*, New York, Harper & Brothers, 1940.

Brown, F. J. and J. S. Roucak, *One America*, New York, Prentice Hall, Inc., 1945.

Kraus, Michael, *Immigration: The American Mosaic*, Princeton, D. Van Nostrand Co., 1945.

Saloutos, Theodore, *The Greeks in the U.S.*, Cambridge, Harvard University Press, 1964.

HONG KONG

The Hong Kong Tourist Association "A to Z" Sheet, A-O-A Ltd., Hong Kong, 1975.

HUNGARY

Barrett, James Wyman, *Joseph Pulitzer and His World*, New York, The Vangard Press, 1941.

Hohenbeg, John, *The Pulitzer Prize Story*, New York, Columbia University Press, 1959.

Lengyel, Emil, *Americans from Hungary*, Philadelphia, J.B. Lippencott Co., 1948.

Szeplaki, Joseph, *The Hungarians in America 1583-1974*, Dobbs Ferry, Oceana Publications, Inc., 1975.

IRELAND

Brand, Oscar, *The Ballad Monger*, New York, Funk & Wagnalls, 1962.

Brown, Thos., *Irish-American Nationalism*, Philadelphia, Lippincott, 1966.

Cavanaugh, Frances, *We Came to America*, Philadelphia, Macrea-Smith, 1954.

Considine, Robert, *It's the Irish*, Your Ancestry Series, 1961.

Duff, Charles, *Ireland & The Irish*, New York, Putnam, 1953.

Emurian, Ernest K., *Living Stories of Famous Songs*, Boston W.H. Wilde & Co., 1958.

Potter, George, *To the Golden Door*, Boston, Little, Brown & Company, 1960.

Shippen, Katherine B., *Passage to America*, New York, Harper, 1959.

Wibberly, Leonard, *Coming of the Green*, New York, Holt, 1958.

Wittke, Carl, *The Irish in America*, Baton Rouge, Louisiana State University Press, 1956.

ITALY

Aikman, Lonnelle, *We The People*, United States Capitol Historical Society, 1963.

Capra, Frank, *Frank Capra, The Name Above the Title*, New York, MacMillan, 1971.

A Documentary History of the Italian Americans, New York, Praeger Pub., 1974.

Hazleton, George C. Jr., *The National Capitol, Its Architecture, Art and History*, J.F. Taylor, 1914.

Murdock, Myrtle Cheney, *Constantino Brumidi, Michaelangelo of the U.S. Capitol* , New York, Grosset, 1953.

National Geographic, Volume 125, January 1964.

Nisenson, Samuel, *Illustrated Minute Biographies*, New York, Grosset, 1953.

Shippen, Katherine Binney, *Passage to America*, New York, Harper, 1950.

St. Johns, Adela Rogers, *Some Are Born Great*, Doubleday, 1974.

Untermeyer, Louis, *Makers of the Modern World*, New York, Simon & Schuster, 1955.

MEXICO

Grebler, Leo, Ralph C. Guzman and Joan W. Moore, *The Mexican-American People*, New York, Free Press, 1970.

Lamb, Ruth S., *Mexican Americans: Sons of the Southwest*, Claremont, Ocelot Press, 1970.

Nava, Julian, *Mexican Americans Past, Present, and Future*, New York, American Book Co., 1969.

THE NETHERLANDS

Bok, Edward, *The Americanization of Edward Bok*, New York, Charles Scribner's Sons, 1922.

Brown, Francis J. and Joseph Slabey Roucek, *One America: The History, Contributions and Present Problems of Our Racial and National Minorities*, Revised Edition, New York, Prentice-Hall, Inc., 1945.

Cavanah, Frances, *We Came to America*, Philadelphia, Mac Rae Smith, 1954.

Einstein, Albert, *Essays in Science*, New York, Philosophical Library.

Morison, Samuel Eliot, *The Oxford History of the American People*, New York, Oxford University Press, 1965.

Mulder, Arnold, *Americans from Holland*, Philadelphia and New York, J.P. Lippincott Co., 1947.

Sandoz, Mari, *Old Jules*, Lincoln, University of Nebraska Press, 1962.

Schilp, Paul Arthur, editor, *Albert Einstein--Philosopher--Scientist,* New York, Tudor Publishing Co., 1951.

Swiss American Historical Society, *Prominent Americans of Swiss Origin*, New York, James T. White and Company, 1932.

NORWAY

Buehr, Walter: *The Viking Explorers*, New York, G.P. Putnam's Sons, 1967.

Malstrom, Vincent and Ruth, *Norway*, Grand Rapids, Fideler, 1962.

Rice, Grantland, *The Best of Grantland Rice*, Franklin Watts, Subsidiary Grolier, 1963.

PHILIPPINES

Nicanor, Precioso M., *Profiles of Notable Filipinos in the U.S.A.*, New York, Pre-Mer Publishers, 1963.

Ramos-Shahani, Laticia V., *The Philippines in Pictures*, New York, Sterling Publishing Co., 1972.

Ritter, Ed and Helen, *Our Oriental Americans*, St. Louis, McGraw-Hill, 1965.

POLAND

Antin, Mary, *The Promised Land*, New York, Houghton Mifflin Co., 1912.

The Bellaire Texan, September 20, 1972.

Maisel, Albert Q., *They All Chose America*, New York, T. Nelson, 1957.

Yezierska, Anzia, *Children of Loneliness, Stories of Immigrant Life in America*, New York, Funk & Wagnalls, 1923.

PORTUGAL

Angle, Paul M., *The American Reader: From Columbus to Today*, Rand McNally & Co., New York, Chicago, San Francisco, 1958.

Beck, Horace, *Folklore of the Sea*, American Maritime Library, Weslyn U. Press (Maritime Historical Association) Middletown, 1973.

Campbell, Roy, *Portugal*, Chicago, H. Regenery, 1958.

Dos Passos, John, *The Portugal Story: Three Centuries of Exploration and Discovery*, Garden City, Doubleday & Co., Inc., 1969.

Fendler, Grace A., *New Truths About Columbus*, London L. N. Fowler & Co., 1934.

Gordon-Brown, A.H., *Madeira and the Canary Islands*, Union-Castle Steamship Line, London R., London, 1963.

Hart, A.B. *American History as Told by Contemporaries*, London, MacMillan Ltd., 1924.

Lovell, John, Jr., *Black Song, the Forge and the Flame*, New York-London, MacMillan & Co., 1972.

Merriman, Roger, Bigelow, *The Rise of the Spanish Empire in the Old World and the New*, MacMillan, New York-London, 1918.

Sachs, Curt, *World History of the Dance*, New York, W.W. Norton & Co., 1937.

Sheperd, W.R., *The Hispanic Nations of the New World*, Chronicles of America Series, New Haven, Yale University Press, 1919.

Soares, Celestino, *California and the Portuguese*, Lisbon, SPN Books, 1939.

Taft, Donald R., *Two Portuguese Communities in New England*, New York, Columbia Press, 1923.

Wells, H.G., *The Outline of History*, Garden City, Garden City Books, 1961.

RUSSIA

Brown, Francis J. and Joseph Slabey Roucek, *One America: The History, Contributions and Present Problems of Our Racial and National Minorities*, Revised Edition, New York, Prentice-Hall, Inc., 1945.

Edon, Martin, *Svetlana*, New York, New American Library, 1967.

SCOTLAND

Arden, Harvey & Dewitt Jones, *National Geographic*, "John Muir's Wild America", April 1973.

Captains of Industry, New York, "The Happiest Millionaire", American Heritage Pub. Co., 1966.

Cottler, Joseph and Haym Jaffe, *Heroes of Civilization*, Boston, Little Brown & Co., 1969.

de Camp, Sprague L. and Catherine C. de Camp, *The Story of Science in America*, New York, Charles Scribners Sons, 1967.

Evans, I.O., *Inventors of the World*, London and New York, Frederick Warne & Co. Ltd., 1962.

Forbes, (Father Bell), January 15, 1969.

Hill, Napoleon, *Think & Grow Rich*, Greenwich, Conn., Fawcett Pub., 1960.

Judson, Clara Ingram, *Andrew Carnegie*, Follett Publishing Co., 1964.

Norman, Charles, *Father of Our National Parks*, New York, Julian Messner, 1957.

Wall, Joseph, *Horizon*, "Andrew Carnegie & Dunfermlike" Autumn, 1970.

SWEDEN

Borth, Christy, *Pioneers of Plenty. The Story of Chemurgy*. The Bobbs-Merrill Co., 1939.

Brown, Andrew H., *National Geographic Magazine*, April, 1963, p. 455.

Carroll, David, *The Matinee Idols*, New York, Galahad Books, 1972.

Higham, Charles and Joel Greenberg, *Hollywood In The Forties*, New York, A.S. Barnes & Co.

Hughes, Elinor, *Famous Stars of Filmdom (Women)*, Freeport, Books for Libraries Press, 1931.

Kanin, Garson, *Hollywood*, New York, The Viking Press, 1967.

Morison, Samuel Eliot, *The Oxford History of the American People*, New York, Oxford University Press, 1965.

SWITZERLAND

Brown, Francis J. and Joseph Slabey Roucek, *One America: The History, Contributions and Present Problems of Our Racial and National Minorities*, Revised Edition, New York, Prentice-Hall, Inc., 1945.

Einstein, Albert, *Essays in Science*, New York, Philosophical Library.

Morison, Samuel Eliot, *The Oxford History of the American People*, New York, Oxford University Press, 1965.

Prominent Americans of Swiss Origin, Swiss American Historical Society, New York, James T. White and Company 1932.

Sandoz, Mari, *Old Jules*, Lincoln, University of Nebraska Press, 1962.

Schilp, Paul Arthur, editor, *Albert Einstein--Philosopher--Scientist*, New York, Tudor Publishing Co., 1951.

TURKEY

Davis, Fanny, *Getting to Know Turkey*, New York, Coward-McCann, Inc. 1957.

Handlin, Oscar, *The Uprooted*, Boston, Little, Brown, 1973.

WALES

Anstruther, Ian, *Dr. Livingstone, I Presume*, New York, Dutton, 1960.

Deacon, Richard, *Madoc & the Discovery of America*, New York, G. Braziller, 1967.

Farwell, Byron, *Man Who Presumed*, New York, Holt, 1957.

Fehrenbach, T.R., *Greatness to Spare*, Princeton, Van Nostrand, 1968.

Hartman, Edward George, Ph. D., *Americans from Wales*, North Quincy, Christopher Publ. House, 1967.

Keir, Malcom, *Pageant of America--The Epic of Industry*, New Haven, Yale University Press, 1926.

Lens, Sidney, *The Labor Wars*, Garden City, Doubleday, 1973.

McGee, Dorothey Horton, *Famous Signers of the Declaration*, New York, Dodd, 1955.

Richmond, Jack, *Immigrants All-Americans All*, New York, Comet Press, 1955.

Sanderson, John, *Biography of the Signers to the Declaration of Independence*, Philadelphia, Cowperthwait, 1848.

Vaugh-Thomas, Wynford & Alvin Llewellyn, *Shell Guide to Wales*, London, George Rainbird, 1969.

INDEX

A

B

C

D

H

Marconi, Guglielmo, 162

Markova, Alicia, 107

Marquette, Jacques, 109

Marshall, Brenda, 209

Marx, Emil, 122

Marx, Guido, 122

Marx, Joseph, 122

Mason, James, 107

Mata, Jur, 211

Matzeliger, Jan Ernst, 75

May, Karl, 129

Mayer, Louis B., 237

Mayo, Charlie, 105

Mayo, Will, 105

Mayo, William Worrall, 104

Medill, Joseph, 61

Menderes, 275

Mendez, Sergio, 75

Menendez de Aviles, Pedro, 246

Mercouri, Melina, 137

Mies Van Der Rohe, Ludwig, 127

Milhand, Darius, 117

Milland, Ray, 287

Millikan, Dr. Robert A., 197

Mills, Hayley, 107

Mills, John, 107

Mills, Juliet, 107

Mimeux, Yvette, 118

Minuit, Peter, 111

Miro, Joan, 248

Metropolis, Dimitri, 137

Modjeska, Helen, 215

Modjeska, Ed, 214

Molines, Prisicilla, 110

Molines, William, 110

Monasterial, Marcelino, 208

Mondrian, Piet, 191

Montalban, Ricardo, 185

Monteux, Pierre, 117

Montovani, Annuzio, 165

Moore, Roger, 107

Moramarco, Antonio, 159

Moreno, Omar, 73

Morley, Robert, 107

Morris, Lewis, 283

Mozart, Wolfgang Amadeus, 31, 32

Muir, John, 240

Mulder, Arnold, 191

Mulhare, Edward, 157

Murray, Philip, 243

Musial, Stan, 214

N

Nain, Anais, 118

Naismith, James A., 54

Nakahama, Manjiro, 167

Nanjo, Kenzo, 169

Narvaez, Panfilo de, 128

Nast, Thomas, 128

Navarro, Jose Francisco de, 248

Navarro, Ramon, 185

Neagoe, Peter, 228

Negri, Pola, 215

Negulesco, Jean, 228

Neruda, Pablo, 73

Neutra, Richard, 35

Newley, Anthony, 107

Neyman, Jerzy, 227

Nichols, Mike, 129

Nieuwland, Father Julius Arthur, 47

Nobel, Alfred Bernhard, 261

Novaes, Guimor, 73

Nureyev, Rudolph H., 234, 236

O

Oberon, Merle, 17
Obici, Amedeo, 164
O'Casey, Sean, 157
Ochoa, Severo, 248
O'Hara, Maureen, 157

Ohnick, Hutchlon, 172
Oldenburg, Cloes Thure, 260
Olivier, Laurence, 107
Onate, Juan de, 181
O'Neill, Eugene, 157

O'Neill, Jennifer, 73
O'Neill, John, 157
Onuki, Hachiro, 172
O'Reilly, 154
Orozco, Jose, 185

O'Toole, Peter, 157

P

Paderewski, Ignace, 215
Palmer, Daniel David, 61
Palou, Friar Francisco, 247
Papas, Irene, 137
Park, Chung, Yang, 177

Park, Dr. Ro Jeung, 175
Pasternak, Joseph, 149
Paz, Frank, 184
Paz, Octavio, 185

Peerce, Jan, 237
Pei, Ieoh Ming, 79
Penn, William, 122, 123, 231
Peter the Great, 231
Peters, Svetlana A. S., 237

Pettiford, Oscar, 22

Phyfe, Duncan, 243
Picasso, Pablo, 248
Pickering, Kate, 195
Pickering, William Hayward, 125, 195

Pickford, Mary, 57
Pierce, Franklin, 171
Pierkarski, Frank, 214
Pinkerton, Allan, 243
Placzek, George, 84

Player, Gary, 17
Plunkett, Jim, 184
Pohlosky, Tom, 214
Pollack, Jackson, 127
Pompey, 13

Pomutz, Gheorghe, 227
Ponce de Leon, Juan, 246
Ponte, Lorenzo da, 164
Potnaref, Michael, 117
Power, Tyrone, 157

Preminger, Otto, 128
Prince Henry the Navigator, 219
Pulaski, Casimir, 213
Pulitzer, Joseph, 143

Q

Quayle, Anthony, 107
Quinn, Anthony, 185

R

Racz, Andre, 227
Radovan, Jose, 209
Radziminiski, Karol, 215

Wright Brothers, 124
Wright, Frank Lloyd, 287
Wright, Louise, 104

Y

Yankwich, Leon Rene, 228
Yeardley, George, 211
Yeats, William B., 157
York, Michael, 107
York, Susannah, 107

Z

Zaborowski, Oebracht, 212
Zabriskie, 212
Zachos, John, 134
Zenger, Peter, 128
Zeppelin, 124

Zetlin, Erlinda Cortes, 209
Zimbalist, Efrim, 237
Zolnay, George Julian, 227
Zrencia, Karol, 211
Zukor, Adolph, 149

Zworykin, Dr. Vladimir, 231